The Working Man's Reward

The Working Man's Reward

*Chicago's Early Suburbs and the
Roots of American Sprawl*

Elaine Lewinnek

OXFORD
UNIVERSITY PRESS

OXFORD
UNIVERSITY PRESS

Oxford University Press is a department of the University of Oxford.
It furthers the University's objective of excellence in research,
scholarship, and education by publishing worldwide.

Oxford   New York

Auckland   Cape Town   Dar es Salaam   Hong Kong   Karachi
Kuala Lumpur   Madrid   Melbourne   Mexico City   Nairobi
New Delhi   Shanghai   Taipei   Toronto

With offices in

Argentina   Austria   Brazil   Chile   Czech Republic   France   Greece
Guatemala   Hungary   Italy   Japan   Poland   Portugal   Singapore
South Korea   Switzerland   Thailand   Turkey   Ukraine   Vietnam

Oxford is a registered trade mark of Oxford University Press
in the UK and certain other countries.

Published in the United States of America by
Oxford University Press
198 Madison Avenue, New York, NY 10016

© Oxford University Press 2014

Library of Congress Cataloging-in-Publication Data
Lewinnek, Elaine.
The working man's reward : Chicago's early suburbs and the roots
of American sprawl / Elaine Lewinnek.
pages cm
Includes bibliographical references and index.
ISBN 978-0-19-976922-3 (hardback)
1. Home ownership—Illinois—Chicago Metropolitan Area—History.
2. American Dream. 3. Working class—Illinois—Chicago Metropolitan Area—History.
4. Immigrants—Illinois—Chicago Metropolitan Area—History.
5. Racism—Illinois—Chicago Metropolitan Area—History.
6. Chicago Metropolitan Area (Ill.)—Social conditions. I. Title.
HD7287.82.U62C65   2014
307.7409773'109034—dc23   2013040062

1 3 5 7 9 8 6 4 2

Printed in the United States of America
on acid-free paper

CONTENTS

ACKNOWLEDGMENTS

I feel especially fortunate in the number of people I get to thank. This work began in Nancy Cott's research seminar at Yale University and grew into a dissertation supervised by Jean-Christophe Agnew, Dolores Hayden, Michael Denning, and Matthew Frye Jacobson: a dream team of insightful readers. John Demos, Aaron Sachs, Adam Arenson, Amy Reading, Bob Morrissey, and others in Yale's Writing History group regularly inspired me, along with Julia Ott, Bethany Moreton, and Michael Jo in Yale's Consumer Culture colloquium. Along with all that academic support, Andrea Becksvoort, Robin Bernstein, Francoise Hamlin, Brian Herrera, Victorine Shepard, and Heather Williams in Yale's quilting group taught me how to work on large projects step by step. Matthew Feiner's Sunday bike rides sustained me. The many activists in Elm City Cycling and our partners in New Haven's City Planning Department kept me convinced of the importance of spatial politics, while the Urban Resources Institute at the Yale School of Forestry provided further evidence of the intriguing cultural politics of urban ecology. In New Haven the community gardeners near East Rock, the extended family neighborhood around Killam's Point, and the backyard of Tracy Earnshaw's house in West Rock all helped me think better about spatialized communities. In southern California, the 07 Cardiff Playgroup and Room 6 of Cardiff Elementary have further taught me about neighborhood communities.

My colleagues at California State University, Fullerton, are perhaps the only academic department that can sincerely joke about retiring to a commune together. I hope we will. Allan Axelrad, Erica Ball, Jesse Battan, Adam Golub, Wayne Hobson, John Ibson, Carrie Lane, Karen Lystra, Terri Snyder, Michael Steiner, Pamela Steinle, Susie Woo, and Leila Zenderland have all inspired me with their friendship as well as their scholarship. Carrie, Mike, and Erica have been especially helpful readers of sections of this book. A CSU junior faculty research grant and sabbatical gave me time to complete this book, and departmental research funds generously helped offset the cost of acquiring images. Fellowships from Yale's Graduate

School—including a John J. Abernethy fellowship and two John F. Enders grants—also supported my research, along with the generosity of the Piotrowski family in Oak Park, who kindly housed me during my very first summer exploring Chicago's archives.

I am indebted to the many other scholars who have preceded me in a way that footnotes only begin to express. For instance, the philanthropists of Chicago's Relief and Aid Society kept careful records in 1871, numerous anonymous librarians collected and preserved those Relief Society reports, Edith Abbott quoted the Relief Society in her study of Chicago tenements in 1936, Paul Groth quoted Edith Abbott in his study of San Francisco hotels in 1994, and Dolores Hayden recommended that I read Paul Groth. That is only one example of a single chain of intellectual debt. There are many others, for which I am grateful. Librarians at the Chicago Historical Museum, Newberry Library in Chicago, University of Chicago Regenstein Library, the Canadian Centre for Architecture, Sterling Memorial Library at Yale, Mudd Library at Yale, Pollack Library at CSU Fullerton, and Interlibrary Loan at both Yale and Fullerton made this project possible.

Carole Angus, Michael Hoyt, Michael Kenny at the University of Chicago Library, Brian Maughan at the Chicago Title and Trust Company, Edna Williams at the University of Chicago alumni association, and the staff at the Chicago History Museum all helped with the images. Anna Souchuk translated articles from the *Illinois Staats-Zeitung*, while Yvonne England prepared an early index. I am grateful to all of them for their assistance.

Becky Nicolaides generously introduced me to the supportive world of urban historians. Carl Abbott, Parker Everett, David Goldfield, Richard Harris, Brad Hunt, Hilary Jenks, Donald Waldie, Alexia Yates, and Sandy Zipp have all deepened my ideas, as have numerous conference audiences, especially at the Urban History Association, American Historical Association, American Studies Association, and Urban History Seminar at the Chicago History Museum.

An earlier version of chapter 2 appeared in the *Iowa Journal of Cultural Studies*, and earlier versions of chapters 4 and 5 appeared in the *Journal of Urban History*. Some information from chapter 4 also appears in "'I Consider It Un-American Not to Have a Mortgage': Historic Perspective on the Housing Crisis," in *Debt: Ethics, the Environment, and the Economy*, edited by Peter Paik and Mary Wiesner-Hanks for Indiana University Press.

At Oxford University Press, Susan Ferber has been a terrific editor: deft, patient, and wise. Matthew Klingle and an anonymous reviewer greatly improved this work with their insights. Any faults that remain are, of course, solely my own.

Perhaps most important, my students at both Yale and Fullerton have continually motivated me with their thoughtful questions and their insistence on clarity. This book is dedicated to my students and my family. Ben Jones, Sophie Love, and Everett Love have done their best to keep me aware of the world beyond my computer screen. I look forward to seeing the housing choices that Sophie and Ev and my students will make.

The Working Man's Reward

Introduction

Forging the Suburban Dream in Early Chicago

Chicago's first product was real estate. Before becoming a processing center for lumber, grain, and meat; before becoming a business center for banking, retail, and corporate conventions; before becoming a transportation center of canals, railroads, and then airlines, Chicago was a place to make money by selling plots of land. Chicago's earliest European settlers also sold furs and wild garlic, but mostly they sold the idea that a city would grow at this portage point. They transformed land into real estate by promoting an image of a frontier city where landownership would be accessible to laborers as well as the elite. They probably did not know it, but in marketing their city, nineteenth-century Chicagoans also created the model for modern American cities surrounded by diverse and sprawling suburbs.

In order to extract the greatest value from their prairie land, nineteenth-century Chicagoans chose to encourage single-family homeownership for a wide range of classes. "Chicago is America's dream, writ large," Studs Terkel wrote.[1] The American dream can mean hopes for class mobility, economic security, political rights, or religious freedoms, but ever since the turn of the twentieth century, single-family homeownership has constituted a significant aspect of the American dream, as evidenced by advertising slogans like that of the mortgage lender Fannie Mae: "We're in the American Dream business."[2] That slogan is a useful reminder that the real estate aspect of the American dream is indeed a business.

During Chicago's first century as an American city, many Chicagoans helped develop the elusive American dream of suburban-style single-family homeownership. The dreamers included a growth machine of city boosters, land speculators, bankers, and builders who hoped to profit from suburbanization, alongside individual immigrants who created their own important versions of this dream. This homeownership version of the American dream had a nightmare side: in Chicago, many land speculators faced bankruptcy, some suburbs became slums, and numerous homeowners suffered foreclosures. Still, Chicago was a space where widely promoted, widespread homeownership served to extend the city outward to suburbs in often complexly segregated diversity. Chicagoans' developing ideas about property ownership merged with ideas about race and class that hardened in the early twentieth century.[3]

One of Chicago's developers, Samuel Eberly Gross, called the homeownership aspect of the American Dream "the working-man's reward."[4] This book argues that suburbs were the working man's reward in several distinct senses. As late nineteenth-century workers relinquished control over the processes of production, they were promised control over issues of consumption, especially housing, which elites imagined to be a purely residential respite from work. That consumption-oriented reward for work is one sense of this book's title. Yet to workers themselves, houses were also tools for productive self-provisioning, opening boardinghouses, running small businesses, and, increasingly in the twentieth century, hoping for rising property values. Workers perceived housing as a productive space that they hoped to control. That is the second sense of the working man's reward: workers used homes as a bulwark to help them navigate the vicissitudes of industrial capitalism. Third, as other scholars have pointed out, in America the term *worker* is often perceived to be exclusive to white males.[5] "The working man's reward" had subtly racist implications that increased as the twentieth century progressed. Fourth, the promised reward was not always delivered. When Chicago's diverse workers felt their tenuous control over their homes was threatened, they rioted, in 1872 and 1919. These two housing-based riots frame this story and emphasize how contested America's early suburbanization was.

Beginning in the 1830s Chicago's earliest real estate investors bought bare plots of prairie. They subdivided each acre into sixteen standard lots in narrow rectangles of 25 by 100 feet, marked off by wooden stakes gridding the ground. Speculators bought these standard lots, often reselling them to other speculators without ever erecting buildings there. By the mid-nineteenth century, some subdividers offered "construction discounts" to any buyer who would actually build a house on these lots.[6]

Construction discounts worked to lure other buyers by helping customers imagine that each bare rectangular plot would eventually become a home.

Before any plot of land can be sold, it must be imagined. It may also be mapped and connected to transportation routes, water and sewage lines and dependent on local governance, credit financing, and other infrastructure undergirding the built environment—but it does not necessarily need actual sewers or roads or anything else except a willing buyer who agrees to imagine that such infrastructure will eventually be in place.[7] The value of land in early Chicago depended on buyers believing that this portage point would eventually become a metropolis where many people would want to own land. Chicagoans imagined their city stretching across the prairie, sprawling outward, because of a shared vision of widespread single-family homeownership. Chicagoans imagined suburbs, then created them.

This book investigates the creation of Chicago's early suburbs by focusing on that imagining in suburban marketing, financing, mapping, critiquing, and building. Because this is an analysis of ideas as well as actions, its sources will include novels and poetry as well as bank records and real-estate maps. "Chicago is the *known* city," Richard Wright wrote.[8] Chicago's social realist novelists, like Wright, join many others who documented the growth of Chicago. Discussing the development of Chicago's built environment, Chicago's bankers, boosters, builders, guidebook authors, tourists, insurance adjusters, members of the foreign-language press, novelists, parish historians, muckrakers, real-estate journalists, realtors, reformers, sociologists, social workers, and urban planners collectively participated in a complex conversation imagining how Chicago should grow. They helped create a city that became a model for America's suburban growth.

Studying suburbanization requires attempting to define this slippery word. Popularly, the word *suburb* calls to mind the setting of a post-1950s sitcom: houses where no one but the maid or plumber does waged labor, and no one (except maybe the maid) is black, elderly, or poor. Many historians recognize that the seeds of those postwar middle-class residential enclaves—seeds such as the invention of the automobile, governmental subsidies for developers, mortgage tax breaks, and ideas about separating home and work—were all actually pre–World War II phenomena that awaited postwar prosperity in order to flourish.

Defining suburbs is particularly complicated because legal political boundaries do not always match community boundaries. The city of Chicago annexed its suburbs so often that the city grew from three square miles in 1835 to thirty-seven square miles in 1864, then 174 square miles in 1889, and eventually 211 square miles today. After the largest suburban annexation, in 1889, a Chicago guidebook writer predicted, "Like London, the parent community will probably always in the future be known as 'The City,' while the annexed districts will continue to bear their distinctive names."[9] From Andersonville to Edgewater, Lake, and Hyde Park, many of the annexed suburbs did preserve their names and some of their suburban character well into the twentieth century.

How to define *suburb*, then? In fourteenth-century England, where it was first used, the word originally meant subpar spaces on the periphery of a city. Outside the walls of many medieval cities, poorer people lived among small farms and noxious industries, in areas with less policing and lower taxation. The Chicago poet Carl Sandburg implied this older meaning of suburbia when he wrote, "I've been to this suburb of Jerusalem they call Golgotha."[10] Some *faubourgs* of Paris and shantytowns of Mexico City still recall this earlier meaning of suburbs as non-elite areas. Sandburg may have been familiar with this vision of suburbs as subpar because he saw the Golgotha-like suburbs of Chicago.

In the early United States, despite widely available land, many Americans chose to settle quite close together, clustered at the southern tip of Manhattan, around New England town greens, or close to the fort that was early Chicago. A new vision of suburbia emerged in the United States during the mid-nineteenth century, as industrial capitalism encouraged the separation of home and work while also encouraging separating the homes of the wealthy from those of the poor. Suburbs began to be imagined as prestigious spaces for white-collar commuters. No longer necessarily subpar, suburbs began to grow faster than the cities they surrounded. Boosted by car culture and governmental subsidies in the twentieth century, this idea of suburbs as middle-class residential space is now Americans' dominant impression of suburbia.[11] Yet both visions of suburbia continually overlapped.

During the nineteenth century the phrase *suburban sinner*, referring to a prostitute, was replaced with *girl on the town*. American spatial values were flipping, as the space for unsanctioned activities like prostitution switched from suburbs to towns. Suburbs gained prestige that towns lost. But that reversal did not happen all at once or everywhere at once. In his statistical analysis of national census records, Todd Gardner has found that as late as 1940, central cities had a higher status than their suburbs. The older idea of suburbs lingered, and poor people, vice districts, and industries remained in suburbs.[12]

Out of Town, Jason Runnion's 1869 guidebook to Chicago, defined "true suburbs" as "quarters where urban and rural advantages are agreeably combined . . . where gentlemen doing business and having all of their interests in Chicago live with their families." Runnion was using the then-new definition of suburbs as residential spaces for white-collar commuters. His summary of Chicago suburbs included the elite suburbs of Hyde Park, Riverside, Evanston, and Lake Forest. Yet he also included Austin, "the pioneer of the recent suburban towns," an industrial suburb whose clockworks factory had attracted workers to its small and inexpensive lots, a space that did not fit his own definition of "true suburbs" for gentlemen commuters. Runnion repeatedly ignored his own definition throughout his guidebook by listing suburban towns built around brickyards and beer halls. Like many others, he noted "the important fact that economy is one of the objects of suburban life." He mixed the older idea of suburbs as subpar with the newer idea of suburbs as relatively elite residential spaces. Both types surrounded Chicago and contributed to the city's sprawling metropolitan geography.[13]

Kenneth Jackson's seminal study of suburbanization defines suburbs as spaces of low density and high rates of homeownership, encompassing residential areas in socially homogeneous communities of single-family houses on the edges of a city, spaces far enough away from work that it is difficult to go home for lunch. Yet these seemingly specific requirements are surprisingly hazy. What does *single-family* mean, when *family* may stretch to include grandparents and adult children or live-in servants and long-term houseguests? Why not also include boarders? What constitutes a relatively low density, and how important is it, given that nineteenth-century suburbs often centered around resort hotels or factories and twentieth-century suburbs included condominiums, retirement centers, and dense gated communities? If social homogeneity is important to a suburb, can this include the homogeneity of poorer suburbs? What does social homogeneity mean for spaces like Chicago's Riverside, which included housing for servants and gardeners next to wealthy elites? In a related question, whose journey to work should scholars measure: a middle-class office worker, his unwaged wife, the family's gardener, their teenager with a part-time retail job, or their teenager's schoolteacher? Even limiting the criterion to only full-time waged work, it is difficult to account for the gardeners, schoolteachers, plumbers, writers, doctors, child care providers, police, and others whose work often takes place in putatively residential zones. Finally, what is a high rate of homeownership, and how much does it matter, given that Progressive-era housing reformers recognized that Chicago's immigrant poor often owned their own small homes at much higher rates than Chicago's wealthy, belying ideas of suburbs as a "bourgeois utopia"?[14]

In 1925 the University of Chicago sociologist Harlan Douglass defined "a true suburb" as any space with less density than nearby cities and with transportation links to cities. He noted that this definition included industrial suburbs because they are just as attached to cities as residential suburbs are, since they rely on urban centers for ideas, credit, transportation, and supplemental jobs. Yet even the categories of industrial, residential, and mixed suburbs were insufficient, in Douglass's view. "The industrial suburb may be either foreign or American. In either case its dominant population may be either young or old, its origins ancient or recent, its development planned or unplanned, its physical structure centralized or scattered." Its industry may employ more women than men, he added, and it might house both whites and blacks. Douglass also distinguished between educational suburbs, resort suburbs, political-capital suburbs, truck-farming suburbs, suburban "colonies of domestic servants," and "asylum suburbs," by which he meant suburbs near prisons or hospitals. Among planned suburbs, he described "communistic would-be utopias," exclusive private retreats, and planned company towns. He proposed the labels "stranded suburbs," which had been abandoned by speculators; "older-community" suburbs, where a preexisting enclave exerted social control over incoming residents; and "spill-over" suburbs, which were urbanized extensions of an ever-expanding metropolis. Any of those suburbs might be wealthy, middle class, or working class, he asserted. After listing all of these types, Douglass added, "Few suburbs are of any pure type."[15]

Chicago's suburbs were complex. If we think of suburbs as simply a synonym for homogeneous middle-class residences, we cannot see the working-class immigrants' struggles for homeownership on the city's periphery. Turn-of-the-century Chicagoans saw this and participated in it. America has inherited a model of metropolitan expansion that was developed in Gilded Age Chicago, a model of diverse spaces of homes as well as work, a model that was never monolithically middle class.

In the 1920s Herbert Hoover famously declared, "The sentiment for homeownership is embedded in the American heart," even as he instituted numerous government supports for homeownership, first as secretary of commerce and then as president. Hoover added, "Those immortal ballads, 'Home Sweet Home,' 'My Old Kentucky Home,' and 'The Little Gray Home in the West' were not written about tenements or apartments. They never sing songs about a pile of rent receipts." Yet Hoover himself lived in a hotel, both as a politician and during his thirty years of retirement. But this is not simply a case of yet another hypocritical politician. Hoover's hotel living raises questions about what the alternatives to owning suburban-style detached houses were and why those alternatives have been discouraged both by institutional policies and cultural representations.[16]

It may seem that Americans have a natural penchant for a pastoral home, that the U.S. government has a natural desire to encourage home-owning citizenship, and that technology naturally progresses to allow people to live ever farther from work in suburbs. Yet historically Americans lived in dense cities for centuries before shifting to a sprawling city form. Economically the U.S. government does not have a natural reason for subsidizing what is an inefficient environment for which to provide sewers, schools, and many other government services. Cities and suburbs do not evolve naturally: they are socially produced spaces.[17] Chicagoans between 1865 and 1919 extensively documented their own social production of suburbia.

The suburban ideal has not always been the dream of most Americans. The early fort of Chicago and the boardinghouses, hotels, and shops that eventually surrounded it exemplify the ways that many early American villages mixed home and work as well as rich and poor in houses built close together and often containing apprentices, servants, and others not part of a nuclear family, no matter how much land was available. The American suburban dream did not develop until the middle of the nineteenth century and did not gain wide popularity until the later nineteenth century.[18]

Suburbanization came with industrialization, but it was not only new technologies that caused Americans to decentralize their housing. The authors of *Streetcar Suburbs, Down the Asphalt Path*, and *Electrifying America* all belie their titles by explaining that technology alone does not determine an outcome. It is easy for readers to miss those caveats and simply conclude that streetcars caused suburbia, or automobiles did, along with highways or the decentralizing tendencies of electrification or some combination of technologies, but this ignores the frequent decades-long gaps between the invention of a technology and widespread use of that technology. It evades questions of why Americans chose to use electricity to decentralize, while Europeans did not. Looking again at Chicago's suburbanization adds social and cultural pressures to any technological or natural explanations.[19]

During America's industrialization, an emerging middle class began to assert its family values. Architectural advice books encouraged separation of home and work, private and public, female and male spheres, consumption and production, although none of those binary oppositions was ever complete.[20] Also suburbanization was never simply a middle-class phenomenon: workers too chose to suburbanize both because of access to suburban work locations and because of the income-generating possibilities of suburban property. This book takes a fresh look at America's suburbanization by examining the intriguingly complex suburbs of one paradigmatic American city.

Recently suburban historians have produced superb single studies of working-class owner-building, industrial suburbs, and minority suburbanization, collectively proving that the supposedly bland, white, middle-class reputation of suburbia actually obscures an interesting range of classes and races and conditions of labor. Other scholars have uncovered the extensive institutional buttressing required for the seemingly natural but actually precarious modern American model of a central business district surrounded by residential suburbs. Yet so far only anthologies have attempted to pull together the strands of this new suburban history. With its attention to suburban diversity and analysis of regional power dynamics, the new suburban history is too important to be left fragmented.[21]

Another set of recent scholars has perceptively analyzed the often hidden racial agendas of property-based social movements in the latter half of the twentieth century, exploring the capacity of homeowners' "rights" to subvert American civil rights.[22] As Robert Self explains, "The most significant political, economic, and spatial transformation in the postwar United States was the overdevelopment of suburbs and the underdevelopment of cities."[23] Yet we know from the new suburban historians that suburbs were also places of refuge for people on the margins of power, both before and after 1945. This book aims to connect two important strands of American urban history: the diversity of urban growth and the inequality that growth both reflects and reinforces.

This book aspires not only to synthesize the new suburban history but also to reperiodize it. While post–World War II urban politics have their own specific contours, earlier metropolitan development not only set precedents for what was to follow but also indicated alternative routes not taken. This book examines the time when diverse Americans first learned to identify as homeowners.[24]

Why focus on Chicago, when American cities from Florida to California have similarly begun with real estate booms? "Chicago is distinctly American," a visitor wrote in 1891, echoing a London journalist who had called Chicago "that concentrated essence of Americanism." Similarly a recent Italian critic declared that Chicago exhibits "that quintessentially American, quintessentially capitalist ideal, that the ultimate human aspiration is to own a single-family dwelling, separated from neighboring dwellings by a lawn." While Chicago's growth and suburbanization can be seen as typically American, the particularity of any city defies any assertion of representativeness. What is fascinating about Chicago is that the city proclaimed itself to be a typical American city and, through this claim, eventually affected the rest of the United States.[25]

Throughout its first century as a city, Chicago led and magnified national trends in real estate. It positioned itself as the model for America through spectacles like the 1893 World's Fair Columbian Exposition, for which one guide explained, "The city stretches into suburbs, which themselves widen away and exhibit the outlines of new suburbs. Chicago will be the City of the Twentieth Century." The architecture of Chicago's 1893 World's Fair led to Daniel Burnham's nationally known *Plan of Chicago* (1909), a paradigmatic example of the City Beautiful movement and an indirect spur to suburbanization. Chicago scholars like Ernest Burgess and the Chicago School of sociologists, as well as Edith Abbott at the University of Chicago School of Social Services, also affected national ideas about urban growth. Their lesser-known colleagues, such as the sociologist and settlement-house founder Charles Zueblin, gave revival-like speeches around the nation, encouraging Chicago-style city planning.[26]

Chicago's leading realtors were some of the first to organize into a board of realtors, in the 1870s. Chicago's Real Estate Board became the model for other American realtor boards, especially after 1908, when Chicago realtors helped found the Chicago-based National Association of Real Estate Boards (NAREB), creating a powerful national lobby. In the 1910s it was Chicago realtors and Chicago property owner's "protective" associations that pioneered the market-based, putatively race-neutral resistance to black presence in white neighborhoods. It was also a Chicagoan, Frederick M. Babcock, who wrote the first standard realtor textbook, *The Appraisal of Real Estate* (1924), popularizing and nationalizing the idea that land achieved its highest value in homogeneous areas, separated by race, class, and business or residential use. Frederick Babcock later became the chief appraiser for the Federal Housing Administration, working alongside another powerful Chicago realtor, Homer Hoyt, to make these ideas national.[27]

Hoyt, Babcock, NAREB, Burgess, and the many bankers, builders, and legislators they inspired were extrapolating from a hazy interpretation of Chicago's nineteenth-century growth. The policies they developed helped impose a simplified Chicago model on twentieth-century America. As the guide to the World's Fair had predicted, nineteenth-century Chicago did indeed influence the built environment of twentieth-century America.

In addition to experts among Chicago's sociologists, real estate appraisers, real estate lobbyists, and city planners, Chicago businesses also helped nationalize Chicago models of urban geography. Chicago had some of the first distinctly suburban factory districts, while the Chicago-based Sears Roebuck Company pioneered the suburban location of retail stores, and the Chicago-based Curt Teich Postcard Company produced popular, idealized postcards of Main Streets around America, pseudo-documentary images that encouraged Americans to imagine retail-oriented downtown districts, separated from residences and streamlined according to modern city planning ideas.[28] The popular painters at the Teich Postcard Company joined the academics and realtors of Chicago who based their visions of urban growth on their understanding of Chicago's past growth. Through all these overlapping educational forces, Chicago positioned itself as a model for America.

An overview of Chicago's first century as a city forms chapter 1, tracing the growth of Chicago's real estate business, literary reactions to that growth, and the growth of American ideas of suburbia. Chapter 2 focuses on conversations about homeownership during the year of reconstruction after the Great Chicago Fire of 1871. With one-third of the city left homeless and winter rapidly approaching, Chicago's leading philanthropists chose to tear down emergency barracks and instead erect 8,033 "isolated" suburban-style houses on the edge of the city. With suburbanization, Chicago's leaders hoped to forestall what they perceived as the physical threat of disease, the moral threat of too-easy sexual relations, and the political threat of property-less people. Chicago's aldermen instituted "fire limits," an early form of zoning, attempting to separate home and work as well as rich and poor. In January 1872 thousands of German and Irish residents marched from Chicago's North Side to City Hall to protest these fire limits. They demanded single-family houses within the city limits. They shared the elite penchant for single-family homes, but they resisted building those homes in the suburbs.

Other workers did voluntarily move to the suburbs throughout the era of Chicago's industrialization. Chapter 3 focuses on the assembly-line factory as a force for suburbanization by examining Chicago's Town of Lake, founded just after the Civil War and flourishing after the 1880s. This chapter analyzes two classic representations of the Town of Lake: Samuel Eberly Gross's advertisement "The Working-Man's Reward" (1891) and Upton Sinclair's novel *The Jungle* (1905). Reconsidering *The Jungle* as a story of suburbanization means reconsidering why American cities have expanded.

Workers moved to the suburbs for proximity to factories, while they also used houses to escape from sole dependence on factory wages. They kept boardinghouses, grew market gardens, nurtured small animals, opened backyard laundries, and used other strategies of productive homeownership in order to resist dependence on industrial capitalism. This is the subject of chapter 4, which analyzes the records of Chicago's immigrant-led building-and-loan associations as well as social workers' critiques of the stringent economies that immigrants practiced in order to achieve a precarious domesticity. Buying a home, especially for Chicago's mostly immigrant working class, meant buying an elusive respectability along with hopes for an investment that they could control.

Chapter 5 investigates the various ways Chicagoans tried to explain their suburbanizing region. This chapter examines the relationship between cartographic maps on paper, cognitive maps in people's minds, and actual conditions on the ground. Many Chicago land speculators, tourists, sociologists, city planners, and city reformers imagined their city as a series of concentric circles, radiating outward like ripples from a pebble dropped in water, but others offered contrasting views of the city's expansion. The sociologist Ernest Burgess's famous bull's-eye diagram of city growth is contradicted by the neglected starfish model of Burgess's student Lewis Copeland. This contrast helps reveal the contested nature of urban growth, even as many, including Burgess, asserted that their city's growth was natural.

Chapter 6 builds on the ideas of W. E. B. DuBois and the historian David Roediger, who have pointed out that whiteness brings with it a psychological wage, entitling whites to leisure space, dignity, and respect. I argue that these psychological wages of whiteness were magnified by expectations about white property values: the mortgages of whiteness. Because of both the racially divided property market and the racially divided mortgage markets, white Americans have often benefited from real estate profits far more than nonwhites. However, the promise of the mortgages of whiteness has not always been fulfilled, especially for working-class and ethnic whites. By the early twentieth century, in the space that Chicago developer Samuel Eberly Gross had advertised as "the working man's reward," residents recognized that the reward of upward mobility through homeownership had eluded many of them. They felt their property values were threatened, they blamed African Americans, and in July 1919 they rioted. Chicago's week-long riots of 1919 were a contest over the mortgages of whiteness in which the children of immigrants consolidated their own sense of race and their own theories of urban expansion. It was a riot between people who were already working together but violently opposed to living together. The white immigrants and black migrants who fought each other in 1919 could have avoided confrontation by moving to newer suburbs—as others, both black and white, did—but many chose to defend their urban neighborhoods in the former suburb of Lake, resisting resuburbanization.

All Chicagoans faced limited housing choices constrained by class, race, ethnicity, access to credit, sites of labor, and the built environment they had inherited from an earlier era. Chicago's two antisuburban riots of 1872 and 1919 help reveal how much spatial politics mattered to many ordinary Chicagoans who recognized that spatial and social distinctions magnify each other. Chicago's suburbanization required resistance as extreme as riots because there were so many other pressures encouraging suburbanization: pressures of real estate marketing and financing, factory locations, leaders' desires to keep people in isolated houses, and workers' own strategies for self-provisioning. By considering these interdependent factors from above as well as from below, this study aims to broaden explanations of why America suburbanized and who was left out.

"The pig-wallows are paved," Nelson Algren wrote in his vivid description of Chicago in the middle of the twentieth century, but "the place remains a broker's portage."

> Hustlertown keeps spreading itself all over the prairie grass. . . . Most native of American cities, where the chrome-colored convertible cuts through traffic ahead of the Polish peddler's pushcart . . . where the all-night beacon guiding the stratoliners home lights momentarily, in its vast sweep, the old-world villages crowding hard one upon the other. Big-shot town, small-shot town, jet-propelled old-fashioned town.[29]

Chicago was a city of startling juxtapositions and fascinating self-promotion. Most Chicagoans thought their sprawling city was natural, but they left glimpses of their growth that allow for reconsideration of who encouraged it, who resisted it, and why.

One Chicago booster criticized those who insulted "the neat wooden structures constantly filling the suburbs, five or six thousand of them every year, to become pleasant, independent homes of the laboring and middle classes." Those inexpensive, often flimsy homes far out on the prairie could appear to a pessimist to be "a mere shell . . . a moment of unhealthful growth, which the city must speedily slough off, and stand before the world in her repulsive nakedness."[30] Yet the city kept her outskirts on. In the latter half of the nineteenth century, while Americans invented the idea of a suburb as a bedroom community for the elite, Chicago's poor were also moving out of town. The suburbs were diverse, and they were not freely chosen. Some workers resisted moving out of town, while others embraced the suburbs' opportunities for self-provisioning and their proximity to jobs in factories that were also suburbanizing. Chicago's boosters and elites encouraged workers to aim for the respectable domesticity of a single-family home with a garden, while Chicago's economy left workers few other options for saving or for striving to enter the middle class.

Chicago's first product was real estate, and real estate is a particularly interesting product, offering to produce further profits while providing shelter, class status, community, access to jobs, and investment equity.

Real estate decisions can affect health, educational opportunities, physical mobility, and ultimately class mobility. Real estate matters, so much so that riots erupted over it. As Chicagoans sorted out what a modern city would look like—through land speculation, boosterism, two riots, and many barely conscious, often-constrained choices—they developed a city form that affects the sprawling and often racially divided spaces that all Americans have inherited.

CHAPTER 1

✧

"Vast and Sudden Municipality"

Boosting and Lamenting Chicago's Growth

Chicago is a portage point offering a link between the Great Lakes and the rivers flowing into the Mississippi. Planning a canal to improve this connection between America's eastern cities and western frontier, at a time when water travel was more efficient than most overland routes, Chicago's earliest English-speaking settlers envisioned their city as the fulcrum connecting New York to New Orleans. At the intersection of lake and river routes, at a harbor just dredged in 1833, near proposed canals, on land recently taken from Native Americans and the French, the city of Chicago began with a real estate boom. It was a village of only a few hundred people, it was a military fort, and it was an outpost where wolves occasionally walked on downtown streets. Speculators proclaimed that a city would develop here. They proclaimed this so persuasively that a house lot that had sold for $33 in 1829 was resold for $100,000 in 1836.[1]

As a nineteenth-century Chicago realtor recalled, "The country whose trade was to support Chicago had not yet been sufficiently developed to buy merchandise or sell produce to any great extent," so real estate was what was for sale. "The muddy reaches called streets, the wretched shanties dignified with the name of 'hotel,' swarmed with capitalists and speculators of every grade," as even barely solvent settlers speculated in Chicago land. Land that sold for $1.25 an acre in 1830 could generally be resold for $50 in 1833 and $100 the next year. Another Chicago realtor explained, "It did not take long under such circumstances to develop a strong speculative fever, which infected every resident of the town and was caught by every newcomer. At the close of 1834 the disease had become fairly seated. Whatever might be the business of a Chicagoan or however profitable, it was not considered a full success except it showed an outside profit on lots bought and sold." This might seem to be a realtor's self-interested exaggeration, but in both memoirs and literature from Chicago's first century as a city, it is difficult to find any adult who did not speculate in real estate.[2]

In Chicago's early years as an American settlement, the total value of its land rose more than sixty-fold in six years, from $168,800 in 1830 to $10,500,000 in 1836. "The mechanic and laboring man is on an equal footing with the capitalist," declared an advertisement for one of the earliest Chicago real estate auctions in 1835. "A few hundred dollars here, in the course of two years at the fartherest, will make him worth thousands." Of course, most laborers had less access than capitalists to "a few hundred dollars" to invest in speculative real estate, but many did manage to invest in Chicago land. "Canal terms" allowed them to pay one-fourth down, then one-fourth of the remaining balance each year for three years, at 8 percent interest. This early form of financing benefited both cash-strapped pioneers as well as the government, which needed the proceeds from land sales in order to begin construction of the proposed Illinois and Michigan Canal, which would reduce the need for unpacking, portaging, and then repacking boats.[3]

Chicago's nineteenth-century historian A. T. Andreas wrote that in the 1830s "every man who owned a garden patch stood on his head and imagined himself a millionaire."[4] It is a wonderful image and a hint that investing in Chicago real estate offered tantalizing possibilities for class mobility but also did not benefit everyone. When Chicago landowners stood on their heads, some of them toppled over.

Chicago's first real estate bubble burst in the national banking crisis of 1837. Land prices dropped an average of 87 percent from their height in 1836, and "foreclosures were the features of the day" for the next decade. In 1841 Chicago's mayor wrote to a friend, "It often happens that property which sold for hundreds, even thousands, is not now worth even ten dollars. . . . Very few of the old stock of '36 are otherwise than deeply embarrassed," deeply in debt. Bankruptcies were common.[5]

After the Illinois and Michigan Canal was finished in 1848, Chicago's overall land values increased by almost 9,000 percent in the second of several nineteenth-century real estate booms. Still, real estate depressions regularly punctured the bubble of Chicago land values. Another depression began in 1856, then again in 1873 and 1893. During the late 1870s, as in the late 1830s, virtually all of Chicago's real estate sales were for mortgage foreclosures and property tax forfeitures. A reporter for Chicago's *Real Estate and Building Journal* wrote that these were "years strewn with the wrecks of fortunes and the destruction of hopes."[6]

In between these depressions, there were booms. Chicago's 1869 "park boulevard boom" encouraged elite suburbs near picturesque parks, while the "car-shop booms" after 1865 encouraged industrial suburbs near assembly-line factories. These dual booms reveal the early diversity of Chicago's sprawling cultural geography, as elites moved to suburbs to be near parks and workers moved to suburbs to be near factories. There was a railroad boom in the 1860s and an electric transit boom in the 1890s, but technology was not the cause of suburbanization so much as people were, people seeking the potential profits of real estate in Chicago.

In the first three decades of Chicago's city government, 70 percent of aldermen were booster businessmen—realtors, lumber dealers, and land speculators—whose booster system of government worked toward the primary goal of enhancing land values. In the next three decades, other booster Chicagoans wrote books about increases in real estate values, spurring on further investments in land. It was because of this boosterish bragging, and not its breeze, that a New York City newspaper labeled Chicago "the Windy City."[7]

Chicagoans put immense energy and engineering inventiveness into improving the value of land. "So overpowering was the commercial necessity that here should be a great *entrepot*, that one would have been constructed, even if the ground had had to be reclaimed from Lake Michigan," one of Chicago's boosters declared. The ground was indeed reclaimed from the lake. The space that became the city of Chicago began as a swampy bog that today probably would be labeled wetlands and protected from development. Wagons, horses, and people regularly sank waist-high in the mud. Chicagoans raised their streets and buildings between six and twelve feet during the mid-nineteenth century in order to get themselves out of the muck. Engineers also reversed the flow of the sluggish Chicago River to keep the city from being swamped by its own garbage.[8]

In the 1840s and 1850s new streets, sidewalks, and buildings were constructed at a grade elevated above the swampy, sewage-strewn ground. As Chicago's boosters explained, "The very streets have been reclaimed from the bubbling sloughs of a mucky prairie." But not everything was elevated. "Some spirited owners raised old buildings to the proper level; but many houses were upon the grades previously established, and a large number were down upon the original prairie. The consequence was, that the plank sidewalks became a series of stairs." Chicago grew so rapidly that it became a city built, literally, on several levels at once. Visitors complained of constantly walking up and down varied levels of sidewalks in this flat city. Those uneven sidewalks reflected an uneven class mix: some owners had the "spirit" or wherewithal to raise their buildings, while others did not have the money, access to credit, or shared vision of Chicago's growth. Even today it is possible to find older houses in Chicago that appear to be sunken below ground level. They were built before the ground was raised all around them and are physical evidence of the city's sudden growth and also of class disparities, of those who fell behind while the city raised itself up.[9]

In the early twentieth century an anonymous Chicagoan wrote:

> Boost your city, boost your friend
> Boost the lodge that you attend
> Boost the street on which you're dwelling
> Boost the goods that you are selling.[10]

Chicago's bragging had a conscious commercial purpose, boosting its businesses and land values, helping the young city compete with Cleveland, Milwaukee, St. Louis, Pittsburgh, and all the other possible claimants to the title of doorstep to America's West. Early Chicagoans were outspoken about working to produce property values just as they produced processed pork and Pullman railroad cars in their expanding city. As another booster explained, "In no direction has Chicago made history more rapidly than along the line of material development and enhancement of real property values."[11]

A few of Chicago's boosters admitted that real estate could be a risky investment, especially for the inexperienced and the poor, who had the most to lose. In 1872 one Chicago-based real estate journal warned:

A sharpie in this city, who pretends to call himself a real estate agent, lately sold a woman a lot for $400, to which he had no other claim than that given by a tax title which cost him $3.17. The woman discovered the fraud when it was too late. Many such swindles are perpetrated, of which the public know nothing, by fellows who make a pretence of engaging in the real estate business here, in little six-by-nine rooms resembling dry goods boxes. They wait like spiders for victims.[12]

Such warnings benefited already established realtors, keeping those with lavish offices from having to compete with upstarts in cheap offices. Still, such warnings also reflected the real dangers of real estate transactions. With few start-up costs to prevent people from becoming realtors, Chicago had more real estate executives, according to its 1890 census, than any other category of professional workers. In 1870 Chicago's leading real estate executives formed the National Board of Real Estate Agents, declaring in the first article of their constitution that they were organizing because dishonest amateurs threatened public confidence in real estate agents. This first board did not last, but in 1883 Chicago's realtors tried again, creating the Chicago Real Estate Board to ensure "integrity among real estate agents" and to protect "the interests of property owners." One realtor explained that the "curbstone broker" who has his office "in his hat," the "bird dog" decoy, the "'shark,' 'fly-by-night,' 'rate-cutter,' 'high-power salesman,' the 'commission-thief,' the 'get-rich quick' are irregulars of one sort or another," from which Chicago's "polite real estate society" attempted to separate themselves by patenting the name of realtor. They were protecting themselves from competition while also promising to protect their customers from swindlers.[13]

Only about 10 percent of Chicago's realtors ever belonged to the Chicago Real Estate Board, but they conducted an average of 75 percent of the city's real estate business and wielded a great deal of power. They succeeded at regulating not only realtor practices such as standardized commissions but also standardized leases, eviction procedures, property taxes, public improvements, early forms of zoning, and even janitor's wages. "Only the hoboes escape[d]" its power, an early official history explained, ominously communicating the importance of real estate for all Chicagoans except for homeless hoboes. In 1908 the Chicago Real Estate Board helped found the Chicago-based National Association of Real Estate Boards to "furnish the machinery of making control general."[14]

Chicago realtors were powerful partly because the city had grown tremendously quickly, doubling its population at least every decade of the nineteenth century, sometimes more frequently. From thirty-five eligible voters in 1825, Chicago mushroomed to a population of 350 in 1833 and 3,200 in 1835. Nineteenth-century Chicago resembled numerous other small American cities but succeeded in attracting the newest transportation technologies, allowing the city to process raw materials from its hinterland and then sell finished products to the frontier. Chicago had 30,000 residents by 1850, then 110,000 in 1860. "The city has come to pass in thirty-three years," the *Atlantic Monthly* declared in 1867, reporting that European visitors were advised, "See two things in the United States, if nothing else,—Niagara and Chicago." Chicago's growth seemed as tremendous as Niagara Falls, and the boosters, advertisers, and land speculators who promoted that growth liked to imply that Chicago grew outward as naturally as the waters of Niagara fell downward.[15]

By 1870 Chicago's population was 300,000 and its booster journalists enjoyed placing bets on how soon the population would pass one million. "There is a vitality to this city which demands for it almost infinite expansion," boosters believed. Chicago had a half million residents in 1880, and in 1889 Chicagoans annexed 125 square miles of suburban land to help fix the statistics so that the 1890 census showed the population to be over one million. Without that large annexation, Chicago would have had only 800,000 residents in the 1890 census and would not have been able to claim its desired status as America's second-largest city. But with the annexation of the suburbs of Hyde Park, Jefferson, Lake, and Lake View, Chicago's population in 1890 was counted as 1,098,570: ten times as many residents as it had held just one generation earlier, in 1860.[16]

Chicago kept growing rapidly, although not at such a dizzying pace. The population was 1.7 million in 1900, 2.2 million in 1910, 2.7 million in 1920, and 3.4 million by 1930. These numbers are nearly unimaginable, a disorienting growth, as Chicago filled with immigrants, expanded its borders, and became "a vast and sudden municipality." Lest visitors miss this story, in 1881 menus at the prestigious Palmer House Hotel featured an illustration. "On one side was depicted a pigstye [*sic*] and a hovel—'Chicago forty years ago.' On the other was a wonderful city—'The Chicago of to-day.'" Boasting of past growth was one way to ensure future growth, by recalling how much real estate values had already increased and enticing newcomers to invest in more of Chicago's land.[17]

CHICAGO, IN 1820.

Images juxtaposed Chicago's earliest wooden fur-trading buildings, situated haphazardly around the Chicago River, with the orderly gridded streets and imposing brick buildings that would quickly develop. This engraving of "Chicago in 1820" appeared in Frank Luzerne, *The Lost City! Drama of the Fire-Fiend, or, Chicago, as It Was and as It Is!* (New York: Wells, 1872), 27. Reproduction courtesy of the University of Chicago Library Preservation Department.

Throughout the second half of the nineteenth century, a majority of Chicago's newcomers were immigrants from Europe. The city's population had not only doubled every decade since 1830; it had also diversified, so that by 1870 European-born immigrants made up more than 66 percent of the city's residents. By 1890 41 percent of Chicago's population was foreign-born, and 75 percent had foreign-born parents. Until 1920 Chicago's foreign-language press had a wider circulation than its English-language journals, since Chicagoans preferred to read their newspapers in Czech, German, Greek, Italian, Polish, Swedish, and Yiddish. In 1900 Chicago had the second-largest population of Czechs gathered in any city in the world, including the cities in Czechoslovakia. It had the third-largest population of Norwegians, the third-largest population of Swedes, the fourth-largest population of Poles, and the fifth-largest population of Germans.[18]

"The white men, the natives who've spoken English for three generations or even two, are so few," lamented one visitor, sharing a widespread notion that nineteenth-century European immigrants were not white or, more precisely, not quite white. Chicago's twentieth-century African American, Latino, and Asian newcomers would face a more solid color line than the movable line of "probationary whiteness" that confronted its nineteenth-century European immigrants. Still, Chicagoans in the Gilded Age and Progressive era perceived themselves as a multiracial, turbulently divided society in which "whites" were a minority. Their ideas about race were exacerbated by the extreme overlap between ethnicity and class that existed then; in nineteenth-century Chicago, while 41 percent of the overall population was foreign-born, more than 80 percent of the working-class was foreign-born. Most of Chicago's blue-collar workers were immigrants or the children of immigrants.[19]

It was these immigrants who led Chicago's suburbanization. In every North American city where researchers have investigated turn-of-the-century rates of homeownership—Boston, Chicago, Detroit, Toledo, Toronto, Johnstown (Pennsylvania), New Haven (Connecticut), and Newburyport (Massachusetts)—the immigrant working-class owned homes at far higher rates than the wealthy, who preferred to rent. In Chicago in 1939, only 21.7 percent of native-born white residents were homeowners, while 41.3 percent of immigrants were. In 1913 in the notoriously poverty-stricken, immigrant-filled stockyards district of Back of the Yards, even 30 percent of female-headed households owned homes, 47 percent of male-headed households earning less than $2 a day owned homes, and, of the rest of male-headed households, a remarkable 95 percent owned homes. As David Roediger declares, "Immigrant[s] did not so much 'buy into' the American dream of home ownership as help create it."[20]

Chicago's immigrants and leaders both spurred suburbanization. "The tendency is to enlarge the city in all directions," announced an 1869 journalist. He predicted that Chicago would "swell" because "there is nothing in natural circumstances to prevent it from being coterminous with Cook County, or even the State of Illinois." A half-century later Chicago's leading housing reformer, Edith Abbott, echoed this idea: "In a prairie city . . . the distant horizon offered the only limits to city growth." Many others shared this assumption. "Chicago, for its size, is more given to suburbs than any other city in the world," a Chicago *Times* reporter bragged in 1873. "Few cities anywhere are so well adapted to the fostering of suburbs as this. There is no impediment to trains in any direction—except the lake, and that will be tunneled some day." Until the imagined tunnel under Lake Michigan, the enthusiastic journalist declared, "the enterprising real-estate dealer meets with some difficulty in disposing of water-lots [eastward under the lake], but westward there is unlimited space, bounded only by the swamps of the Calumet, the British provinces, and the imagination. Some day the Queen's dominions will be annexed, and then there will be absolutely no limit to Chicago enterprise." Chicago has not yet annexed Canada, despite these early ambitions, but its current metropolitan area does spread from Wisconsin to Indiana.[21]

The diverse and sudden city of Chicago grew at the same time that the idea of suburbs grew in America. Rapid developments in transportation allowed Chicagoans to imagine a fantastic vision for future commuters:

> Several sanguine minds are confident that in another decade a man somewhat in a hurry will be able to telegraph his corporosity to New York within a matter of a single hour, stoppages for wind included. When this plan is thoroughly a-going, the business man of Chicago can build his villa on the banks of the Mississippi, at the foot of the Rocky mountains, or among the pictured rocks of Lake Superior, and still attend to business as readily as does the man who now jogs down to Thirtieth street in a blundering one-horse car.[22]

Twenty-first-century airplane shuttle services, and even telecommuting, do not quite live up to these extravagant hopes, but the dream of a picturesque suburban retreat is still familiar, and the hope that this would be possible by 1883 is a reminder of just how rapidly so much was already changing in Chicago. Many Chicagoans were choosing to live in suburbs after the Civil War, and they expected to invent the technology that would allow them to do so.

They wanted this transportation technology partly because Chicago was shrouded in smoke between the Civil War and World War I. Coal pollution blackened clothing and buildings. After visiting Chicago in the 1890s, Rud-yard Kipling declared, "Its air is dirt." The lake was the color of café au lait, an Italian tourist added. "The sky is a stain," another visitor explained, and from this dark sky, pollution descended like "black snow . . . blanketing the prairie." Plants withered in urban gardens, smothered by smog. The Chicago River, pristine in 1840, had become undrinkable by 1870.[23]

The pollution from Chicago's factories was one spur to suburbanization, encouraging the separation of elite residential quarters from industrial business quarters, but the process of suburbanization was more compli-cated and more interesting, as the factories were also moving to suburbs. Assembly-line factories require horizontal space and often welcome the af-fordability of suburban land as well as the chance to avoid city building codes and city taxes. Workers followed the factories to the suburbs, while other middle-class suburbanites leapfrogged over the factories, so that the desire to be close to factories and the desire to be far from factories both led to Chicago's suburbanization.

The picturesque suburbs of the elite had such a complex relationship with the economical suburbs of the poorer that it can be difficult to sepa-rate the two. An evocative 1897 ad for Edgewater explains, "After business hours it's different; the city isn't quite the place to spend the remaining two-thirds of a man's life. A good many of Chicago's businessmen live in Edgewater." The ad claimed Edgewater had "the best roads, best scenery, best surroundings of any suburb of Chicago, and without the disagreeable features that cause the other 'home spots' to fall short of perfection." Those "disagreeable features" are a subtle acknowledgment of the diversity of Chicago's early suburbia; they included poor transportation links, limited municipal services, polluting industries, and poor people. Edgewater's ads insisted that, unlike other suburbs, Edgewater was a residential retreat for businessmen. One concluded, "For your children's sake: You can't afford to live in the city. You can't afford to live in any *less best* place than Edgewater." Edgewater marketed itself as a refuge for middle-class families who wanted to save money, producing a profit from their real estate investment while also reproducing high-class status for their children, even while retreating from the commerce of daytime business into a space that boasted it would be both elite and affordable. It seems a quintessential suburb.[24]

Yet in 1897, at the time of these advertisements, Edgewater was already part of the city of Chicago, having been annexed in 1889 in order to boost the census numbers for 1890. Edgewater's middle-class residences were neighbors to truck farms and the humble homes of immigrants. Within another decade Edgewater would include apartment houses, a reform school for wayward children, and a large hotel.[25] The idea of a middle-class pastoral retreat was one spur to the development of Edgewater, but it also grew by adding urban amenities, varied institutions, and inexpensive land for market gardens and other small businesses.

Like Edgewater, Chicago's other suburbs developed around large industries and small businesses, beer garden resorts, domestic-service enclaves, and inexpensive working-class housing as well as more elite residential areas and institutions such as summer resorts. Along with famous residential suburbs like Riverside and elite institutional suburbs like Evanston (developed around Northwestern University), Chicago had working-class residential suburbs like Robbins and Ford Heights, working-class industrial suburbs like Lake and Cicero, and working-class enclaves of domestic servants even in seemingly elite, seemingly residential spaces such as Riverside and Evanston.[26]

An observer of Chicago after the Civil War commented on the popularity and diversity of the city's suburbs:

> Along the lake, south of the river, for two or three miles, extend the beautiful avenues which change insensibly into those streets of cottages and gardens which have given to Chicago the name of the Garden City. . . . In all Chicago there is not one tenement house. Thrifty workmen own the houses they live in, and the rest can still hire a whole house; consequently seven tenths of Chicago consist of small wooden houses.[27]

It was a common boast that Chicago had no tenement houses because so many classes of people lived in single-family homes on the outskirts of the city. A real estate booster of 1874 bragged:

> Children of Chicago compare with those of eastern cities almost as health contrasts with disease . . . [because] in all Chicago there is not one regular "tenement house," nor will there ever be one. . . . Chicago workers are now flocking into the suburbs to live. The fact is thoroughly established that ninety-nine Chicago families in every hundred will go an hour's ride into the country, or toward the country, rather than live under or over another family, as the average New Yorker or Parisian does.[28]

Another real estate journalist bragged about the diversity of Chicago's sprawl: "In no other large city does so large a proportion of the laboring classes enjoy the luxury of a homestead. Instead of huddling in loathsome tenements, our poor, to a very large extent, live in their own houses."[29] On the edges of the ever-widening city, Chicago's blue-collar workers could live in detached houses.

By the early twentieth century Chicago's reformers began to note that their city's many single-family houses could be as uncomfortable as a multiple-family tenement. Progressives worried that Chicago's lack of tenements might weaken their calls for housing reform:

> Chicago has no tenement-house problem, if by that be understood a consider-able area where there are crowded upon every lot one or two high buildings, enclosing within their walls from six to thirty tenements. . . . But Chicago has a very serious housing problem. The statement that it has no tenement-house problem does not mean that its housing of the poorer classes is necessarily better than that of New York, London, or Boston. Chicago's problem is one of small wooden residences . . . dilapidated frame structures . . . cottages and two-storied houses. Many of these are little, unpainted tenements, rickety and awry from age and poor building.[30]

While admitting that Chicago had "no tenements" by New York standards, this reformer redefined tenements to include modest single-family housing. Similarly the reformer Edith Abbott defined tenements by class and race, not architecture. She noted that Chicago's legal definition of a tenement was any building housing more than three families, a definition that potentially included a "fashionable apartment." Anxious to find a def-inition that excluded rich apartment-dwellers but included all substandard housing, Abbott repeatedly insisted that "insanitary conditions are just as bad for the family living alone as for the family that occupies a flat," so a tenement, to her, was any building whose inhabitants were "people of small incomes . . . frequently immigrants and Negroes."[31] Abbott taught her stu-dents at the University of Chicago's School of Social Service that tenements exist wherever poor people and nonwhite people live. Of course, assuming that any dwelling place of poor or nonwhite people is a tenement slum is as inadequate as assuming that any single-family dwelling is a middle-class suburb. Actually Chicago's slums and suburbs overlapped.

"I think what makes the slums of Chicago more dreadful than any other is that they are so flimsy, so shallow, so open and so bleak," one visitor wrote in 1931. She was describing slums, but her description could be read as a portrait of suburbia. "I saw no crowded buildings. . . . Instead, there are thousands upon thousands of new, shabby, square wooden boxes, no more solid than packing cases, perched on the hard ground. They look as if the icy wind would blow them away, and round them, between them, are vacant lots, ragged patches of prairie littered with scrap-iron, stones, and gar-bage."[32] Remove the condescension and what remains is a view of single-family houses surrounded by yards, flimsy but nonetheless suburban.

These were areas on the fringes of Chicago, occasionally annexed into the city limits. Chicago's poorest residents lived in crowded urban apartments; the richest lived on the South Side near Michigan Avenue until the 1880s, and on the North Side near Lake Shore Drive after that, as well as in the most prestigious suburbs along the North Shore. The people in between lived in the many other suburbs and almost-suburbs. Chicago's fringes were filled with places in which diverse people struggled to own their homes.

WITH THE PROCESSIONS

Chicago's social realist novelists documented the complex forces of Chicago's suburbanization. In Theodore Dreiser's novel *Sister Carrie* (1900), Carrie Meeber's sister and brother-in-law live drably pinched lives partly because they are saving to build a house on two lots that they own "far out on the West Side," on Chicago's suburban fringe.[33] They are two of Chicago's many literary characters engaged in real estate investing, as they aspire to build a home in one of the working-class suburbs. Carrie herself takes a different trajectory. Despite a romantic drive with one of her lovers across an unbuilt suburb, her own social rise is a series of moves closer to the center of town. She moves into an apartment in a three-flat brownstone, then eventually to a hotel in New York City, seeking to avoid the dreary ordinariness of her brother-in-law's suburban dream.

Carrie's brother-in-law, if he ever succeeded in saving enough for his suburban lot, would have been joined by many other characters from Chicago's turn-of-the-century literature.[34] The question of whether to move to the suburbs is the central conflict of Henry Fuller's 1895 novel *With the Procession*. This story features the Marshalls, a wealthy family who consider themselves among the original settlers of Chicago, conveniently forgetting the French and Indians. Mr. Marshall is the successful owner of a dry goods store, and his son is a lawyer, but, like many other characters in Chicago literature, they both make most of their money through real estate investment. Despite the knowledge of urban expansion that must have been necessary to achieve their real estate profits, the Marshall family struggles to accept how much Chicago has changed in their lifetimes, both physically and socially.

"The Marshall house had been built at the time of the opening of the [Civil] War, and as 'far out' as seemed advisable for a residence of the better sort," Fuller writes, conscious that in the 1860s suburbanization was not yet fully fashionable.[35] The Marshall house is located in the 200 block of

Michigan Avenue, an area now in the heart of the city. In the decades after the Civil War,

> the day came when the church jumped from its old site three blocks away to a new site three miles away. And by that time most of their old neighbors and fellow church-members had gone too—some southward, some northward, some heavenward. Then business, in the guise of big hotels, began marching down the street upon them, and business in all manner of guise ran up towering walls behind them that shut off the summer sun hours before it was due to sink; and traffic rang incessant gongs at their back door, and drew lengthening lines of freight-cars across the lake view from their front one; and Sunday crowds strolled and sprawled over the wide green between the roadway and the water-way, and tramps and beggars and peddlers advanced daily in a steady and disconcerting phalanx, and bolts and bars and chains and gratings and eternal vigilance were all required to keep mine from becoming thine; until, in the year of grace 1893, the Marshalls had almost come to realize that they were living solitary and in a state of siege.[36]

Tall buildings, congested traffic, urban pollution, and class disparities all push the Marshalls out of town in a process that Fuller describes with the imagery of warfare. Marching phalanxes lay siege to the Marshalls. Sparks and soot constantly fly into their open windows, while urban pollution kills their prized cherry trees and currant bushes. "I believe things get dirtier every year," Mrs. Marshall observes. A passing train makes it impossible to hear her, and a passing tramp interrupts by knocking at the door. Strangers break in at night, beat the Marshalls' coachman, and wreck their carriage. Taxes increase, which the Marshalls blame on the city's struggles to deal with "an alien and rabble populace." A warehouse and a boardinghouse are built next door.[37]

In addition to these physical pressures, there is social pressure: the Marshalls' adolescent children are embarrassed by their "old and dismal," unfashionable house. "How much longer have we got to live down here among all these savages and hoodlums?" whines young Rosy, a debutante. Yet her older sister, Jane, attempts to convince the family to stay rooted:

> We have lived right here in this one house over thirty years. . . . We started in a good neighborhood, and we've always stayed here—the only one in all the town that has anything like an old-time flavor and atmosphere of its own—the only one where nice people have always lived, and do live yet. Isn't that better than a course of flats up one street and down another? Isn't that better than a grand chain through a lot of shingle-shangled cottages in the suburbs? I should say so.

What are they doing in the East now? They're going back to their old neighborhoods, and the people who haven't left them at all are the ones who are right on
top of the pile.

Both arguments are based on class and space: both sisters long to live with
"nice people," "on top of the pile," and away from "savages and hoodlums."
Yet it is unclear to the Marshalls where to find "nice people" and how to
understand their city's growth. Fuller carefully observes that there is no
nice gentrification of traditional neighborhoods, as Jane had hoped, but
there is also no nice suburb, as Rosy longed for.[38]

Their brother Truesdale dismisses his hometown after returning from a
European tour: "The great town, in fact, sprawled and coiled about him like
a hideous monster."[39] It is a monster that is not easy to understand, coiling
around itself in a confusing commercial diversity. Truesdale prefers to join
the leaders of Chicago society, who spend their summers at resorts in Wisconsin, shuttling between city and country, instead of living year-round in
a suburban compromise.

Another sister, Alice, has moved to Riverdale Park, a suburb whose name
echoes Chicago's actual suburb of Riverside. "Riverdale Park!" Jane scoffs.
"There isn't any river; there isn't any dale; there isn't any park." The houses
are flimsy, she reports, the trees are too new to have any leaves, and the
space is emptied of men every weekday, left with only babies and bored
women. Jane's scorn prefigures the twentieth-century critical dismissal of
cheaply built, overfeminized suburbs, except that Fuller also describes
"suburban grocers"—small farmers and wholesalers who supply the father's dry goods store—as well as suburban hotels and picnic grounds. This
is a diverse view of suburbia that does not fit into a linear procession out of
town.

Fuller constructs his story around two main processional scenes: there
is the procession of elites at a society ball, and then there is the more diverse procession of the confusing city, beginning with the novel's opening
scene of a mixed-class traffic jam in downtown Chicago. The effort to keep
up with both of these processions eventually kills David Marshall, the
family patriarch, who loses control of his business and his urban home.

In Fuller's story the social procession and geographic procession are in-
tricately linked. Knowledge of good neighborhoods, good architecture, and
good house decor all help keep the Marshall family within the procession of
Chicago's high society. To stay in this procession the debutante daughter,
Rosy, embraces what the University of Chicago sociologist Thorstein Ve-
blen would soon label "conspicuous consumption," while the philanthropist daughter, Jane, embraces conspicuous donations, erecting an urban

boardinghouse for working girls as well as a student dormitory at the University of Chicago—and eventually marrying an architect, underscoring the importance of buildings to this Chicago story. Jane encourages her family to participate in small acts of architectural charity for urban dwellers while also moving their own home three miles south to the edge of town.

The Marshall family does eventually join the centrifugal procession to the outskirts of town, to the neighborhood now known as the Prairie Avenue Historic District, at the edge of Chicago's old city limits, though within the new city limits after 1889. Prairie Avenue was known as Millionaire's Row in the 1880s, but—as Fuller's contemporary readers would have recognized—its popularity was already beginning to wane by 1895, as Chicago's most fashionable wealthy moved to the North Shore after the World's Fair. On the South Side, next to the Marshall's new villa, Fuller writes that there were commercial billboards and the "gaunt framework" of an elevated train line that had preceded them "among the stark weeds of last year that swayed and rustled on every vacant lot." This is far from a positive image. Like weeds, the financial and technological signs of a modern city grow up around the Marshalls no matter how far they flee. In the new house Mrs. Marshall feels "homesick, heartsick, as lost and forlorn as a ship-wrecked sailor on the chill coast of Kamchatka." The strain of building the new house and keeping up with his progeny eventually leads to Mr. Marshall's death in this drafty new space that does not feel like home to him. The final procession in *With the Procession* is a funeral procession.[40]

To a casual reader there may not seem to be much difference between *With the Procession* and the literature excoriating America's post–World War II suburbs, such as *The Crack in the Picture Window, Revolutionary Road,* and *The Man in the Gray Flannel Suit*.[41] Yet Fuller's novel shifts the beginning of suburbia back more than half a century, from 1945 to 1895, while also ascribing suburbanization to the upper class and not just the middle class. Fuller is aware of the industry that surrounds the elites in complex suburbs that are actually within the city limits. Most significantly, he takes a different tone than the more well-known post-1945 stories of suburbanization. Instead of scorn for characters who mistakenly strive for suburban homes, Fuller writes with a spirit of lamentation for characters who are unable to resist the forces that push them to the suburbs.

In the very different *Studs Lonigan* trilogy, James T. Farrell portrays a blue-collar Irish Catholic family who begin their story a few miles south of Chicago's center, close to where the Marshalls ended up. Comparing these two stories helps emphasize that working-class immigrants like the Lonigans participated in Chicago's suburban growth along with wealthy "natives" like the Marshalls. Farrell's trilogy is a coming-of-age story about a macho Irish boy, written three decades after Fuller's story of the upper-class Marshalls, yet these two different novels share a narrative of reluctant suburbanization.

Farrell's story begins in 1916 with the reflections of Studs's father, the elderly Mr. Lonigan, a house painter who owns his own three-story apartment building near Wabash and Fifty-eighth Street, on the South Side of Chicago. He thinks to himself, "Things just change. Chicago was nothing like it used to be, when over around St. Ignatius Church and back of the yards were white men's neighborhoods, and Prairie Avenue was a tony street where all the swells lived, like Fields [and the fictional Marshalls]; and the niggers and whores had not roosted around Twenty-second street, and Fifty-eighth street was nothing but a wilderness." This was a "wilderness" where Mr. Lonigan had taken his wife-to-be on a ride in a rented carriage during their courtship. Echoing the Marshalls' concern with living in a "nice" neighborhood, Mr. Lonigan reflects, "When he'd bought this building, Wabash Avenue had been a nice, decent, respectable street for a self-respecting man to live with his family. But now, well, the niggers and kikes were getting in, and they were dirty. . . . And when they got into a neighborhood property values went blooey. He'd sell and get out." Despite this resolution, he delays his family's move. Neighbors and his own daughters periodically remind him that the neighborhood is losing respectability, but he still lingers. The priest builds a new church in 1926, yet this elaborate edifice fails to halt the Irish Catholic exodus from the parish. In 1927, more than ten years and four hundred pages after the elder Mr. Lonigan's opening resolution to move, the family finally sells their building to an African American and relocates to the far suburbs.[42]

The move leaves them heartbroken, disconnected from their friends and familiar places. Blacks "will never get out where we are going," the Lonigans hope, yet they also remember that Fifty-eighth Street once seemed far out. It is nearly one hundred pages before readers glimpse the Lonigans' new suburban home. Before that, readers see Studs riding on trains, going downtown, and twice wandering wistfully among the new black residents of his old neighborhood, imagining he hears the voices of friends.[43] The loneliness of suburbanization, combined with Studs's alcoholism, machismo, and pool room street gang culture, lead to his death from pneumonia at age thirty.

The Lonigans are unlike the Marshalls in class, ethnicity, and even generation, but both novels are about social position as it is reinforced by geographic position. Both novels also include a startling specificity of street addresses. Studs never goes for a walk down any old street: he walks down Fifty-fourth Street near Cottage Grove Avenue and then under the el station at Fifty-fifth. Real estate possessions identify characters at least as much as clothing, physiognomy, or job titles, so that many of Chicago's social realist novels abound with addresses. It is possible to organize walking tours of the novels of Henry Fuller, James Farrell, Nelson Algren, Theodore Dreiser, Frank Norris, and Richard Wright, not only because many of these novelists were inspired by literary realism combined with the ethnographic methods of the Chicago School sociologists but also because these novelists recognized that they lived in a city obsessed with real estate, a city whose central product was still its own dirt.[44]

Critics have debated whether Studs Lonigan is a working-class juvenile delinquent or a middle-class child of homeowners. He is both. Farrell allows another character to call Studs and his friends "ragamuffins from the slums," while Farrell also deliberately shows that the parents of these ragamuffins own their own homes on the fringes of the city. Farrell described his own characters as "well-to-do working class." He understood that a range of classes owned homes on Chicago's fringes and his story reflects that, in Chicago, suburban homeownership did not necessarily mean middle-class domesticity.[45]

In both Fuller's 1895 *With the Procession* and Farrell's 1932–35 *Studs Lonigan,* the plot pivots on whether the main characters will move to the suburbs. They do move—pushed by industries, pulled by snobbery and racism—yet they do so reluctantly, highlighting how difficult it could be to resist suburbanization, both for the elite and the working class. The Marshalls and the Lonigans are profoundly reluctant to suburbanize, so much so that in each of these stories, suburbanization leads to a protagonist's death. Both these novels were written at a time when suburbanization was not yet perceived to be the dream of almost all Americans. Both have a tone of lamentation about suburbanization, while identifying the multiple forces—beyond individual choice—that propelled Chicago's suburbanization. Real estate speculators promoting land, booster businessmen in government, factory owners' decisions about where to locate their industries, elite pressures for homeownership, and workers' own desires for homes that could be used as small businesses and as investments they could control were all part of Chicago's early growth machine.

CHAPTER 2

✧

"Domestic and Respectable"

Property-Owner Politics after
the Great Chicago Fire

Chicago's Great Fire of 1871 left 100,000 people homeless. At first, city authorities erected barracks for emergency shelter, but within a week they changed their tactics, "the barrack style of life proving unhealthy, both morally and physically."[1] Chicago's elite philanthropists decided that barracks posed not only a physical threat of disease but also a moral threat to economic industry, political stability, and sexual propriety. They believed that in the apartment-like barracks "so large a number, brought into promiscuous and involuntary association, would almost certainly engender disease and promote idleness, disorder, and vice." Chicago's Relief and Aid Society was especially worried about "mechanics and the better class of laboring people, thrifty, domestic, and respectable," who had owned their houses before the fire and for whom they believed only single-family houses could restore "hope, renewed energy and comparative prosperity."[2] At stake, according to the Relief Society, were the values of Chicago's lower middle class and, with these, the prosperity of the whole city.

Winter was approaching, lumber was scarce, fire had just destroyed the center of the city, one-third of Chicago's population was homeless, and the Relief and Aid Society chose to tear down most of the barracks and replace them with single-family homes. Chicagoans had been burned out of apartments, boardinghouses, brothels, and hotels, but for the safety of their city, the Chicago Relief and Aid Society decided to build suburban-style cottages. Over the exceptionally cold winter of 1871–72, the Relief

Society built 8,033 of these cottages on the outskirts of Chicago, while businessmen erected a new downtown commercial district.[3] It was a remarkable feat of organization, buttressed by leaders' surprisingly open discussion of suburban housing as a tactic of social control. Instead of demonstrating responsible domesticity, though, Chicago's working-class homeowners actually engaged in fierce political activism months after the Great Fire. Their determination to protect their investments in homes threatened the interests of Chicago's elites and revealed the potential radicalism of property-owner politics.

Chicagoans engaged in conversations as they decided how to rebuild after the fire. These were both elite conversations encouraging suburban homeownership as well as some workers' own desires for a different homeownership closer to the city center. Chicago's leaders did not actually use the word *suburban* to describe their goals after the fire; instead they wrote about "isolated houses."[4] Isolating one family from another, isolating the flammable wooden buildings of the lower class from the brick and marble of the upper class, isolating many residential areas from Chicago's commercial center: these isolated houses were suburban houses, created in the context of Victorian industrialization, immigration, and suburbanization, as well as some immigrant homeowners' vehement resistance to that suburbanization.

"BARRIERS BURNED AWAY"

It had been exceptionally dry in Chicago in 1871, with no rain since early July and daily fire alarms throughout early October, exhausting the city's small department of firefighters. Chicagoans agreed that the "proximate causes" of the Great Fire included this hot, dry weather, the overextended fire department, and the swirling, hurricane-like winds on the night of October 8, but they naturally sought to identify an immediate cause. Their theories about the origins of the fire exposed fears about Chicago and other Victorian-era booming cities. Chicago had grown more rapidly than almost any other nineteenth-century American city, and such speed frightened many people.[5]

The fire story most widely circulated, then and now, is that an Irish immigrant named Catherine O'Leary was milking her cow at 9:30 p.m. in a barn on DeKoven Street, southwest of what would later be called the downtown Loop, when the cow kicked over a kerosene lamp and started a fire. The first official alarm was rung from DeKoven Street, but the O'Leary barn was still standing after the next three days of flames. The popular story of Mrs. O'Leary's cow seems to offer an obvious moral: Beware of poor foreign women who pursue rural professions in urban settings. Contemporary Chicago journalists drew a slightly different moral: "If the woman who was milking the cow had not been late with her milking, the lamp would not have been needed. If she had plied the dugs of the animals with proper skill, the lamp would not have been kicked at all. . . . The blame of setting the fire rests on the woman who milked, or else on the man who allowed her to milk."[6] This was a moral about engaging in punctual and gender-appropriate behavior.

Neighbors swore that the O'Leary family had been in bed an hour before the fire began. Some reported a suspicious man lurking near the barn when the fire started, and soon the *Chicago Times* printed "A Startling Story," purporting to be the confession of a Parisian communard revealing his secret organization's "diabolical plot for the destruction of the city."[7] Frustrated after months of "fruitless attempts to stir up strife between the mechanics of the city and their employers," the communard claimed he had burned Chicago "to humble the men who had waxed rich at the expense of the poor." Other newspapers reprinted this story "without the expression of any opinion as to its authenticity," but they did print it. "That many of our prominent citizens believe in the genuineness of these revolutions, is demonstrated in daily conversation; and it is by no means impossible that they are founded on truth," one journalist mused.[8] Perhaps he meant to write *revelations*, but perhaps he was genuinely worried by the Paris Commune of 1871 and other revolutions then stirring in Europe, at a time when no one could forget that European immigrants made up a majority of Chicago's population.

Chicago in 1871 was a world in which people could believe that a vengeful French radical or a careless Irish woman had destroyed an entire American city. In the words of a popular song of the time, "A cow could kick over Chicago."[9] Chicagoans felt unstable in 1871, torn by growing divisions of class and ethnicity. The potential for strife between mechanics and their employers that was visible in the rumor about the communard, the dangers from insufficiently bourgeois immigrants like Mrs. O'Leary, the risks from placing wooden structures like the O'Learys' house and barn too close to marble mansions: all these tensions might be alleviated, Chicago elites hoped, with suburbanization.

Nineteenth-century cities had been developing increasing spatial segregation between classes and genders, a spatial segregation that the fire disrupted.[10] Part of the horror of the fire was the resultant crowd of people without places, a crowd wherein classes had become less recognizable, without the familiar status markers of fashion and architecture. Consider

Reverend E. P. Roe's account of the LaSalle Street tunnel under the Chicago River on the night of the fire:

> There jostled the refined and delicate lady, who, in the awful democracy of the hour, brushed against thief and harlot. . . . Parents cried for their children, women shrieked for their husbands, some praying, many cursing with oaths as hot as the flames that crackled near. Multitudes were in no other costumes than those in which they had sprung from their beds. Altogether it was a strange, incongruous, writhing mass of humanity, such as the world had never looked upon, pouring into what might seem, in its horrors, the mouth of hell.[11]

Roe's popular novel about the fire was titled simply *Barriers Burned Away*. Prostitutes no longer confined by brothels, millionaires no longer sheltered in their mansions, immigrants no longer contained by slum districts, all joined the mixed-class, mixed-gender, multiethnic throng fleeing the fire.

Witnesses described white people blackened by smoke. Even without soot, lack of shelter threatened people's whiteness, as they wandered "as homeless as, and much more haggard than, the Gypsies or the Arabs." While noting these racial slippages, accounts of the fire dwell most often on violations of class and gender norms. "Men of iron were completely

PANIC STRICKEN CITIZENS CARRYING THE AGED, SICK AND HELPLESS AND ENDEAVORING TO SAVE FAMILY TREASURES.

During the fire, crowds of different genders, classes, and ages filled the streets. Emphasizing lost domesticity, Frank Luzerne titled this engraving "Panick Stricken Citizens Carrying the Aged, Sick and Helpless and Endeavoring to Save Family Treasures." From Frank Luzerne, *The Lost City! Drama of the Fire-Fiend, or, Chicago, as It Was and as It Is!* (New York: Wells, 1872), 97. Reproduction courtesy of the University of Chicago Library Preservation Department.

unmanned," according to the *Chicago Times*. And women were shockingly unfeminine: "half-clad" or "dressed in the apparel of the opposite sex," carrying an assortment of heavy items with masculine strength. Even more often than cross-dressing women, chroniclers of the fire reported women in shock, giving birth out of doors and alone to babies who quickly died of exposure. They disagreed on the number—somewhere between 150 and 500 babies were rumored to have been born in Chicago that night—but agreed that women and newborn children were suffering without shelter.[12]

There was real cause for terror. Sparks fell from the sky like red rain, swirled by the gusting, hurricane-force winds. Piles of metal spoons fused together from the heat of the fire, financial records and property deeds burned away, and nearly the entire city center and North Side turned to rubble, "one vast blackened smouldering plain of desolation."[13] One hundred thousand people, suddenly homeless, spent the night standing in the lake water or shivering together on the prairie. This would have been traumatic to anyone at any time, but Chicago's Victorians were particularly disturbed by the loss of spatial signs of social divisions. One man reported spending the night of the fire following his sister-in-law as she ran out of her unburned house into the crowd, losing her children and jewelry in the confusion, until he finally "hauled her, shrieking with hysterics, in a baker's wagon, some four miles, over much debris, to the home where she ought to have stayed in the first place."[14] Homes were the place to properly maintain gender, class, and racial norms—norms already threatened by industrialization, immigration, and sudden urbanization in Chicago in 1871.

Just three hundred people died in the fire, according to official reports, while 17,450 buildings burned. "That first night after the fire—that fearful Monday night of the 9th of October in Chicago—was as complete a picture of social, moral, and municipal chaos as the wildest imagination can conceive. . . . Men were like ships which had lost their anchors,—adrift in mid-ocean, without chart, compass, or destination." Homes were the anchors that had been lost, leaving people adrift in social chaos. "Like thistle-down ten thousand homes went drifting through the air / And dumb Dismay walked hand in hand with frozen-eyed Despair." Chroniclers of the fire reached for multiple images: it was Babel, Bedlam, Sodom, Pompeii; it was, perhaps, the end of the world.[15]

On the night of the fire, "away sped the crowd, afar off to the bleak prairie, to the lake shore, to parks, cemeteries, anywhere remote from combustible material."[16] The places that people fled for safety were picturesque parks and suburban enclaves. The *Chicago Times* predicted, "There will be a very general demand for property in the numerous suburban villages that surround Chicago. . . . This demand will be the natural result of the recent fire, which has shown the danger of building frame dwellings too close together."[17]

This suburban impulse intertwined with the Victorian ideology of domesticity. To many survivors, the loss of homes meant the loss of objects that had helped them adjust to the dislocations of the nineteenth-century American West:

> We had a nice little cottage . . . with a little yard in front, where I had planted the rose tree mother gave me from our dear old home. Mother is dead now, and the homestead sold. . . . The honeysuckle over the door came from a far-away sister's grave at the East. The mementoes on the mantel, the pictures of those gone before, the playthings of some little ones who are lying still and peaceful in Rose Hill, the golden locks cut from their curly heads, and the little clothing that they wore—where is it all? What a horrible dream! We didn't save anything.[18]

Such sentimentality is familiar to any reader of nineteenth-century fiction. It is also often suburban. This woman missed her decorated cottage and picturesque yard; she missed the horticulture that suburban architect Andrew Jackson Downing had called "a labor of love offered up on the domestic altar."[19] She had used her suburban cottage to feel connected to loved ones despite the disruptions of commercialization and the increased mortality that may have resulted from urbanization and industrialization. She had used her suburban cottage to ease herself through the dislocations of the 1870s.

She was not the only one to rely on real estate. The first Chicago business to reopen after the fire was the shop of Chicago realtor William D. Kerfoot, who stood in a quickly built shanty under a sign declaring, "All gone but wife & children & ENERGY!"[20] Energized by domesticity, Kerfoot encouraged others to be similarly energized and to buy homes from him. The image of his real estate shop in the ashes was one of the most widely circulated images after the fire; for Chicagoans, it was an image of hope. Another popular woodcut showed a couple getting married in the ruins. These images insisted that the nuclear family and the real estate associated with it would continue in Chicago. Such sentimental domesticity was institutionalized through the Chicago Relief and Aid Society.

THE BUSINESS OF CHARITY

"More remarkable than the fire itself are the events that have followed it," several Chicago journalists agreed. While the embers still smoldered, Chicagoans were so confident about rebuilding that they repeated jokes about

KERFOOT'S BLOCK AFTER THE FIRE.

Realtor William D. Kerfoot built one of the first of many "shanties" to spring up after the Great Chicago Fire: a one-room wooden structure that probably served as both home and business. Kerfoot advertised his real estate business as "first in the burnt district," announcing that he and his customers were motivated by domesticity: "All gone but wife and children and ENERGY!" From Frank Luzerne, *The Lost City! Drama of the Fire-Fiend, or, Chicago, as It Was and as It Is!* (New York: Wells, 1872), 229. Reproduction courtesy of the University of Chicago Library Preservation Department.

it: "The editor of the New York *Commercial* says he read it just 47 times in 48 hours that 'Chicago will arise like a phoenix from the ashes.'" Chicago could rise like a phoenix because, although homes had burned, commercial networks of credit remained. As *Harper's Magazine* explained, "The telegraph has made us all of one nerve. . . . While Chicago burns New York trembles." Because of the unburned infrastructure of communication, transportation, and banking, copious philanthropy flowed to Chicago from friends and creditors. Boston, Berlin, Cincinnati, Dublin, Milwaukee, New York, Philadelphia, and St. Louis together sent millions of dollars for Chicago's relief.[21]

At first this relief was distributed by a Citizens' Committee formed of recently elected immigrant politicians as well as businessmen representing each ward of Chicago. They distributed water and food while providing shelter in churches, schools, and barracks. Their "relief was necessarily conducted without system, and relief was given to all who asked."[22] This was a problem, Chicago's native-born elites worried, because "indiscriminate" charity might create a permanently dependent underclass. On October 12, four days after the fire began, Chicago's mayor took responsibility for relief disbursement away from the city's aldermen, transferring the $5 million relief funds from public control to a private philanthropic society headed by leading Chicago gentlemen. Instead of immigrant politicians, only native-born elites would guide the distribution of Chicago relief.[23]

The gentlemen philanthropists of Chicago's Relief and Aid Society— including the millionaires George Pullman and Marshall Field—believed in what they called scientific charity. Using a board of directors modeled on boards of businesses, they divided the charity work into bureaus and the city into districts, creating an extensive bureaucracy of superintendents, sub-superintendents, clerks, and inspectors and held weekly staff meetings to manage this endeavor. Scientific charity meant carefully examining each request for charity, using bureaucratic forms that eventually cost Chicago's Relief Society $22,000 to print. They believed that those who asked for charity might be dangerously prone to dependency, while they imagined the ideal charity recipient as a poor but respectable widow, too proud to ask for a handout. They saw their task as "perform[ing] the double service of guarding against imposition and hunting out deserving cases who were too sensitive to apply in person."[24]

The paradoxes are fascinating: while discouraging anyone who asked for aid, the philanthropists of Chicago's Relief and Aid Society also encouraged people who had not requested aid to take it, and while practicing an explicitly masculinized, supposedly unsentimental form of charity, the Relief Society also strove to reestablish the domestic sphere, implicitly acknowledging the

public, political nature of private homes. They paid female inspectors to examine others' homes, thus turning sentimental domesticity into waged
work. Some Chicagoans complained about the excessive bureaucracy of relief
administration, but many journalists agreed with the committee's goals.[25]

The committee on shelter especially "illustrate[d] the intelligence, energy, business-like economy, and prompt dispatch" of the Relief and Aid
Society, observers enthused.[26] To any family who already owned a plot of
land, the relief committee gave one bed frame for the whole family, one
mattress, stove, table, and cooking pot, one half-ton of coal, and all the
lumber necessary to build a house. They gave this outright to widows,
while they asked for $125, a remarkable bargain even in 1871, from those
who they believed could afford to pay. They rejected about one-third of the
housing applications they received, "of course," the *Chicago Times* explained, "as the vouchers of endorsement will not always hold water, and
again many others are unable to furnish satisfactory proof of their being in
any way worthy objects for help in this direction."[27] Those who deserved
the most generosity, the Relief Society believed, were people of good character who already owned a house lot.

To those deemed worthy, the Relief Society provided lumber for one of
two basic houses: a twelve-by-fifteen-foot one-room house for families
of three or fewer, or a sixteen-by-twenty-foot two-room house for families
of four or more. These were small but not unusually small houses. Andrew
Jackson Downing's most basic design for a suburban cottage was a two-
room building, eighteen by twenty-six feet, with only a few closets and a
slightly overhanging roof to distinguish it from the plain plan of the Relief
Society.[28] The Relief Society cottage was stark, but it was not much different from the lowest level of suburbia in America then.

Chicago's Relief and Aid Society also distributed food and water, especially in the weeks immediately following the fire. Initially they gave free
rail passes to people wishing to leave the devastated city, explaining, "We
hope to reduce the houseless and idle population," equating lack of property with a lack of work ethic. Later the Relief Society also furnished tools,
including sewing machines for seamstresses and hammers for carpenters,
to help Chicagoans resume their professions. They endowed hospitals and
a home for orphans with $354,000, while keeping about $1 million to fund
their own charitable institution for the next fourteen years, despite public
agitation, especially during the depression of 1874, when Chicago politicians complained that the money had been donated to assist individual
Chicagoans, not to support the bureaucrats of the Relief Society. The Relief
Society believed they were doing Chicagoans a favor by withholding money,
withholding the chance to become dependent on welfare.[29]

The funds they did distribute were focused on housing. The Committee on Shelter spent $925,668.50 on basic wooden cottages, while the Department of General Relief spent another $557,980.85 on furniture, stoves, and beddings, so that one-third of all funds dispersed went to housing.[30] It was their largest expenditure because the Relief Society believed that single-family homes on the outskirts of Chicago would contribute best to the city's recovery.

When the earlier Citizens' Committee erected barracks, the *Chicago Tribune* had advised bringing in an army quartermaster to oversee more barracks construction, and even the first general plan of the Relief Society had assumed that barracks would be built, titling its housing committee the Committee on Shelter, with a mandate "to provide tents and barracks."[31] Then, a week after the fire, the gentlemen leaders of the Relief Society announced they would replace most of the barracks with tents, where "families can be more isolated, each occupying its own house, thus avoiding in a great measure the very bad feature of herding together."[32] They declared that these single-family tents would lead to more permanent, isolated single-family homes. It is worth quoting at length from the Relief Society's *First Special Report* of November 1871, in which the philanthropists explained their enormous emphasis on shelter:

> Some rude barracks were, at the outset, put up by the Citizen's Committee which could only answer for immediate protection from the weather, but such structures, even if well built, were open to grave objections as the homes of forty or fifty thousand people in the winter. So large a number, brought into promiscuous and involuntary association, would almost certainly engender disease and promote idleness, disorder and vice, and be dangerous to the neighborhood in which they might be placed. Such buildings could only be put up by sufferance upon land to which the occupants could obtain no title, could have no interest in improving, and from which they would undoubtedly be removed in the spring, if not sooner, by the actual owners. To construct barracks for the houseless, therefore, was only to postpone the solution of the problem for a few months, to find us then with a large class of permanent poor still without homes and demoralized by a winter of dependence and evil communications. A small number, under stringent police and sanitary rule, might be kept in health and comfort and order in the barracks, but the system would be manifestly a bad one for so large a number of people, and particularly for the class who made much the larger proportion of those who were sufferers by the fire. These were mechanics and the better class of laboring people, thrifty, domestic and respectable, whose skill and labor are indispensable in rebuilding the city, and most of whom had accumulated enough to become the owners of their own homesteads either as

proprietors or leasees of the lots. To restore them to these homes would be to raise them at once from depression and anxiety, if not despair, to hope, renewed energy and comparative prosperity. With all the incentives to industry left them, and with the conscious pride and independence of still living under their own roof-tree, they would thus settle for themselves, and in the best way, the question of title to land, and restore value to their real estate.[33]

Since property titles had burned, there was understandable concern over issues of land ownership. Abstracts listing exchanges of property titles had survived in Springfield, and though searching these chronologically arranged records was tedious, by July 1872 the question of landownership had been settled in a more orderly manner than this early Relief Society report feared.

The question of class proved more thorny. Barracks should be reserved for "the class who have not hitherto lived in houses of their own, but in rooms in tenement houses," the Relief Society explained. "As a rule, none but permanent paupers will stay in the barracks," the *Chicago Times* reported. The Relief Society believed this pauper class of former renters was only 5 percent of the fire sufferers, eventually sheltered in four barracks, where, the philanthropists explained patronizingly, "under the constant supervision of medical and police superintendents, their moral and sanitary condition is unquestionably better than that which has heretofore obtained in that class." This supervision included compulsory smallpox vaccinations for all barracks "inmates," despite the dangerous side effects of vaccinations then. But the pauper class was not the class the Relief Society wanted to serve. In January 1872 the Society reported to Chicago's aldermen, "In regard to the Barracks, we are glad to be able to say they have begun to disappear."[34]

Another class, 40 percent of the sufferers, the Relief Society recognized as the "mechanics and the better class of laboring people, thrifty, domestic, and respectable." For this middle group of former home-owners, the Relief Society gave lumber to build isolated, single-family houses. In the Society's view, 5 percent of Chicagoans needed barracks and supervision, while 40 percent merited basic houses and respect, and the remaining 55 percent were either too immoral or too wealthy for charity. Single people disappeared from the Relief Society's view, but what remains is a remarkable record of elites' hopes for class formation. Analyzing census data from 1870, historian Robin Einhorn has found that property-less Chicagoans were not 5 percent of adult males, as the Relief Society asserted, but actually 78 percent. Labor historian Karen Sawislak has described a two-tiered class system during the Great Chicago Fire, divided between workers and capitalists, albeit complicated by overlapping categories of ethnicity and gendered respectability. Chicago's Relief and Aid Society hoped that encouraging respectable, home-owning mechanics would further blur the class lines between workers and employers by creating an almost impossibly wide middle class. "Respectable" meant middle class, then as now, while "mechanic" meant manual laborer, especially one with basic skills. Being "domestic . . . owners of their own homesteads" was what made these blue-collar mechanics respectable to the leaders of the Relief Society.[35]

It was more than blurred class lines that the Relief Society hoped to accomplish with its isolated houses. The Society had worried about the "dependence and evil communications" of a winter in the barracks. They worried that "promiscuous and involuntary association, would almost certainly engender disease and promote idleness, disorder, and vice." In the nineteenth century, *promiscuous* meant being crowded together indiscriminately. Promiscuity posed a physical risk of disease due to overcrowding, while also posing a moral risk as urban residents mingled without small-town systems of supervision. City hotels, boardinghouses, and apartments—like Chicago's post-fire barracks—were perceived as "insidious, family-wrecking" spaces. If busybodies could not tell who was entering a home, it was assumed, the members of that home might be tempted to commit adultery. If nonrelated adults lived in close proximity, especially in lower-class homes, they might also be tempted to adultery. Servants and visitors in upper-class homes were exempt from this logic, although live-in female servants, who were vulnerable to sexual harassment from their employers, had more frequent pregnancies than any other unmarried women at the end of the nineteenth century. Families living alone in isolated houses also had the most incidents of domestic abuse and incest. Perhaps unaware of those statistics, moralists did not worry about servants in elite homes or isolated families in respectable homes. Instead there was widespread concern for "women adrift" from nuclear families.[36]

Some of those drifters found housing within the homes of poorer families who took in lodgers to supplement their incomes. At least 20 percent of turn-of-the-century households took in lodgers. Housing reformers worried that this "lodger evil . . . prevails chiefly among the foreign elements of the population. . . . It frequently leads to the breaking up of homes and families, to the downfall and subsequent degraded career of young women, to grave immoralities—in a word, to the profanation of the home."[37] In other words, taking in lodgers might lead to extramarital sex. "What are the chances for morality when members of more than one family, or even of a single family with grown up children live in one or two rooms?" asked one Chicago reformer, who worried that girls' "natural safeguard of modesty and reserve has been broken down by the overcrowding of tenement house life." Even without lodgers, working-class housing included dark hallways, dark stairways, and shared bathrooms, which "furnish most plausible excuses for personal familiarities of the worst kind between the sexes." Young women's "virtue is in peril, if it has not already been lost."[38]

Moralists also worried about "Parisian flats," what we now call apartments. The very term *Parisian* had subtle sexual connotations. Living in a Parisian flat "saps self-respect, weakens the resistance to temptation, aggravates the evil passions, and breeds the habit of unmanly and unwomanly conduct," the *New York Times* declared in 1894.[39] Edith Wharton illuminates this idea in her novel *The Age of Innocence*, when she describes an 1870s New York City apartment where the bedroom could be glimpsed from the sitting room: "Her visitors were startled and fascinated by the foreignness of this arrangement which recalled scenes in French fiction . . . and architectural incentives to immorality such as the simple Americans never dreamed of. That was how women with lovers lived in wicked old societies, in apartments with all the rooms on one floor, and all the indecent propinquities that their novels described."[40] If visitors could see the bed, it was feared that they might be unable to resist leaping into it.

Given these widespread ideas about the sexual temptations of the built environment, Chicago's relief barracks were shocking to the city's elites. The relief cottages were also only one story and only two rooms, but they were isolated from other families, unlike the relief barracks, which were full of multiple families. The cottages offered the possibility of later respectable architectural expansion, as suburban architect Andrew Jackson Downing had explained: "The American cottager is no peasant, but thinks, and thinks correctly, that as soon as he can afford it, he deserves a parlor, where he can receive his guests with propriety."[41] Downing, like Wharton's characters and Chicago's reformers, believed that the built environment could invite propriety with a parlor, or it could invite impropriety with a bedroom visible to guests, a bathroom shared with other families, a dark hallway, or the presence of lodgers. Chicago's Relief and Aid Society went to great expense to build isolated single-family houses that would have architectural incentives to morality.

The Relief Society worried not only about propriety but also about disease. Physical illness could easily spread in congested neighborhoods, and reformers worried that crime, intemperance, political radicalism, vice, and poverty itself might also be potentially contagious. The germ theory of disease was still new in the late nineteenth century, alarming people with the idea of invisible infectious agents. Whether they believed in the new theory or older notions of miasmic vapors or a version of Spencerian

Darwinism that emphasized environmental influences on personalities, many Americans agreed that light and air were necessary sanitary agents.

"Tight sleeping-rooms and close, air-tight stoves are now poisoning more than half of this nation," Catherine Beecher wrote in her popular 1869 textbook of household hints. She recommended sleeping with open windows because she believed oxygen aided brain development. A generation later Chicago's housing reformers demonstrated the same priorities by counting windows and measuring ceiling heights in order to calculate the cubic feet of air space per sleeper in the bedrooms of the poor. They went door to door in tenement districts, attempting to note how far from a window it was possible to read a book around noon on an ordinarily sunny day, in a valiant attempt to scientifically measure what they called "the dark room evil." They did so because they believed that lack of light and air would lead to disease and perhaps poverty. As a Chicago businessman declared in 1891, "To shut off the sunbeams from the earth is to encourage the bacteria, to breed fevers, to sap vitality, to make men and women pale cellar plants."[42]

Extending this discussion of health, America's leading housing reformer, Lawrence Veiller, wrote in 1910, "We know now that poverty too is a germ disease, contagious even at times; that it thrives amid the same conditions as those under which the germs of tuberculosis flourish—in darkness, filth and sordid surroundings." Adopting this germ metaphor, one Chicago housing reformer lamented that, in poor neighborhoods, "the child lives constantly in a morally contaminated atmosphere, breathing the very germs of delinquency." Another Chicago housing reformer declared, "The state is losing annually thousands of lives through crime, drunkenness, and disease directly traceable to bad housing. Discontent, the germ of which lies in the home, is recognized by modern penologists as the underlying cause of much wrong-doing." Reformers believed houses might contain germs of crime, alcoholism, poverty, and general unhappiness, as well as germs of disease. They hoped to eliminate both poverty and disease by eliminating congested urban housing.[43]

After the Great Fire, Chicago's Relief and Aid Society worried that epidemics might spread easily in the barracks. "Isolated homes were promptly furnished by the Shelter Committee for such families as in the judgment of the medical officers were most exposed to disease from over-crowding."[44] Other housing reformers agreed, in a remarkably pervasive and long-lasting discourse. "The isolated home is the true home," a minister had written in 1855. Reiterating similar ideas in different language, a social worker explained in 1919, "The American standard in housing [is] the single-family detached house surrounded by a yard." Another reformer added, "The ideal city is, of course, one in which every family should own and occupy a separate house." The ideal city looked like a suburb. When it didn't, as in late nineteenth-century New York and, increasingly, Chicago, "every effort should be made to encourage people to leave the crowded quarters of the large cities and return to country or suburban life." In 1872 the Chicago Relief and Aid Society made this effort by erecting 8,033 suburban cottages. Not all of these housing reformers were Chicagoan, but they all shared similar views in a common intellectual conversation, reading the same books, attending the same conferences, and reaching many similar conclusions about housing. All these reformers imagined homes that were geographically isolated but politically central.[45]

"Whether we approach the subject from the point of view of health, morals, family life, child welfare, juvenile delinquency, industrial efficiency, or Americanization, the housing problem is fundamental," housing reformers asserted.[46] "When a man has to live year in and year out on a dirty, narrow apology for a street in a row of . . . tenements begrimed with smoke and soot, divided into little boxes of rooms into which his family must be huddled . . . he is not apt to look on the bright side of life."[47] Instead he might go to a saloon to drink alcohol, brood with other workmen, or plan a strike.

Chicago's Relief and Aid Society declared that they gave away 8,033 cottages in order to provide "incentives to industry [and] the conscious pride and independence of still living under their own roof-tree . . . to raise them at once from depression and anxiety, if not despair, to hope, renewed energy, and comparative prosperity."[48] They believed a domestic refuge in an isolated house would inspire "the better class of laborers" to work at rebuilding Chicago. With Relief Society lumber,

a handy man [can] build in ten days a comfortable dwelling which thousands of Illinois pioneers forty years ago would have coveted. He will thus obtain a new home for his family; a home which he can call his own; a home which comfort, cheerfulness, and contentment can then make glad with blessings and from which he can go forth with a heart full of hope to battle against the world, to assist in rebuilding Chicago.[49]

This home was built by men, maintained by women, planned for families only, and meant to serve as a refuge from work in order to energize men to go forth into the nineteenth-century workplace.

The Relief Society's vision was a falsely nostalgic one, with its reference to pioneers. Chicagoans may have already forgotten that most of Illinois's pioneers had lived in a fort before the 1830s. In the 1840s, according to early settlers as well as city directories, "half of [Chicago's residents] boarded in the taverns and boardinghouses, and the other half were crowded into small dwellings in rooms over the stores."[50] Some of Chicago pioneers' sixteen-by-twenty-foot wooden homes did outwardly resemble relief society cottages, but they housed unrelated residents and commercial businesses in a way that mixed uses and classes. Still, by 1871 Chicagoans, along with other Americans, believed in the false nostalgia of the cult of domesticity.[51]

The Relief Society expected their cottages to provide "incentives to industry" not only because of women's unwaged domestic work in the cult of domesticity but also because of the waged work spurred by homeownership. As historian Lendol Calder argues, any single-family home "calls for the satisfaction of a thousand wants," from furniture to household tools. Buying a house leads to the need for ever more consumption. Home mortgages also can keep workers obediently laboring in order to pay off their debts. As an Illinois banker explained, "It is for homes that we labor and which inspire our being." This may explain why the Relief Society required most recipients of cottages to pay back the cost of lumber within twelve months.[52]

"It requires character to save money; it forms prudent habits to lay aside money for a home in early life," a guide to Chicago's 1893 Columbian Exposition declared, so a "model working-man's house" from a Philadelphia suburb was, according to this guide, the most "useful" display at the entire World's Fair. Those prudent habits of homeownership were part of what Chicago's Relief Society sought to encourage. As Chicago's Progressive housing reformers later declared, "The unstable, irresponsible, shiftless family is most likely to begin living in furnished rooms; and the influence of that type of living . . . is in the direction of increasing their instability and shiftlessness," a downward spiral. Reformers worried that furnished rooms and apartments, like Chicago's post-fire barracks, would allow women to do less housework and "shiftless" people of all classes to preserve mobility without the responsibility of owning a great deal of property. Lodging houses often lacked proper sanitation, but social workers declared, "The great evil of the furnished rooming-house, however, is not that of inadequate or filthy sanitary arrangements, dark halls, or danger from fire, but the degradation that comes from a family living in one room with broken, dilapidated furniture, without responsibility or a sense of ownership." Such shiftless nonconsumption, Chicago's social workers believed, was caused not simply by poverty but by "bad management on the part of the wife" and a "disorderly method of living" on the part of families who chose to pursue vices while shirking housework.[53]

Social workers had heavily gendered expectations of domestic respectability, yet they noted that their clients seemed to prefer another arrangement, in which furnished apartments and residential hotels could become zones of opposition to middle-class mores: "A case-worker on the West side said that in her opinion many of her families lived thus because they liked it. The desire for excitement that can be found in many of the rooming-house neighborhoods, for change, anonymity, for drink and narcotics, and for easier housework, combine in influencing families to adopt this manner of life. . . . It involves very little responsibility and much freedom."[54] Later, in Progressive-era Chicago, "whenever it seems probable that a family will settle down . . . the United Charities makes an effort to get them out of furnished rooms." Switching to even a rented apartment "is clearly more wholesome and normal for the family." Yet such rehabilitation to a "normal" middle-class style of domesticity often failed. "It takes only the slightest hardship to cause them to return to furnished rooms," sell their furniture, pay rent weekly instead of monthly, and return to what social workers saw as shiftlessness but what their clients must have seen as lighter housework and greater flexibility. Social workers were baffled by their clients' preferences for what seemed to them to be "a harmful and degrading mode of living."[55] After the Great Chicago Fire, Chicago's immigrant aldermen had erected barracks, but Chicago's elite philanthropists did not want people to choose this shiftless, non-middle-class mode of living. They tore down the barracks and substituted isolated houses in order to create incentives to industry.

Friedrich Engels theorized in 1872 that owning a house could not only foster middle-class consumption but could also restrain workers' radical politics: "For our workers of the big cities freedom of movement is the prime condition of existence, and land ownership can only be a fetter to them. Give them their own houses, chain them once again to the soil, and you break their power of resistance to the wage cutting of the factory owners." Engels feared that homeowners would be reluctant to go on strike and risk missing a mortgage payment, less able to vote with their feet by moving to jobs with better conditions, and less free to demand political change. Workers might be able to own inexpensive houses at a city's suburban fringe, including a small food garden, but Engels saw this as a "reactionary . . . idealized restoration of small enterprise," giving employers an excuse to lower wages while attempting to turn workers into the petit bourgeoisie. Engels believed that housing reformers wanted "*a bourgeoisie without a proletariat*" and hoped to eliminate the proletariat simply by eliminating lower-class housing.[56]

Chicago's housing reformers shared Engels's view of the conservative effects of homeownership, but without his dismay. As the Citizens' Association of Chicago declared in 1884, "Furnish a man with good lodgings and surroundings and he at once becomes a better citizen. Provide him with a good home at a moderate cost and he becomes healthier and happier, a better workman, more contented and reliable, a saving man instead of a spendthrift; every condition of his existence is bettered."[57] Similarly, in 1888 the Chicago Real Estate Board congratulated itself:

> Because the ownership of land is almost thrust upon its citizens, communistic theories are unwarranted [in cities like Chicago]. . . . In this distribution of property real estate men have been performing a mission equal in magnitude and importance to the greatest conquests of history, because this distribution has brought about a result that might have cost the lives of half a million, and a sum of money equal to the national debt. Foreign socialistic elements congregated in the large cities in the U.S. have propagated much dissatisfaction among the laboring classes, causing the majority of the strikes and riots. . . . And what has been the brake upon this headlong rush to revolution? What has preserved us from the horrors of anarchy? It was the distribution of land among this very class, acting like oil upon a turbulent sea. In fact, it is fast becoming apparent that there is no power that will convert foreigners into American citizens faster than warranty deeds.[58]

With related logic, in 1871 the *Chicago Tribune* praised the post-fire Relief Society cottages: "With this plan 30,000 people, hitherto householders, will still be in their own homes, surrounded by the sacred and conservative elements of family, of independence, of respectability, and of individual responsibility which are so immense a moral force in the community."[59] Housing, it was hoped, would be a moral force of social control. Chicago's police commissioner was blunt about this: "Men who own the house and lots where their families live are not very likely to engage in bloody riots or in destroying the property of other people."[60]

If the Relief Society had given out only food and clothing, it was feared that Chicagoans might have sunk into "hopeless despondency" and become "helpless paupers." Giving alms might have hurt the alms recipients by making them dependent, in the view of Chicago's mainstream journalists. On the other hand, giving "a cheap but comfortable house . . . made them again independent citizens, giving them once more the proud sense of being property-holders, of having a share in the well-being of the community, bestowing upon them a renewed incentive to good order, industry, and thrift." The housing program cost one-third of the relief fund, but "the money could have been put to no wiser or more beneficent use, both in its material and moral influence."[61]

The year of reconstruction after the Great Fire was unique to Chicago, but the discourse about domesticity that it exposed was shared by many elite Americans in the second half of the nineteenth century, in a wide-spread conversation in which suburban-style housing was the perceived solution to numerous urban problems. Suburban-style housing was expected to reduce sexual immorality, prevent the disease of poverty, encourage women's domesticity, promote capitalist consumption, and help turn the proletariat into the bourgeoisie.

In spite of all the rhetoric of housing as a force of social control, Chicago's working-class homeowners had their own surprisingly volatile politics of property ownership. Protecting their investments in housing actually led them to aggressively challenge Chicago's leaders.

"LEAVE A HOUSE FOR THE LABORER"

In 1870 Chicago houses had a median value of $2,500 and Chicagoans born in the United States had houses whose median value was $7,000, but houses on Chicago's North Side were worth a median of only $1,500. On the North Side three-quarters of the homeowners were German immigrants. On the semisuburban fringes of the far North Side, these immigrant workers had managed to own homes at nearly twice the rate of Chicagoans overall. Boat traffic on the busy Chicago River kept drawbridges up, cutting North Siders off from the rest of Chicago, so this was a fringe area filled with small wooden cottages.[62]

The North Side was the neighborhood most devastated by the Great Fire. It was a neighborhood of immigrants, a neighborhood where four out of every five residents were foreign-born, a neighborhood so predominantly German that the English-language press mockingly called it the *Nord Site*. All but one of their humble houses had burned in the Great Fire. Photographs show open vistas of barren, charred land. Most owners of those burned houses did not have fire insurance or did not have fully paid-up fire insurance or did not have fully paid-up fire insurance with a large company outside of Chicago that was stable enough to pay back everyone whose property had burned. These poorest homeowners had to rebuild their homes on their own, without the benefit of insurance.[63]

Given the widespread discourse encouraging homeownership, one would expect Chicago's elites to applaud these immigrants' ownership of small homes, but in addition to Mrs. O'Leary's cow and the mysterious Parisian communard, Chicagoans blamed the fire on the great number of wooden houses in the city. The fire was due "less to the judgment of God than the folly of man," some Chicagoans complained, and they set about to undo that folly.[64] Since 1845 Chicago had set fire limits that prohibited new wooden construction in central neighborhoods. After November 1871 a new board of aldermen, elected on a popular bipartisan "Fireproof" ticket, proposed extending Chicago's fire limits to the city limits.

The leader of the "fireproof legislators," Mayor Joseph Medill, was also the owner of the *Chicago Tribune*. All of Chicago's English-language press supported his proposed fire limits. The *Chicago Times* explained, "Those who had the welfare of the city really at heart . . . with justice asked of the city for some guarantee that if they erected $100,000 marble fronts some other person did not squat $500 tinder-boxes beside them." The rich, for their safety, wanted Chicago's housing more clearly segregated by class. They perceived the poor not as property owners but as squatters whose buildings might become kindling. Even if not all wealthy shared this view, many insurance companies did, and their insurance policies helped structure the rebuilding of the city.[65]

The poor defended their small wooden urban homes. Chicago's German-language newspaper, the *Illinois Staats-Zeitung*, explained that brick houses required expensive foundations that made them cost two to four times as much as wooden ones. Brick houses cost more than the land on the North Side was then worth, so North Side landowners would not be able to borrow enough money to build in brick. "Men of small means . . . if obliged either to build brick houses or not build at all, would have to forego all hope of ever improving their property." They could try to hang on, paying taxes on cheap lots left vacant, or they might have to sell at a time when there were few buyers. "Thus the value of property in all those districts in which our laboring population used to live, would be depreciated," the German paper concluded, "and the earnings of thousands of thrifty and industrious citizens would melt away." Such language was similar to the Relief Society's discussion of thrifty and industrious homeowning citizens, but their proposed solution was quite different. Chicago's German and Irish North Siders demanded the right to live within the city of Chicago and to build as they pleased on their own land.[66]

Anton Hesing, the editor of the *Illinois Staats-Zeitung*, joined with the North Side's Irish alderman Tom Carney to lead meetings opposed to the proposed fire limits. The English-language press called these meetings "North-Side stupidity" when they reported them at all. The *Tribune* opined, "We trust that the Council will not listen to the demagogues who are interesting themselves in the nefarious movement to burn up the City of Chicago as soon as there shall be enough of it rebuilt to make a good bonfire."[67]

This was strong language, especially since Hesing and Carney's meetings had explained that the proposed fire limits would not actually protect Chicago from fire: "So far as safety against fire is concerned, the ordinance now before the council is a delusion and a snare, since, while prohibiting frame cottages, it permits the building of wooden, bay, and oriel windows up to the height of the third story; and of wooden sheds, and, worse than all, of wooden cornices, and does not prohibit wooden sidewalks."[68] A large mansard roof was more flammable than a small cottage, but Chicago's fire limits permitted the fashionable roofs while prohibiting the humble cottages. Fire limits also applied only to new buildings and to significant repairs on old buildings, so they did not really remove all flammable structures from an area. What they did remove was the all-wooden houses of the poor. Fire limits were a sort of zoning ordinance, using the excuse of fire safety to impose a class uniformity, limiting new construction to brick houses and brick office blocks. Fire limits were an attempt to reconstruct some of the barriers that had burned away in the Great Fire. The "fireproof legislators" wanted to make the fire limits coextensive with the city limits, thus imposing a sort of regional planning that would limit humble wooden houses to the suburbs.[69]

Chicago's immigrant workers protested. On Monday evening, January 15, 1872, a crowd gathered in front of Alderman Tom Carney's house on the western edge of Chicago's near North Side. "Shortly after seven a loud drumming began and streams of citizens came from all sides," the *Staats-Zeitung* reported. By 7:30 the crowd filled the whole street, swelled by delegations led by various North Side leaders with German surnames: Schlotthauer, Hahn, Zirngebel, Beder. The *Staats-Zeitung* reported that eventually ten thousand people marched down Michigan Street (now known as Hubbard Street), eight abreast, carrying torches. At a time when it was still unusual to see a city lit at night, "they made a spectacular impression as the many [fire] ruins, on which the freshly fallen snow lay like a shroud, were lit up by their torches." They traveled the route that, for many of them, would be their journey to work. From Carney's place at Illinois and West Orleans Streets, they marched down Hubbard Street, crossed the river by descending through the LaSalle Street tunnel, and kept on marching to City Hall. "The people wore no lace gloves or diamond brooches, one could see immediately that they were working-class men who had come to stage a demonstration for their right to their modest houses."[70]

At least that is what the German press reported. The *Chicago Tribune* reported that two to three thousand people had gathered at Alderman Carney's grocery store. The *Chicago Times* reported that four thousand had gathered at Alderman Carney's gin shop. It was probably a house from which Carney sold groceries and gin in the mixed use typical of Chicago immediately after the fire. The protestors marched four abreast, according to the *Times* and six abreast according to the *Tribune*, in a confusion of basic details that calls into question the reliability of all these accounts. These were not workers demonstrating in defense of their modest homes, according to the English-language press. The *Times* called them "a horde of ruffians ... mongrel fire-bugs ... drunken North-Siders." The *Tribune* described them as "the scum of the community. . . . men who never owned a plot of ground, and never will," and simply showed up for the "fun" of shouting. There is fear underlying this name-calling, along with an oblique acknowledgment that if the protesters were actually property owners, then their concerns might merit more consideration.[71]

The English- and German-language press did agree on the banners that the marchers carried, although the *Times* insisted that the banners had misspellings:

No Barrocks.
No Tenment Houses.
No Fire Limitz at the North Site.
Voice of the People.
Harmany of all Nations.
The Relief Tem Prance and Fire Lim Its Svindle Must be Cut Down.
Don't Vote Any More for the Poor Man's Oppressor.
Leave a House for the Laborur.[72]

As these signs implied, the multiethnic, working-class, and anti-Prohibition marchers believed that the proposed fire limits would keep them from building wooden houses on their own lots, thus forcing them to rent space in tenements or remain in the Relief Society barracks. They did not want either, nor did they want to move outside the city limits, where wooden houses were permitted. Seeking to avoid both apartments and suburbs, they marched to City Hall.

The marchers carried a black, red, and white German flag. Their most controversially aggressive banner depicted a person hanging from a gallows, above the statement, "This will be the lot of those that vote for the fire ordinance." They sang "Macht am Rhein" (Watch on the Rhine) as they marched past the Chicago River. When they reached City Hall, they pushed inside with their banners. The English-language press wrote that the marchers "invaded" City Hall, squeezing in "suffocatingly thick," in a crowd surging with "yelling riotous persons . . . howling indignant gutturals" of German.[73] The six or ten policemen on duty were overwhelmed, unable to close the council doors. "Desks were overturned. . . . Aldermen were jostled about. . . . The crowd struggled here, there, everywhere. Their dirty, greasy fingers seized upon any scrap of paper they could find. They broke open drawers and abstracted the printed proceedings of previous meetings. They tore valuable documents to pieces, and scattered the fragments on the floor."[74] They threatened the orderly governance of Chicago.

With all the noise, the *Tribune* reported, it was difficult to hear the chairman of Chicago's City Council, "but at least he was understood to say that not being able to keep order, and the further transaction of business being impossible, the Council was prorogued," adjourned for the evening. Some remaining aldermen, police officers, and German community leaders stood on chairs to make speeches, urging the crowd to calm down and leave peacefully, but it was hard to hear those speeches. Some feared the building would collapse, as the city government headquarters—hastily constructed after the Great Fire—"quivered" under the weight of "at least 1500 men" on its second floor. With the crowd still pressing through the doors, the *Times* reported, "it was impossible to leave the room, and it seemed ALMOST CERTAIN DEATH TO REMAIN." Seeking a safe exit, people moved toward the windows. Other people in the crowd still outside began throwing bricks and stones at those windows. Six windowpanes were broken, according to the *Staats-Zeitung*, while the *Times* reported, "ALL THE WINDOWS BROKEN." All the papers agreed that one policeman, Sergeant Louis J. Lull, was hit in the face by a brick.[75]

Eventually the janitor turned out the lights and the crowd dispersed, leaving behind at least two trampled lecterns and a great deal of alarm. The *Staats-Zeitung* admitted that the banner showing an alderman hanging from a gallows was "scandalous" and added that when the marchers reached City Hall, they should have appointed a committee to deliver their petition "politely." The *Staats-Zeitung* wrote that there had been "confusion and noise that were horrible, but still not a riot in any sense of the word." In contrast, the *Times* declared it had been "the most disgraceful riot which ever visited Chicago," as City Hall was filled with "mongrel fire-bugs" who carried the Prussian flag while trampling the American flag underfoot. The *Staats-Zeitung* insisted that no American flag had been trampled, but all three major newspapers agreed that this protest left a strong anti-immigrant feeling in Chicago.[76]

From the distance of more than a century, it is difficult to know whether there were two, four, or ten thousand protesters that night at City Hall. It is difficult to know whether they marched eight or six or four abreast, whether they broke six windowpanes or all the windows, and whether the American flag was physically trampled or only metaphorically trampled in the minds of *Times* reporters attempting to express their outrage. What is clear is that many Chicagoans felt quite passionately about the fire limits. The vitriol that the *Tribune* and the *Staats-Zeitung* leveled at each other reflects the division between Joseph Medill and Anton Hesing, between native-born and immigrant, and between those who insisted on building brick houses and those who could not afford brick.[77]

The *Times* declared that the protesters had "struck almost as much terror to the souls of right-thinking and law-abiding members of the community as did the terrible fire of which they were the sequel."[78] The march to City Hall on January 15 was the first mass demonstration since the Great Fire. Under the subheading "HIGH TREASON," the *Times* reported that Hesing had declared that if the fire limits were passed, they could not be enforced, because "we can bring 5,000 citizens against their 300 policemen . . . I SCHWEARS TO IT."[79] His foreign accent and his formidable numbers intimidated native-born Chicagoans, who were becoming a minority in the city.

The *Times* criticized "those who wish to erect hovels on the North side," those whom the *Tribune* called "the North Side incendiaries." The *Republican* announced that anyone who tried to build with wood "trifles with the life of the city" and "is no better than a traitor and an incendiary." The *Tribune* declared this was not a movement for property rights but a movement of people wanting "to squat wherever they choose with wooden shanties," driving up insurance rates, discouraging others from building "first-class edifices," and thus "rendering good architecture in Chicago impossible." High insurance premiums and low, unimpressive buildings would cause potential settlers to move on to Milwaukee or St. Louis, the newspapers feared. The question of fire limits concerned so many Chicagoans because, as they saw it, the future shape of Chicago was at stake.[80]

The *Staats-Zeitung* responded that fire limits themselves would limit the growth of Chicago: "The rebuilt Chicago will only be a medium-sized city. Chicago owes its first growth spurt to its wooden constructs and—fire here, fire there—it cannot spare them if it wants to become again what it once was." Occasional fires were necessary, the *Staats-Zeitung* argued, shockingly soon after the terror of the Great Fire, because it was humble wooden houses that had made Chicago thrive.[81]

Homeownership made workers proud and industrious, the *Staats-Zeitung* explained, echoing the ideas of the elite Relief and Aid Society. Without access to wooden houses, the "German, Scandinavian, and Irish workers that lived under their own roofs before the fire will be reduced to poor proletariats that must live together in huge, filthy barracks, all while losing their self-confidence and pride." Homeownership blurred class lines, the paper asserted, and it prevented proletarianism. Without wooden houses, Chicago risked becoming like "the European large city, in which the differences between rich and poor are clearly visible." Homeownership also attracted responsible workers; it was "the main 'selling point' that Chicago had used to attract immigrants."[82] "The naturalized citizens of the north side that want Chicago to remain a city in which a worker can live in his own house are better Americans than any fresh bullies who maintain that our working classes should [herd] in large filthy barracks in order to sink to the level of the European proletariat."[83] The German, Irish, and Scandinavians of the North Side seem to have wanted the same independent houses that the native-born elites of the Relief and Aid Society promoted. But the workers wanted to choose the location of these houses and to control their private property without government interference. Homeownership was their American dream, but it was not a suburban dream, nor one of passive subservience to elites.

Where the *Staats-Zeitung* saw respectable homeowning citizens striving to avoid proletarianization, the *Times* saw German and Irish immigrants carrying clubs while wearing the red neckerchiefs of the Internationale and threatening the stability of the city. Under the headline "COMMUNISM," the *Tribune* wrote that this housing protest was "one of the rare tastes of Communism that has been thus far vouchsafed to the American people." Earlier the *Chicago Tribune* and the Relief Society had predicted that property ownership would create politically conservative citizens, but in this case, property ownership on Chicago's North Side actually led to noisy, "communistic" protests at City Hall. Instead of housing as a force of social control, defending their investment in their homes led North Side property owners to challenge the city's political leaders.[84]

The North Side protesters of 1872 won their demands, at least in the short term. During aldermanic meetings over the next few weeks, after much debate—and while defended by seventy-eight armed policemen—Chicago's leaders eventually passed modified fire limits. They honored the protesters' request that the fire limits extend to only part of the North Side, stopping at Chicago Avenue and Wells Avenue. Even south of that reduced line, the fire limits ordinance was unevenly enforced. Despite the risk of "fire here, fire there," Chicago's aldermen agreed that it was more important to the future of the city to permit humble homes within the city limits than to force the poor up into apartments or out to the suburbs. By using language similar to that of the Relief and Aid Society, Chicago's poor had preserved their urban homes.[85]

This victory lasted only two and a half years. On the afternoon of July 14, 1874, fire leveled another of Chicago's fringe neighborhoods. Beginning in a "Polish Jew's shanty" next to an oil factory, in what the *Tribune* called a "bad place" at the intersection of Taylor and Clark Streets on the near South Side, this fire burned a neighborhood that was "in great part occupied by colored people." It leveled sixty acres, "strik[ing] those who, though they lose a little, lose everything."[86] A shift in wind kept it from reaching the central business district and becoming as famous as the Great Fire of 1871. This fire nonetheless hurt the poor and led to laws causing the poor to move to the suburbs.

The *Tribune* editorialized, "We have paid a light penalty for allowing our magnificent business-centre to be surrounded with wooden rookeries. We have come off cheap. The great, gilded martyr, around which the fagots have been so profusely piled, has not yet been burned to death. Perhaps this small calamity will show us how to save it."[87] Days after this fire Chicago's elites held their own mass meetings. This time, instead of workers and immigrants, "about seventy of the wealthiest men in Chicago" marched into City Council to ask that the fire limits be extended to the city limits. Chicago's Board of Trade circulated a "mammoth petition" calling for this extension, and, to present this petition to the aldermen, they chose Anton Hesing, the former opponent of fire limits. "Things had changed," Hesing told the aldermen. Whereas before he had stood before them "defending the poverty-stricken people of the North Side," he now had the "honor" of speaking "in the name of an organization representing millions of dollars." Hesing had embraced upward mobility. The *Tribune* complimented him in an editorial: "It is surprising that a man of so much intelligence as Mr. Hesing should have been where he was two years ago." He was now "Mr. Hesing," not a "mongrel fire-bug." His *Staats-Zeitung* developed a reputation as a bourgeois, conformist paper, while other German-language papers in Chicago took up the mantle of speaking for the workers. In 1874 Chicago's aldermen overwhelmingly voted to extend the fire limits to the city limits, thus putting additional centrifugal pressure on Chicago's working class.[88]

Advertisements for some Chicago subdivisions were clear about this government-induced suburbanization: "LOTS! LOTS! OUTSIDE FIRE LIMITS," trumpeted a typical ad for inexpensive $400 lots in 1872. "*OUTSIDE FIRE LIMITS!* You can Build Wooden Houses! NO CITY TAXES!" explained another advertisement in 1880. Buffalo, Cincinnati, Philadelphia, and Pittsburgh all had fire limits resembling Chicago's, while many other cities also regulated lot sizes and sewage disposal, making urban construction more expensive than suburban. The protests around Chicago's fire limits reveal an underrecognized cause of suburban sprawl: government rules have often made it cheaper to build outside the city limits.[89]

Chicago's real estate journalists were conscious of their government's influence on suburbanization. A few years after the Great Fire of 1871, a real estate booster wrote, "The fire ordinance which followed the fire . . . drove beyond the limits named all persons who desired to build homes for themselves and who had not the means to put up a structure of brick or other fireproof material. Hence a brisk demand for building just outside the city limits. . . . Indeed, the feature of the Chicago market for the past two years has been the suburban trade."[90] Chicago's *Real Estate and Building Journal* reported that the fire limits had led so many "mechanics" to purchase "lots on monthly payments" in the suburbs that, within another year after the fire, the limits of metropolitan Chicago would extend "six or eight miles further" in every direction. Approvingly the *Journal* wrote, "The fire drove many thousands of our citizens into more remote sections, and in doing this it also drove the interests of land men and speculators."[91]

Some journalists complained the poor had not moved far enough: "Let a block get well on fire towards the Stock Yards in some densely settled locality, in the face of a gale, and all the apparatus of the fire department must prove futile. Nothing but acres of solid brick or stone buildings that are virtually fireproof can stop it." Instead of medieval city walls, elite Chicagoans envisioned a modern wall of expensive brick and stone buildings surrounding their city. In 1874 the *Tribune* also suggested that Chicago build a swath of open park space surrounding the city, to protect it from the wooden houses of the poorer people on the fringes of the city.[92]

In 1872 the signs of the North Side protestors had declared, "No Tenements," not "No Suburbs." Perhaps they were unaware that the fire limits would push them into suburban cottages as well as urban apartments. Perhaps suburbs had already achieved enough cachet that it was difficult, in 1872, to publicly oppose suburbanization while simultaneously invoking the domestic ideal. The protesters did strategically use ideologies of domesticity. Hesing told a meeting of North Siders on the day before the protest march, "This was no political or religious movement, but it was ONE OF HOME PROTECTION." Afterward Hesing told the *Times*, "If the laborers are not allowed to go on and rebuild their little homes in their own way, the next demonstration will be of women carrying their babes upon their breast." They claimed domesticity in order to claim the sympathy of Chicago's leaders. Hesing and his fellow protesters did not carry signs saying, "No Suburbs," but they did march boldly into City Hall to protest policies that eventually resulted in their suburbanization.[93]

SEGREGATING THE CITY

The North Side Protest of January 1872 came in the middle of a winter of construction. "The ashes were still hot when the first frost came," but freezing temperatures did not halt the tremendous project of rebuilding

Chicago. Workers labored through the exceptionally cold and unusually long winter of 1871–72. Masons kept "a fire on every mortar-board, which keeps the mortar plastic and the blood of the bricklayer uncongealed." Such hasty work in harsh conditions led to improperly set mortar. Many walls tumbled down just after they went up, and the number of deaths at worksites exceeded the number of deaths from the fire itself. The *Chicago Tribune* even complained that building workers spent too much time attending their fellow workers' funerals. The bricklayers union briefly went on strike, just ten days after the Great Fire, but Chicago's leaders threatened that the same telegraphic and railroad links that had brought charity relief to fire sufferers might also bring strikebreakers to the city.[94]

At least thirty thousand people moved to Chicago that winter, hoping to find construction work and helping to keep wages stagnant even as rents doubled in the year after the fire. Chicago's newspapers consistently urged workers—but not landlords—to avoid taking unfair advantage by demanding higher wages. Chicago's building unions did not manage to have a successful strike until October 1872, one year after the fire, but they did recruit thousands of new members and held a peaceful rally of twenty thousand on May 15, 1872, when Mayor Joseph Medill advised them that homeownership was a better strategy than strikes: "Work steadily at the best wages offered; practice economy . . . drink water instead of whiskey . . . put your surplus earnings at interest until you have enough to make a payment on a lot, build a cottage on it at the earliest day possible, and thus be independent landlords."[95] It was yet another reiteration of the pervasive discourse encouraging respectable, suburban homeownership, despite the evidence from January's City Hall protests that showed independent landowners might threaten the city's elite.

The rebuilding that winter was also a re-separating of Chicago's built environment. "Out of the ruins rose workshop, business block and dwelling," wrote one Chicago booster a generation later. "The foundations of Chicago as we know it were laid deep and well." Workshop, business, and dwelling: these were foundations that separated industrial, commercial, and residential space more than ever before. A Chicago magazine declared, "There has been but one parallel to the mighty creation recorded in Genesis. That parallel is the rebuilding of Chicago in twelve months." The city was indeed created while it was rebuilt. "Chicago rose sublime from its ashes," Chicagoans claimed and proudly called it New Chicago. "In fact, the great disaster of last year is beginning to be regarded as a blessing in disguise," *Harper's Magazine* wrote, since public interest in the fire served as an "advertisement" for Chicago and because the fire cleared space for new building.[96] Poet John Greenleaf Whittier wrote:

Men said at vespers, "All is well!"
In one wild night the city fell. . . .
Fair seemed the old; but fairer still
The new, the dreary void shall fill.[97]

What would this new city look like? The fire had destroyed 27,800 "shacks" that were not rebuilt, instead "changed to a higher use," in the words of a 1930s Chicago realtor who became a geographer. "The fire ended the residential occupancy of the downtown area," he concluded, and "accentuated rather than reversed the trends already in evidence before the fire."[98] The Great Fire of 1871 expedited Chicago's suburbanization.

The fire had "cleared" downtown lots "of incumbrances in the way of buildings," one real estate journalist wrote with patronizing disdain for the people whose homes were encumbrances. The housing hierarchy in post-fire Chicago placed hovels, shanties (rickety wooden buildings), rookeries (multi-unit wooden buildings), and tenements (any housing for the poor, but especially for multiple poor families) all on the lowest rung. "The rookeries . . . made a magnificent kindling material, and had never distinguished themselves half so well as habitations of man as they did as fuel for the fiend," one journalist wrote.[99]

Before the fire, frame shanties, brothels, "jew clothiers," and cheap boardinghouses had filled Fifth Avenue (renamed Wells Street in 1871, and later the site of the Sears Tower). A *Chicago Times* journalist observed that this street had

a reputation so odious that nothing less than our fire could have remedied it. . . . In fact Wells street contained a class of buildings and population that Chicago could not feel sorry at the loss of. The property occupied in this objectionable way was valuable, being eligibly situated in respect to some of the most important thoroughfares in the business [district]. . . . The fire, with all its train of misfortunes, did not do so badly in solving this difficulty for Chicago. It swept away all the obnoxious features of the street, and forever.[100]

The fire let Chicago's business leaders replace downtown neighborhoods housing poor immigrants with more prestigious commercial uses. Purchasing centrally located land at fire-depressed prices and having the access to capital to build with the now mandated brick, elites redesigned the center of their city. The central business district "has been rebuilt in a style far more solid, imposing, and beautiful than originally," a journalist boasted one year after the fire. Like later urban renewal, Chicago's reconstruction pushed poor people out of the central city. "Instead of large numbers of uncouth and flimsily constructed buildings in the very business heart of old Chicago, which were not improperly called 'balloons,' 'fire-traps,' and 'shaky affairs,' there will be very few of that style of structures in New Chicago's business streets."[101]

Those houses called shaky fire-trap "balloons" had previously been called "Chicago construction" from the 1830s until the 1870s. Balloon-frame construction was simpler, faster, less expensive, and more flexible than traditional heavy-timbered mortise-and-peg carpentry. Balloon frames were wooden houses built of slender lumber easily nailed together, collectively invented by America's pioneers who needed houses before they had access to expert carpenters. Daniel Boorstin has written a paean to the ingenious American innovation of balloon-frame construction. Yet Boorstin's admiration was not shared by Chicago's elites, who often dismissed these structures as insubstantial shanties and "rickety . . . old fire-traps." The *Lakeside Monthly* explained that the city's progress required moving these houses of poorer people out to the suburbs: elite residences of "good taste" objected to being "side by side" with balloon-frame houses, "which would fail to ornament an insignificant country village. . . . As business increased and more massive and less inflammable structures were required, these houses were moved to the less populous districts." As Chicago rebuilt itself after the Great Fire, it built in a class segregation that sent humble dwellings to the suburbs.[102]

The poor were pushed out by fire limits and downtown development, while also pulled by jobs in industries that relocated to the suburbs after the Great Fire gave some factories the chance to reevaluate their business locations. In the year after the fire, Chicago developed a new Southwestern Manufacturing District where the McCormick Reaper factory, the Chicago Stove Works, the Swan, Clark & Platt factory, and several train car factories all built in new suburban locations. Three miles from the center of town, this district offered cheap land, convenient canals, and railroad access. Other industries moved to the suburbs because Chicago's new fire ordinances forbade woodworkers, planing mills, carpentry shops, and wagon makers from working in the city. Workers followed the factories. After the fire, the O'Leary family moved from their DeKoven Street neighborhood to a cottage at Forty-seventh and Halsted, in what was then a suburb known as the Town of Lake, a suburb that further defies elite notions of respectable housing.[103]

Chicago's stockyards had already relocated to the Town of Lake in 1865. The lumber docks followed them there after the fire, then relocated farther south to the Calumet area during the 1880s. The fire had destroyed six of seventeen grain elevators and thirteen of 121 lumberyards within the city of Chicago, burning tens of millions of bushels of grain and 60 million feet of lumber. Chicago's enormous grain elevators all moved to Calumet between 1872 and 1890. The fire contributed to the already existing centrifugal movement that had been pushing industries into the suburbs.[104]

While factories dispersed over a wider metropolitan area, managers of these increasingly complex corporations concentrated their offices in a new downtown office district, in the Board of Trade and the Chamber of Commerce, and in smaller groups like the Lumberman's Exchange and the National Retail Lumber Dealers' Association. In the confusion immediately after the fire, button sellers had reportedly crowded next to dentists in residential parlors, in a mixture of businesses and residences that contemporaries labeled "whimsical." Permanent rebuilding reorganized the city's commercial and industrial districts. As the fire limits pushed out factories and the wooden homes of the poor, as elites developed prestigious retail and office use for a new downtown, the city of Chicago began to feature a new spatial separation that many twentieth-century urban planners call "rational" and that planning reformer Jane Jacobs later called "unbalanced."[105]

The fire did not cause these changes, but it did accelerate trends that had begun with industrialization. A few years before the fire, Frederick Law Olmsted asserted that the "strong and steadily increasing tendency" to separate business and residence reflected what he believed was the "law of progress," a progress toward segregation. The increasing separation of central business district, industrial areas, and residential areas sorted by class meant that the fire "hastened the removal" of many Chicagoans to the suburbs, and prices of suburban real estate rose 10 to 50 percent during the year after the fire. Real estate prices rose with a growth that "astonished all, and exceeded the predictions of the most sanguine; the tendency being chiefly to outside and acre property." On the one-year anniversary of the fire, a *Chicago Times* journalist declared, "There has never been a season of greater land activity in the suburbs."[106]

Notions of health, morality, sexuality, capitalist consumption, citizenship, and the supposed flammability of humble homes all helped displace Chicago's immigrants to the suburbs, where elites hoped the workers would be domestic and respectable. Yet homeownership did not always work as leaders imagined. The persistence of "the lodger evil" and overcrowding in putatively single-family homes demonstrated that workers had their own views of housing. The thousands of North Side immigrants who marched into City Hall in January 1872 showed that, instead of leading to respectability, homeownership could lead workers to confront their city leaders.

CHAPTER 3

ᴄᴧᴐ

Lake and Jungle

The Assembly-Line Factory as a Force
for Suburbanization

"The Working-Man's Reward" is a classic image of America's early suburban-ization that first appeared in the *Tenth Annual Illustrated Catalogue of S. E. Gross's Famous City Subdivisions and Suburban Towns on Easy Monthly Payments* (1891), a seventy-four-page advertising pamphlet. In the image, a worker sits with his lunch pail in a dark, bleak landscape while an angel floats above him, pointing to a burst of light containing a suburban-style house in an Arcadian grove. The facing page shows floor plans and elevations of actual houses in the "New City" subdivision of Chicago developer Samuel Eberly Gross. These floor plans lack the bay windows, front porch, two stories, low density, and mature trees that the angel offered. Gross's "handsome cottage" is a tiny seventeen by twenty-two feet, available for a $100 deposit plus "long time and monthly payments of $9 to $11, same as rent," for a final purchase price of $1,050 to $1,500.[1] Gross's description foreshadows the offers that William Levitt would make a half-century later, for a small but comfortable single-family house with a yard, in a mass-produced design, built by non-union labor, available for about the same cost as rent, extensively advertised, and aimed at workers hoping to enter the middle class.

Suburban historians often reprint "The Working-Man's Reward" because it seems to perfectly illustrate the forces that led to America's suburbanization.[2] There is the religious imagery associating housing with morality, an easy financing plan, and an illustration of the American dream of a British-style villa in a pastoral setting. But this is not actually a pastoral setting. None of

Samuel Eberly Gross's advertisement illustrates oppositions between home and work, trees and concrete, light and dark, domestic and industrial—yet the actual location of the advertised homes was just outside the gates of Chicago's stockyards, revealing that factories and suburbs were more interlinked than oppositional. From Samuel Eberly Gross (Firm), *Tenth Annual Illustrated Catalogue of S. E. Gross' Famous City Subdivisions and Suburban Towns on Easy Monthly Payments* (Chicago: S. E. Gross, 1891), 62. Image courtesy of the Chicago History Museum, ICHi-03656.

A HOME FOR $100

In my Ashland Avenue and 47th Street Subdivision.

Hall
Bed Room
Parlor
Bed Room
Kitchen
Pantry

FIRST FLOOR.

LOCATION.

These handsome cottages are located on 45th St. and Laflin St., between 45th and 46th Sts., (see plat of property on page 61)

DESCRIPTION.

They are well built and thoroughly finished throughout. Have seven foot basement, lake water, sewers and large lot. Sidewalks laid and fences built.

BASEMENT

BASEMENT.

TERMS.

Price $1,050 to $1,500; $100 cash, balance on long time and monthly payments of $9 to $11, same as rent.

BRANCH OFFICE AND HOW TO GET THERE.

Branch Office corner of 47th St. and Ashland Ave. Open every day. Take Archer and Ashland Aves. cars, or Halsted and 47th Sts. cars; either will take you to the office door; or take Grand Trunk R. R. trains to Ashland Ave. station and go two blocks north; or call at Main Office and you will be taken free to see the property.

South-east corner Dearborn and Randolph Sts.

The image facing "The Working-Man's Reward" in Gross's brochure makes it clear that actual homes in his "New City" subdivision lacked many of the middle-class amenities that the angel offered. These seventeen-by-twenty-two-foot homes were conveniently located near the gates of Chicago's stockyards and available for only $100 down. Workers could contribute their own sweat equity to finish the basement and attic. From Samuel Eberly Gross (Firm), *Tenth Annual Illustrated Catalogue of S. E. Gross' Famous City Subdivisions and Suburban Towns on Easy Monthly Payments* (Chicago: S. E. Gross, 1891), 63. Image courtesy of the Chicago History Museum, ICHi-28172.

the suburban historians who reprint the image mention that the subdivision's address—Forty-seventh Street and Ashland Avenue—is next to Chicago's stockyards. What is being advertised is the opportunity to live close enough to work to go home for a midday meal. The previous pages of Gross's advertising catalogue make this quite explicit, even redundant: "If you buy a home in my subdivision you can go home to your dinner. Why live long distances from your work when you can buy a home within two minutes walk of your work with the money you now spend for rent and car fare? . . . Save your rent. Save your car fare. . . . The money you now pay for rent and car fare will pay for your home."[3] This classic image of suburbia is not of a residential suburb at all. Gross encouraged people to move to his subdivision because of its proximity to multiple sites of industrial employment as well as suburban transportation: "Advantages: Only eight minutes' walk to the Rolling Mills and Lumber Docks. Only five minutes' walk to the Union Stock Yards. . . . Only two blocks to Ashland Avenue station of the Grand Trunk Rail Road and Santa Fe Railroad. Numerous trains. Fare five cents." This was a location from which multiple family members could walk to work in the stockyards, glue factories, canneries, and lumber mills of Packingtown, while other family members could commute to work in central Chicago. Gross proudly proclaimed, "Three hundred fifty men now working in the Packing Houses have bought homes from me in my New City Subdivision. Why shouldn't you?"[4] This was a space of working-class homeownership in an industrial suburb.

The corner of Forty-seventh and Ashland was known as Whisky Point because it had at least six saloons alongside dance halls and Gross's branch office. Whisky Point intersected with a diagonal avenue, which Gross could not resist naming after himself. In the case of Gross Avenue, the name was probably more apt than he would have liked. The streets of this neighborhood were unpaved and potholed, the sewage ditches were open and fetid, and nearby were the large open pits of Chicago's municipal garbage dumps. The head of the nearby settlement house called it a "district segregated for unpleasant things." She reported that the neighborhood around Gross Avenue was so infested with flies from the nearby stockyards that every August all the houses looked black: "the color of the paint was only seen in small spots" beneath the flies. Vacant lots were filled with stinking pig skins salvaged from the packing plants, laid out to decay until the hair could be extracted from the flesh in order to make hairbrushes. These lots were known as hair fields. The nearby river was known as Bubbly Creek because industrial chemicals, grease, and other packinghouse waste caused the polluted water to bubble up and sometimes catch on fire. Newcomers had difficulty tolerating the smell. The extreme industrial pollution of this neighborhood made it a dubious working man's reward indeed.[5]

On the pages preceding "The Working-Man's Reward," Gross did not hide the fact that his subdivision abutted the stockyards, encouraging customers to "buy a home . . . within two minutes walk of your work." From Samuel Eberly Gross (Firm), *Tenth Annual Illustrated Catalogue of S. E. Gross' Famous City Subdivisions and Suburban Towns on Easy Monthly Payments* (Chicago: S. E. Gross, 1891), 60. Image courtesy of the Chicago History Museum, ICHi-64635.

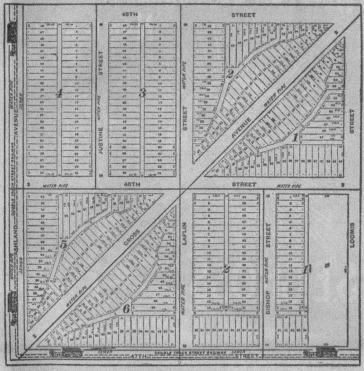

ASHLAND AVE. AND 47TH ST. SUBDIVISION.
400 GOOD AND CHEAP LOTS. Price $625 and Upwards,
HOMES FOR WORKING MEN.   BUSINESS SITES FOR BUSINESS MEN.
INVESTMENTS FOR SAVING MEN.

ADVANTAGES.
1. Lake water, sewers, sidewalk and shade trees.
2. Street cars on two sides of the property
3. Only two blocks to Ashland Ave. station of the Grand Trunk R. R. and Santa Fe
    R. R. Numerous trains. Fare 5 cents.
4. Only 8 minutes' walk to the Rolling Mills and Lumber Docks. Only 5 minutes'
    walk to the Union Stock Yards.
5. Land high, dry and healthful.   **TERMS.**

Price $625 and upwards. $40 to $100 cash. Balance on long time and monthly pay-
ments of $10 to $25 Money loaned for building. No cash payments required if you build
at once,   **BRANCH OFFICE AND HOW TO GET THERE.**

Branch Office on corner 47th St. and Ashland Ave. Open every day.
Take Archer Ave. and Ashland Ave. car, or Halsted St and 47th St. car; either will take
you to the Branch Office door, or take Grand Trunk R.R. trains to Ashland Ave. station and
go two blocks north; or call at Main Office and you will be taken free to see the property.

South-east corner Dearborn and Randolph Sts.

Gross's "good and cheap lots" boasted of proximity to multiple sites of industrial employment and suburban-style transportation. His map does not depict the nearby garbage dumps, hair fields, or Bubbly Creek. Instead he features the dramatic diagonal of Gross Avenue, which would soon become the site of the University of Chicago settlement house, a free public bath, free medical dispensary, and two free day nurseries, alongside small factories that used packinghouse byproducts to produce glue, margarine, and fertilizer. From Samuel Eberly Gross (Firm), *Tenth Annual Illustrated Catalogue of S. E. Gross' Famous City Subdivisions and Suburban Towns on Easy Monthly Payments* (Chicago: S. E. Gross, 1891), 61. Image courtesy of the Chicago History Museum, ICHi-64636. For the actual occupants of Gross Avenue, see Sanborn Map Company, *Chicago: Volume 9* (New York: Sanborn-Perris Map Co., 1894), maps 48 and 49.

How can an advertisement for Packingtown be a classic illustration of suburbanization? This was never a middle-class or purely residential suburb. The working man's reward was a working-class suburb that developed around assembly-line industries and immigrants eager to own their own homes. The name Town of Lake is evocative, since nineteenth-century Chicago land dealers were notorious for selling lake lots—plots whose coordinates turned out to place them underwater—to strangers unfamiliar with the lay of the land. The Town of Lake challenges assumptions not only about what a suburb is but why suburbanization happened and what it accomplished.

THE DISASSEMBLY LINE

In the 1840s realtors had advertised the Town of Lake as an ideal spot for suburban market gardens supplying Chicago with vegetables. The census of 1850 recorded only 349 residents. Realtor Matthew Laflin organized omnibus service to Lake in 1851, which, along with plank roads, a canal, and railroads, helped increase the population to 1,755 by 1860, including farmers as well as a few Chicagoans who had retired to a pastoral retreat. During the winter of 1865 these farmers and suburban commuters were joined by workers constructing the new stockyards, who settled into a "camp" that evolved, with the stockyards, into a "bustling settlement of about one thousand residents" by 1870.[6] Industrial workers settled next to commuters and farmers, vastly increasing the population of Lake and transforming it into an industrial suburb.

In "The Working-Man's Reward," Gross boasted that his subdivision was "only five minutes' walk to the Union Stock Yards." Chicago's Union Stockyards were a union of various smaller abattoirs that had prospered during the Civil War, butchering meat to supply the Union army. Blockaded southern ports, new railroad connections, and the troops' immense need for preserved meat all helped Chicago become the nation's major pork-packing center. As their industry grew, Chicago's pork packers complained about the inefficiencies of driving packs of pigs over crowded city streets to scattered butcheries. They were also facing expensive municipal regulations. After cholera epidemics in 1849 and 1851, Chicago prohibited new packinghouses within the city limits. In the 1870s the city also banned driving animals through city streets between 8 a.m. and 5 p.m. In 1863 Chicago's aldermen pressured packers along the North Fork of the Chicago River to pay to clean up the water pollution they had caused, while Chicago's Bridgeport-area packers were forced to pay new municipal taxes in their recently annexed neighborhood.[7]

Faced with mounting regulation and increasing urban congestion, in 1864 the Chicago Pork Packers Association joined with nine railroad companies to organize a new stockyards center five miles south of the city in the Town of Lake. The *Chicago Tribune* reported that this was a space "out on the prairie, beyond the line ever to be reached by the expanding city." The Union Stockyards built superb railroad connections to the Town of Lake, 345 acres of pens, a large hotel, and a bank that soon handled half a million dollars' worth of transactions each day.[8] A year after the Union Stockyards opened in 1865, a guidebook called it "a suburban city—the great bovine city of the world." It went on to describe the view from the hotel next to the packing plants: "On a warm summer day, this is one of the most enjoyable of our suburban retreats." Actually, on a warm summer day, the stench of the stockyards would have been sickening.[9]

Many of Chicago's packinghouses followed the pork packers and railroads to what would become known as Packingtown. By 1877 Lake held forty-four packing companies, thirteen fertilizer manufacturers, and three glue works that together operated 292 rendering tanks.[10] After the invention of the refrigerated railcar in the late 1870s, Packingtown's beef packers surpassed the output of the pork packers, whose salt-cured products had required less refrigeration. But meatpacking was not the only industry in the Town of Lake. In 1867 companies began manufacturing bricks there, led by J. B Legnard, who commuted from the North Side suburb of Waukegan, a particularly early example of an intra-suburban commute. In 1868 the Chicago, Rock Island, and Pacific Rail Road began building rail cars and locomotives in Lake, employing up to a thousand workers. The following year the American Bridge Company moved to Lake, employing between 150 and 400. In 1871 the Lake Shore and Michigan Southern Rail Road built its machine shops there. In 1880 the New Albany and Chicago Rail Road located its machine shops in the Town of Lake, and in 1882 the Chicago and Atlantic Rail Road followed.[11] Thus transportation was crucial to the development of Lake, but not necessarily for residents commuting to central-city jobs. Railroads were more frequently used to ship meat, bricks, and other rail cars.

In addition to the many jobs available in the packinghouses, brickyards, and rail car manufacturers of Lake, the town's 1886 directory lists 203 saloons; ninety contractors, carpenters, and builders; sixty-nine boardinghouses; thirty-five real estate offices; thirteen hotels; six lumber dealers; and three "house raisers and movers." This was an expanding place, full of realtors and builders and house movers, reeking of the stockyards and the factories that used the stockyards' byproducts to make glue and fertilizer and lard. The most frequent job title for heads of households in Lake was simply "laborer," but other residents were skilled blue-collar workers, including box makers, cigar makers, drivers, engineers, machinists, masons, and switchmen. Lake also housed low-level white-collar workers: bookkeepers, grocery store owners, peddlers, and saloonkeepers.[12]

Middle-class businesspeople and packinghouse managers lived in the part of Lake known as Englewood, south of Fifty-fifth Street (later Garfield Boulevard). Wealthy packinghouse owners lived in an elite "nook of sylvan quietness and verdant beauty" just east of Halsted, in villas on Emerald and Winter (later Union) Streets.[13] By the 1890s the stench of packing and the disparities between Packingtown's owners and workers drove the owners to more quiet, more verdant retreats elsewhere. This created a leapfrog effect. While Chicago's workers moved out of the city, businessmen were also moving out, "to skip the intermediate areas partially filled with obsolete houses occupied by the poorer classes and seek homesites where the houses were new and the neighborhood had not acquired an adverse character."[14] That elite search for space untainted by workers competed with the workers' own search for homes near peripheral factories, both influencing the dispersed nature of Chicago's built environment.

"No respectable person goes near the stockyards after dark if he can help it," a British traveler explained in 1880, when the population of Lake was 44 percent foreign-born. The residents of Lake were mostly Irish and German by 1880, along with Poles, Scandinavians, and Bohemians. They were derided as "pig-stickers" and "bull-whackers," but the meat they packed made up one-third of the value of all the products manufactured in Chicago. They would soon be joined by newer immigrants from eastern and southern Europe as well as Mexico.[15]

In Lake these diverse workers killed a million pigs each year in the 1870s, up to five hundred pigs each hour. This scale was possible because pigs were hooked onto a moving chain, which Kipling called "a railway of death." Workers stood still while the product moved past them, so that up to 126 workers butchered a single pig. "The great sight in Chicago is the stockyards," a British tourist wrote in 1876, because "the scale at which everything is conducted is astonishing." Upton Sinclair sent his novel's characters on one of these tours: "It was pork-making by machinery, pork-making by applied mathematics. . . . It was all highly specialized labor." It was one of the earliest assembly lines in America. Chicago stockyards boasted of being "the largest and in all their arrangements, the most perfect of their kind in the world." Workers performed small divisions of labor, supervised by managers in corporations that mandated the careful use of every animal byproduct ("everything but the squeal"), producing not only packaged meat but also fertilizer, gelatin, glue, hairbrushes, lard, margarine, soap, surgical sutures, violin strings, buttons, and knife handles.[16]

Abattoirs have long been located on the fringes of cities, but Chicago's stockyards had a new reason for moving to Lake in 1865. These were one of the first industries to use an assembly line, employing it to disassemble animals into packaged meat. This disassembly line also helped disassemble the tightly woven fabric of traditionally dense cities. An assembly line requires horizontal space. As early as 1870, land in downtown Chicago was worth from $200 to $3,000 a foot, while suburban land could be had from $4 to $60 a foot. Factory owners chose to locate their assembly-line factories where they could spread out at less expense. Non-assembly-line industries, like garment work, can occupy vertical space in multiple-story buildings or small sweatshops dispersed around a city, so Chicago's clothing, furnishing, and small-scale printing companies remained downtown until the 1940s, while assembly-line work moved out of cities.[17]

Traditional industrial towns such as mining towns, lumber towns, and mill towns were located far from any city, next to natural resources. In contrast, Lake was an industrial suburb, located close enough to Chicago to take advantage of the city's financial networks, large labor pool, access to markets, and railroad and shipping connections. Especially before advances in communication technologies, factories needed close access to credit, expertise, transportation, and workers. As an 1872 Chicago booster explained, "A very large percent of the manufacturing which really centers, in its capital and brains, in Chicago, is done outside of the city limits, where land is cheap, and the workmen can live at less expense and exposure to temptation than in town," adding that the railroads that carried commuters to America's early suburbs also often carried factory materials.[18]

Assembly lines were not the only cause of working-class suburbanization. Lower taxes in unincorporated spaces, the chance to achieve independent homeownership and potentially productive gardens and businesses, and proximity to non-assembly-line employment such as domestic service all contributed. Yet the assembly line was an important and underappreciated factor in America's suburbanization. Lake became the fastest-growing region in Cook County, mushrooming from 3,360 residents in 1870 to 18,000 in 1880, and then 85,000 by 1889. Chicago's factory and tenement inspector identified twenty-one thousand factory jobs in Lake in 1893. Workers moved to places like Lake because they were following their jobs and because they appreciated the same affordable land and lower taxes that had lured factory owners there.[19]

They also appreciated the pastoral ideal. Skilled workers "moved from Blue Island Avenue and Eighteenth Street to the Town of Lake because they wanted more space for grass, trees, and flowers," wrote one turn-of-the-century resident of Gross Avenue.[20] This sounds quintessentially suburban, but those flowers were next to factories, and that resident observer was Mary McDowell, head of the University of Chicago Settlement House, located on Gross Avenue next to the saloons, Bubbly Creek, and the city garbage dumps. McDowell was such an advocate for badly needed "municipal housekeeping" in this neighborhood that she is credited with inventing the term.

In 1889 the city of Chicago annexed the Town of Lake in order to help Chicago's population reach over one million in the 1890 census. Legally, then, Lake was not a suburb at the time of Gross's 1891 advertisement. Yet to the people living there, Lake still felt like a suburb for a generation after 1889. Chicago had so many annexations in these years that the city expanded from three to 211 square miles, while people's sense of community boundaries did not always keep pace with the official city boundaries. Despite the annexation, Lake remained outside the city's fire limits, thus allowing residents to access some municipal services while still building affordable wooden homes. Lake continued to be known as the Town of Lake until 1937, when the local newspaper, the *Journal of the Town of Lake*, changed its name to the *Back of the Yards Journal*, inspired by Saul Alinsky's neighborhood council, which encouraged the community to take pride in the newer neighborhood names that have now become famous: Back o' the Yards and Packingtown. Still, the suburban name Town of Lake lingered until the twentieth century. Lithuanians called it "Taunleikis." Subdividers Edward Dreyer and Samuel Gross also called it "New City," a name that conflated city and suburb.[21]

In 1911 49 percent of the families in the former Town of Lake owned their own homes, giving this area a homeownership rate twice as high as Chicago in general. Reformers warned that this was "likely to give a false impression of prosperity" to people unaware of homeowners' heavy mortgages, paid for by sending wives and children to work, skimping on basic food and heat, and crowding houses with boarders. Lake had homes designed for single families, although they were often occupied by extended families and boarders. It also had homes surrounded by yards, albeit tiny yards abutted by garbage dumps, industrial pollution, and thickets of flies.[22]

In 1913 the reformer Louise Montgomery complained of working girls' "wanderings" as they commuted from Lake to central-city jobs or made intra-suburban commutes to other industrial jobs in West Side suburbs like Cicero, "in spite of the inconvenient distance."[23] Other people had a reverse commute, traveling from the city of Chicago to the Town of Lake, as many African American workers would between 1904 and 1920, after they began to work in the packinghouses but before they were permitted to live in

Packingtown. Lake was a center of employment and a center of white working-class residences. It defies stereotypes of suburbs, yet it is a paradigmatic model of suburbia.

Like Lake on the South Side of Chicago, Chicago's West Side suburb of Cicero developed because of industries: first a limestone quarry, then the Grant Locomotive Works in 1891, then, in 1902, the huge Western Electric Company, which had fifteen thousand employees. By 1922 Cicero had 115 factories. The McCormick Company even built small cottages for their employees at Canalport, creating an industrial suburban enclave so that their workers would have no excuse for arriving late to work. One tourist, recording observations of Chicago for the *London Times*, noted the presence of suburban industry: "A large portion of the city and its suburbs is made up of series of huge stations, car yards, elevators, cattle pens, and storehouses, that almost overwhelm the visitor with the prodigious scale of their elaborate perplexity." The *Chicago Tribune* summarized why factories chose suburban locations: "The advantages afforded to industry by outside locations are low freight rates . . . low taxes . . . cheap land and therefore liberal sites, roomy buildings, mostly low, of modern arrangement . . . together with healthful surroundings for labor." The low, modern buildings of assembly-line factories filled Chicago's suburbs, and the semipastoral setting, it was hoped, would create better laborers.[24]

The U.S. census reported that the number of suburban jobs rose after 1850 and accelerated after 1880, so that, in the second half of the nineteenth century, suburban employment constituted one-third of all manufacturing employment in America. Ignoring those jobs beyond the central business district means ignoring blue-collar workers and ignoring one of the leading forces for suburbanization in America.[25]

THE COUNTEREXAMPLE OF RIVERSIDE

Although tourists visited Lake and other industrial suburbs, Chicago's most famous early suburb may be Riverside, which aimed to be "the model suburb of America . . . a public park for the benefit of private residents." Designed in 1868 by landscape architects Frederick Law Olmsted and Calvert Vaux, Riverside featured curving streets, large lots, architectural restrictions, and plentiful parks nine miles west of Chicago near a new commuter rail line. It is still frequently cited as a quintessential suburb.[26]

Yet in the 1870s Chicago's usually effusive boosters were far from enthusiastic about Riverside. "During the last two years the suburb has made little progress," one wrote in 1874. "Litigation, financial embarrassments, and the reports widely circulated, and having some foundation in fact, of the unhealthy character of the location, have continued to retard its growth."[27] Another described the "low, flat, miry and forlorn character of the greater part" of the country around Riverside.[28] Such accusations of unhealthfulness seem to be part of a larger resentment of the elitist control of the managers of Riverside. The *Land Owner* editorialized vehemently against the Riverside model:

> The Riverside Improvement Company set up barriers against admitting common Tom, Dick and Harry to their silvan retreat on the stagnant Aux Plaines. They gave soirees and garden parties. . . . Even as My Lord Warrick entertained in his grand old castle on the Avon, so did the Riverside nobility dispense hospitality. . . . To their parties were called the sleek beaux of society, the dainty nobodys, the fashionable diners-out. These people gave the place its character, guzzled its wine, and demolished its cold tongue. But as a class they carry their surplus funds in their shirt bosom and on their fingers, and hence they bought no lots. . . . From this collapse managers of suburban towns can draw a useful lesson. It is the people who buy lots, not the ninnies of fashion.[29]

One year later the Riverside Company went bankrupt and the *Land Owner* continued to insult it:

> They won't let you unhitch and feed your horse out of the back end of your buggy at the classic town of Riverside. A gentleman who drove out there to go to church the other Sunday had to cross over into Lyons to bait his beast. This is very much like the few Riverside swallow-tails who still linger around the decaying graveyard their stupidity has made. And still the managers of this concern in their impecuniosity believe themselves still to be the embodiment of all the tone in the West.[30]

This is not simply anti-elitist vitriol. There are some echoes of the commonly understood causes of suburbia in the health concerns over the "stagnant Aux Plaines" and the "decaying graveyard," as well as concerns about transportation facilities. But there is also the clear message that upper-class suburbs were not the main models for Chicago's other suburbs.

Some architects did mimic the Riverside model, and some Chicagoans eventually did settle there, making it a prestigious picturesque suburb today. But many of Riverside's neighbors are sites of working-class homeownership, immigrant settlement, gridded streets, and suburban industries. Understanding Lake as well as Riverside means understating there was no monolithic middle class living in a monolithic suburbia. It means recognizing that at least as much as elite emulation, it was suburban assembly-line factories that caused America's decentralization. From Cicero to Calumet City, working-class people led suburbanization.

"PLACES WHICH THE AVERAGE BUSINESSMAN NEVER SEES"

"If you want to get rich, buy lots in Chicago," Samuel Eberly Gross wrote in one of his many evocative advertisements. He advised investing in neighborhoods housing low-level white-collar workers as well as skilled blue-collar workers, what he called clerks and mechanics. Gross sold lots in suburbs ranging from middle-class Grossdale (now Brookfield) to lower-class Lake, but he guided investors toward the lower end of the suburban scale, where he asserted that clerks and mechanics bought one hundred houses for every three bought by "all other classes."[31]

"As straws show the direction of the wind, these factories coming to this point indicate the great future prosperity of the district and warrant to the real estate investor a promising field for profit," he wrote in one advertisement for Calumet Heights, touting its railroad car shops, steelworks, smelters, foundry, shipbuilders, nickel platers, and Standard Oil works as signs of a profitable residential real estate market.[32] As Gross explained in another advertisement:

> *Established Manufacturing Cities like Chicago are decidedly the Safest*. As the farmer is the producer in the country, so is the factory worker the producer in the city. Without producers we would soon go to the "bloomin" dogs. . . . Chicago is growing faster now than ever before. Where will the more than 100,000 newcomers each year find lots? In places which the average businessman never sees. Bear in mind that the greater part of these new citizens are people who can't afford to pay high prices, and yet they want their own homes more than any other class. When a visitor asks to see "what builds up Chicago so fast" show him the homes of the book-keepers, cashiers, clerks and workingmen—if you know where to find them.[33]

He writes as if he is addressing elite investors, yet he uses frequent underlining, repetition, and colloquial phrasing in order to appeal to less literate readers. He might be just one advertiser, striving to reach an almost impossibly wide range of real estate buyers, but his message echoes what the *Land Owner* wrote about Riverside: "It is the people who buy lots, not the ninnies of fashion."[34] It is the people's lots that deserve attention, "if you know where to find them."

Gross claimed his Chicago business was "the largest real estate business in the world."[35] Trained as a lawyer before switching to full-time real estate development in 1879, Gross followed the then-new "plan of purchasing large pieces of property, subdividing them, and erecting neat and commodious dwellings thereon, which could be sold to persons of moderate means upon monthly payments," a plan that one admirer considered almost "philanthropy," because it supposedly benefited both real estate speculators and working-class homeowners. In gratitude for the workers' suburban homes he built, the United Workingmen's Societies nominated Gross for mayor of Chicago in 1889, although he declined the nomination, citing pressing business demands. Chicago's real estate press praised Gross as "the prime mover in this great matter of improving the city and selling houses on favorable terms to people of moderate means." He was not the only one who developed Chicago's working-class suburbs; he competed with E. A. Cummings & Co., Campbell Brothers, Turner & Bond, and others building modestly priced housing in Chicago—yet he was one of the most creative at advertising. He was reported to be the first realtor to offer customers free railway excursions to view new subdivisions, with free Sunday-afternoon picnics accompanied by real estate auctions. Gross claimed he built more than one million homes, although the actual number was probably less than half that: approximately ten thousand houses and an additional forty thousand lots.[36]

Gross himself lived on Lake Shore Drive, in a grand mansion in the central city, not the suburbs that he touted for workers. His fortune was estimated at $3 to $5 million in 1890, but by 1901 he was suffering tax problems. Buffeted by the depression after 1893 and possibly threatened by more stringent building codes, he was also distracted after 1899 when he sued Edmond Rostand for allegedly plagiarizing *Cyrano de Bergerac* from Gross's play *The Merchant Prince of Cornville*. This odd lawsuit brought Gross expensive legal bills and notoriety. Eventually he filed for bankruptcy in 1908 while living in a sanitarium in Battle Creek, Michigan. His bankruptcy proceedings included the forced sale of one thousand lots, all encumbered by mortgages and back taxes, a sale that brought in only $2,425, though Gross said these lots were worth $200,000 "if properly handled." His wife divorced him in 1909, and a month later the sixty-six-year-old Gross scandalously married the eighteen-year-old daughter of a teamster. Gross died in 1913, leaving a much-diminished estate valued at only $150,000.[37]

Samuel E. Gross appears, thinly disguised, in Theodore Dreiser's novel *Jennie Gerhardt* (1911), in which the slick salesman Samuel E. Ross persuades the naïve Lester Brace to invest $50,000 in a suburban area south of Chicago, an area named Inwood despite its lack of trees. When rumors of a stockyard relocation bring "blight" to Inwood, Brace loses his entire investment, since he believes that only poor immigrants will buy Inwood plots instead of the wealthy suburbanites he had hoped for. Dreiser writes, "From any point of view, save that of a foreign population neighborhood, the enterprise was a failure." Dreiser's representation of Gross as Ross is interesting because it is wrong. When Chicago factories actually moved to suburban areas, real estate prices rose, driven up by speculators eager to sell houses to factory workers. Chicago realtors declared a "car-shop boom" in 1852, 1872, and 1889, when property values more than doubled near any projected railroad car factory. In 1891, when the stockyards considered relocating south of Chicago to Tolleston (near Gary, Indiana), subdividers quickly built nine thousand lots there and prices skyrocketed. Booster images of Greater Chicago portray a railroad diagonally splitting the frame between factories on one side of the tracks and suburban houses on the other, with farmhouses and trees in the distance under billowing clouds of smoke. Those boosters and advertisers understood that factory relocation was a main cause of suburbanization, one that Dreiser missed. Just as it is easy to overlook the wealth of today's slumlords, it was easy to overlook the profits available to investors in Chicago's working-class suburbs and the growth that happened, in Gross's phrase, "in places which the average businessman never sees."[38]

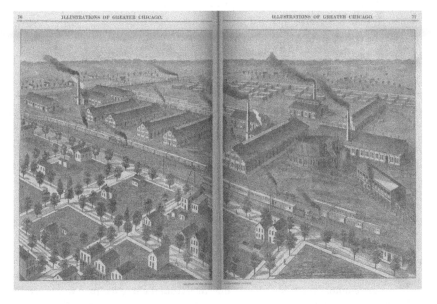

This booster image of the "carshops of the Chicago and Northwestern Railway" shows pastoral suburban housing next to smoke-spewing suburban factories in the West Side suburb of Austin. From *Illustrations of Greater Chicago* (Chicago: J. M. Wing, 1875), 76–77. Image courtesy of the Chicago History Museum, ICHi-64637.

Chicago's real estate boosters claimed that industries could make money simply by buying a large tract of land for a new factory and then subdividing part of it for workers' homes: "This will enhance the value of what they retain of their original purchase sufficiently to pay a very handsome dividend or profit, before they start a loom or forge."[39] The land was inexpensive when the factory decided to move to a new suburb, but by the time workers arrived, prices had often risen, driven up by middlemen, as advertisements explained:

> WEST CHICAGO LAND COMPANY, have purchased and subdivided into Blocks and Lots, about 450 acres adjoining the New Car Works of the Chicago & North-western railway company. . . . In view of the fact that in less than three years there is certain to be a population of at least 10,000 people in immediate vicinity of the Shops, there can be no better investment for capitalists than in some of the blocks of the Land Company's subdivision.[40]

Thus as capitalists speculated in land in industrial suburbs, workers had to move even farther out to less expensive land. These isolated suburbs, such as Harvey, Ford Heights, and Robbins, could end up suffering without any commercial tax base and without urban institutions, flexible transportation routes, or fine housing stock.[41] Industrial suburbs like the former Town of Lake suffered when industries moved on, without the urban amenities that help cities weather capital flight. Despite the promises of the working man's reward, upward mobility could be more elusive in working-class suburbs than in other locations.

THE JUNGLE SUBURB

A decade after Gross's ad for his subdivision outside Chicago's stockyards, a New York newspaper published an article claiming to be the impressions of a Lithuanian recently arrived at those same stockyards:

> We stopped on the bridge and looked into the river out there. It was so full of grease and dirt and sticks and boxes that it looked like a big, wide, dirty street, except in some places, where it boiled up. It made me sick to look at it. When I looked away I could see on one side some big fields full of holes, and these were the city dumps. On the other side were the stockyards, with twenty tall slaughterhouse chimneys. The wind blew a big smell from them to us. Then we walked on between the yards and the dumps and all the houses looked bad and poor. In our house my room was in the basement. I lay down on the floor with three other men and the air was rotten. I did not go to sleep for a long time.[42]

This vivid depiction of stench, overcrowding, and industrial degradation is reminiscent of another story of Lithuanian immigrants struggling in the shadow of Chicago's stockyards: the story that Upton Sinclair famously told in *The Jungle* (1905).

The first half of *The Jungle* describes Jurgis Rudkus and his family attempting to make the mortgage payments on a $1,500 house that they bought after seeing an advertising pamphlet that could have been written by Samuel Eberly Gross: "Why pay rent? . . . Why not own your own home? Do you know that you can buy one for less than your rent? We have built thousands of homes which are now occupied by happy families." They are entranced by the advertisement's portrait of a brightly painted two-story house, with a genteel porch and lace curtains in the windows, though, as in Gross's advertisement, they discover that the actual house they visit is not as grand. It is a single-story house with a basement and attic, like Gross's most common design. It costs $300 down, plus $12 a month, for a total price of $1,500. This is a great deal of money for the Rudkus family, but the house is also a vast improvement over the rows of mattresses they have been sleeping on in a four-room boardinghouse holding fifty people in a filthy space cleaned only by live chickens pecking at the bugs.[43]

Pooling their salaries, pressured by a sales agent, agonizing before signing the deed of sale, the twelve members of the extended Rudkus family move into a four-room house in the suburbs. More than a decade after "The Working-Man's Reward," the Rudkus family cannot live close to Gross Avenue; they can find affordable housing only more than two miles south of the stockyards, or "a long mile and a half," in the phrase of the slick sales agent. The house is unfinished because, the real estate agent explains, purchasers prefer to finish the basements and attics themselves, putting sweat equity into their home instead of cash. Some basic municipal infrastructure is also missing. In the subdivision in *The Jungle*, "the street in front of the house was unpaved and unlighted, and the view from it consisted of a few exactly similar houses, scattered here and there upon lots grown up with dingy brown weeds." There are no sewer pipes near the Rudkuses' new house, although the kitchen has "running water and a faucet, something which Teta Elzbieta had never in her wildest dreams hoped to possess."[44]

This is not the American dream, though; this is the Jungle. The house turns out to be flimsily built, infested with vermin, and previously occupied by three other immigrant families who had been unable to meet the payments. "Cheap as the houses were, they were sold with the idea that the people who bought them would not be able to pay for them," explains a neighbor, who boasts of "fooling the company" by actually paying for her own house.

The Rudkus family discovers that they must pay interest on the mortgage, insurance, and special-assessment property taxes: "As if in a flash of lightning they saw themselves—victims of a relentless fate, cornered, trapped, in the grip of destruction." To make the house payments, Jurgis's wife, Ona, goes to work, then his oldest son, and then the other children, who commute to downtown Chicago to sell newspapers. It is such a long commute that they sometimes do not bother to come home at night. Their house's walls are made of such thin and rotting "weatherboards" that "the cold which came upon them was like a living thing, a demon-presence in the room." The family is weakened by their inadequate shelter from Chicago's harsh weather, along with long journeys to work, brutal factory conditions, impure city food, sudden cuts in wages and hours, workplace injuries, alcoholism, the death of the grandfather, Dede Antanas, and a lost job because of union organizing, but they still keep up the house payments for almost four years.[45]

Eventually Ona's foreman sexually assaults her. Jurgis attacks the foreman and is jailed for one month. When he is released, he navigates his way home by following the smell of the stockyards, then discovers another family living in his house. It turns out that the mortgage was foreclosed while he was in jail. The house has already been resold. Jurgis feels he has lost his manliness as well as his home:

> Why, they had put their very souls into the payments on that house, they had paid for it with their sweat and tears—yes, more, with their very life-blood. Dede Antanas had died of the struggle to earn that money. . . . And Ona, too, had given her health and strength to pay for it—she was wrecked and ruined because of it; and so was he, who had been a big, strong man three years ago, and now sat here shivering, broken, cowed, weeping like a hysterical child. . . . Jurgis could see all the truth now. . . . That first lying circular, that smooth-tongued slippery agent! That trap of extra payments, the interest, and all the other charges that they had not the means to pay, and would never have attempted to pay! And then all the tricks of the packers, their masters, the tyrants who ruled them—the shut-downs and the scarcity of work, the irregular hours and the cruel speeding-up, the lowering of wages, the raising of prices! The mercilessness of nature about them, of heat and cold, rain and snow; the mercilessness of the city, of the country in which they lived, of its laws and customs that they did not understand. All of these things had worked for the [housing] company that had marked them for its prey and was waiting for its chance. And now with this last hideous injustice, its time had come, and it had turned them out bag and baggage, and taken their house and sold it again! And they could do nothing, they were tied hand and foot—the law was against them, the whole machinery of society was at their oppressors' command![46]

The loss of the family home leads to the loss of the family itself. After their mortgage is foreclosed, Ona dies in childbirth in a garret that the unqualified midwife is reluctant to visit. Ona and Jurgis's toddler child drowns in the undrained streets of Packingtown. Jurgis finally leaves this cursed industrial suburb in order to tramp through the countryside, while his cousin becomes a drug-addicted prostitute in the city. Jurgis's not fully convincing turn to socialism in the end is the one bright spot in Sinclair's bleak tale.

Some contemporary reviewers criticized *The Jungle* as exaggerated. The *Chicago Tribune* complained, "Upton Sinclair seems to have been willing to accept as truth nearly every charge that has ever been made against the packers," and added that those anti-packinghouse charges were "95 percent lies." Sales of canned meat had declined by 17 percent after the book was published. A presidential investigation found Sinclair's charges to be substantially true and used this information to help pass the Pure Food and Drug Act and the Meat Inspection Act of 1906.[47]

Sinclair famously complained, "I aimed at the public's heart, and by accident I hit it in the stomach." He had hoped for revolutionary socialism, not the FDA. He had hoped to describe problems with the capitalist system of production, but his readers responded with mild reforms to the process of consumption. He should not have been surprised. Although this novel was first serialized in a socialist newspaper, it dwells on issues of consumption. From the elaborate opening scene of Jurgis and Ona's wedding feast to the many chapters detailing the purchase, decoration, and maintenance of the home, Sinclair implicitly assumes that his readers will identify best with his characters' issues of consumption. He is careful to depict the Rudkus family working in nearly every nook of Chicago's industry, showing them in the steel mills and McCormick reaper factory, as well as meatpacking, canning, and fertilizer making, but he moves them from factory to factory like puppets. They become fully human only at home, buying a sugar bowl.

Few contemporary reviewers even mentioned the family's homeownership. One remarked that "of course" the Rudkuses lose the house and all their savings: this was a well-accepted hazard of "the installment plan." Others seem to have found the novel's plot of a foreclosed mortgage so mundane that it was not worth comment. Sinclair may have exaggerated in his muckraking depiction of industrial meatpacking, but his depiction of working-class homeownership was never accused of exaggeration. Chicago's packing company owners attacked his story; Chicago's housing developers did not.[48]

Historic records of the Town of Lake confirm the general portrait Sinclair drew of its built environment. In the 1890s lots in Lake generally cost $300, houses could cost as little as $600, and packinghouse workers earned an average annual wage of $613. With the help of developers' financing plans as well as immigrant-run building-and-loan associations, homeownership was within the reach of packinghouse workers. In the 1880s three-quarters of all new construction in Lake was residential construction, mostly wooden cottages that were one or two stories tall and only twenty-two-feet wide in order to fit on Chicago's standard 25-by-125-foot lot. These cottages often held extended families like the fictional Rudkuses, as well as boarders, small grocery stores, saloons, and other small home businesses. By the early twentieth century three-story flats were also built in this neighborhood, as the former suburb became more and more urban.[49]

In 1900 infant mortality in this area was five times higher than in nearby Hyde Park. The United Charities of Chicago had more clients from the Back of the Yards than from any other part of Chicago. Most of the neighborhood did not get sidewalks, sewers, or paved streets until after World War I, and as late as 1923 one-quarter of the households still lacked indoor toilets. Houses were "dark, crowded, [and] ill-ventilated," partly because windows were kept closed against the flies. Under pressure from Mary McDowell and neighborhood groups, Bubbly Creek was partially filled in after World War I, but other parts of it remained exposed through the middle of the twentieth century, creating "a pool of stench, slime, and sewage."[50]

The detailed maps of the Sanborn Fire Insurance Company reveal that, despite the general density of this neighborhood, lots on Gross Avenue did not sell well. In 1894, of the one hundred lots available on the two-block-long Gross Avenue, only twenty-five were occupied by any building at all; four lots held a glue factory, and one a free medical dispensary. In 1925 the Chicago University Settlement House, a public bath, two free day nurseries, one margarine manufacturer, and the hide pork press room of the Chicago Packing Company occupied Gross Avenue. This avenue, named after the developer of "The Working-Man's Reward," ended at a fertilizer works. Gross probably sold more small cottages in the streets around Gross Avenue, which—with the exception of the businesses at Whiskey Point— were a largely residential area filled with two-story wooden cottages next to Catholic churches and schools, all in the shadow of the stockyards.[51]

The suburbs of Chicago were filled with working-class residential areas that resembled the residential-industrial mix in the Town of Lake and *The Jungle*. Following the railroads south of Chicago in 1906, H. G. Wells observed

> vast chimneys, huge blackened grain elevators, flame-crowned furnaces and gauntly ugly and filthy factory buildings, monstrous mounds of refuse, desolate, empty lots littered with rusty cans and old iron, and indescribable rubbish.

Interspersed with these are groups of dirty, disreputable, insanitary-looking wooden houses. . . . It is the most perfect presentation of nineteenth century individualistic industrialism I have ever seen in its vast, its magnificent squalor. . . . In 1800 it was empty prairie, and one marvels for its future.[52]

It is a stretch to read past Wells's outrage to see a suburb of single-family houses and open—albeit polluted—space in which industrial assembly lines led to "vast . . . magnificent squalor." It is foolish to view working-class suburbs as simply the "democratization of the American dream," without fully considering the pollution, lack of services, risk of foreclosures, isolation of classes, limited mobility during strikes and layoffs, and other dangers of working-class homeownership, dangers that are not hard to see in *The Jungle*. The Rudkuses' neighborhood, it is worth remembering, could be smelled before it was seen across the flat prairie of Chicago. The fictional story of *The Jungle* is a powerful reminder not to conflate suburban residence with simple middle-class status. The working man's reward did not necessarily signify the workingman's comfort or upward mobility.[53]

The working man's reward does signify just how complex Chicago's suburbs are. America has inherited a model of metropolitan expansion that was developed in Gilded Age Chicago, a model of diverse spaces of homes as well as work, a model that was never monolithically middle class.

PRODUCTION AND CONSUMPTION

Before the Civil War many Americans preferred the independence of self-employment, shunning wage labor as "wage slavery" or "prostitution," terms whose racial and gender overtones were deliberate. Accepting wages meant giving up control over one's work, accepting a dependent relationship that seemed unwhite and unmanly. Before the disassembly line became common in Chicago's stockyards, expert butchers had controlled the pace, quality, and conditions of training of their work. Independent butchers knew how many animals they slaughtered and therefore how much they deserved to be paid for their work. With industrialization, within the giant corporations of Packingtown, workers lost this level of control over production. When a butcher worked alongside 126 others on a single pig, repeating a small division of labor such as slicing the left foreleg, tied into the complex supply chains and marketing strategies of a corporation, it was difficult to articulate how much each worker contributed to the company's profit. Under the surveillance of a manager and the pacing of a mechanical assembly line, workers lost control over the conditions of their labor. They turned, gradually, to issues of leisure.

Instead of objecting to the dependency of wage slavery and insisting on owning the full fruits of their labor—claims based on production—workers began insisting on receiving decent wages, what they called "a living wage" and "an American standard of living," claims based on consumption. Workers who had initially objected to all wages gradually reinterpreted some wages as potentially liberating to themselves as breadwinners, citizens, and consumers.[54]

Suburbanization was part of American workers' shift from issues of production to issues of consumption, as Gross advertised and Sinclair documented. "The Working-Man's Reward" suggested that workers might be rewarded for their dismal labor with a pleasant leisure. Some observers have argued that, by the mid-twentieth century, America's industrial workers could be middle class while at home in the suburbs and also working class while laboring in the factory.[55] Thus "The Working-Man's Reward" indicates two important trends. The first is the assembly-line factory as a cause of suburbanization; the second is the way that suburban home-ownership attempted to blur class lines, promising to reward the working class with a middle-class level of consumption.

Such hopes could be elusive, but workers were not dupes. Within Chicago's housing market, facing limited options, they chose to buy homes close to work, with room for their extended family, near industries in Chicago's diverse suburbs. Workers did not simply adopt the middle-class American family home; their homes were not a sentimental space where the nuclear family retreated from the market. Instead they used their homes as businesses and investments. They bought the working man's reward not only because it was far more comfortable than the tenements and lodging houses that were their few other options but also because it was an investment that they hoped to be able to control.

CHAPTER 4

❦

"Better than a Bank for a Poor Man"

Workers' Strategies for Home Financing

I n 1874 the *Chicago Times* reported that a baker and a tavern hostler had both become millionaires by investing in Chicago real estate. A broadside announced that the price of one lot had increased from $1.25 an acre in 1832 to $75,000 an acre in 1869. Many prominent citizens, from Potter Palmer to John Peter Altgeld, made their fortunes in real estate. Chicagoans could read frequent promises that they too might find upward mobility through real estate investments. Chicago developer Samuel Eberly Gross printed letters he said he had received from customers, in German and Polish and English, such as this one:

> Dear Sir:
>   I am perfectly satisfied with the cottage I bought from you two years ago. I consider I have that much saved. *It is better than a bank for a poor man.*
>   Respectfully, D. H. Brookins, 389 Gross Parkway[1]

Other realtors echoed this sentiment. "A city lot is the natural Savings Bank of a Chicago man that tries to get ahead in the world," declared one subdivision advertisement, ironically written by bankers, slighting their main banking business in order to promote their sideline of real estate development. Similarly the *Land Owner* explained that land ownership was widespread in turn-of-the-century Chicago because it "is the grand arena for investment, a kind of universal bank, in which the surplus earnings of our people are deposited." By the 1880s Chicago's active reformers promulgated strict building codes that limited the possibilities of owner building, so Chicago's working-class suburbs were largely the result of creative home financing.[2]

"Even servant girls and seamstresses and women clerks have caught the fever, put their savings into a lump and become joint owners of suburban property," the *Chicago Tribune* declared in 1889. This was not an empty assertion; a careful accounting in a 1903 sociology dissertation found that, among Chicago's African American property owners, 16 percent were women, including hotel keepers, hairdressers, and teachers, but mostly servants and seamstresses. Chicago's large real estate firms employed "drummers," commissioned salesmen who went door to door through Chicago's factory districts, selling suburban land. One report claimed that half the men and one-quarter of the women of Chicago had invested in lots by 1871. In the 1880s realtor E. A. Cummings held mass picnics at his suburban subdivisions, with band performances, a tent seating two thousand, and a foot race whose winner received a lot of land. Perhaps inspired by Cummings's foot races, in the early twentieth century Chicago's amusement parks offered prizes of a "free lot," which was actually a half-lot, requiring payment on the other half, and bringing even "the *demos* of the amusement park and the movie palace into small-time real estate speculation." Even the *Alarm*, an anarchist newspaper that declared, "Private capital is legalized theft," had back-page ads implying that their readers were homeowners. "Notice to Property Owners and Builders: We are now ready to supply all orders with the best Winter and Summer ventilating coal hole covers," read a typical ad, while the front page gave instructions on using dynamite to destroy private property.[3]

Real estate appeared better than a bank because real estate seemed tangible, apparently improvable, and seemingly permanent, while nineteenth-century banks often failed. Chicago's real estate press hoped, in vain, that periods of banking depressions would be periods of real estate booms. "A home is entirely desirable in times like these," a reporter for the *Land Owner* wrote at the beginning of one depression. Buying a home meant people were "investing in a savings bank they control themselves." This idea was so pervasive that one 1930s observer worried that the New Deal's federally insured bank deposits would improve banking so much that this would hurt the market for real estate. It didn't, but the fear is a remarkable illustration of the discourse that considered homes to be a substitute for banks. Chicago's real estate press declared, "Whatever else a man possess, he cannot afford to do without real estate."[4]

In 1887 the *Chicago Tribune* had printed George Asher Beecher's poem:

> Awake—asleep—'tis all the same,
> Or idle or alert.
> In foreign parts he long may roam—
> It grows as if he were at home.
> There's nothing pays like dirt.[5]

Yet not all dirt paid equally, or equally easily. Elite investors often had better access to credit and better inside knowledge of the future location of streetcar lines and sewers. For smaller investors, title disputes, tax assessments, regular real estate recessions every twenty years, swindling realtors, the uncertainties of neighborhood reputations in a rapidly growing city, the difficulties of reselling houses, and the challenges of paying off a mortgage during sicknesses, strikes, or layoffs, all meant that idle or even inexpert real estate investors took great risks. The real estate columnist of the *Chicago Tribune* observed that those who could least afford to lose money were the ones most likely to lose, especially if they did not spend the money to have a lawyer check the legality of a land title.[6]

Social workers were surprised to find that many Chicagoans seeking charity also owned homes. When a social worker interviewed eighty-four charity-receiving homeowners in 1924, some told her that it was "cheaper to own than rent," it was a "good business," and it allowed them to save money. It was better than a bank. But informants also told her that they had sacrificed "everything" in order to own a home. People bought homes "when their incomes are inadequate to meet the cost of what many regard as the necessities of life." Attempting to save money to pay off their mortgage, poor people would forgo basic home upkeep, adequate heat, food, clothing, and comfort. Even the *Real Estate and Building Journal* admitted, "People compare the amount paid for house rent with the cost of a home, and quite forget the taxes, insurance and repairs," a problem that Sinclair had depicted in *The Jungle*. Like Sinclair, Chicago's social workers noted that in the stockyards district, the relatively high rate of homeownership did not imply prosperity. "Many working people have bought, or have tried to buy, these houses, but before they paid up the installments the houses were in very bad repair and wretchedly dilapidated. Very often workmen have tried to buy them on the installment plan and have lost them again and again." If owning a lot and house was really better than investing in a bank, this may reveal more about the risks of nineteenth-century banking than the benefits of nineteenth-century real estate.[7]

THE CURVE

In 1933, in the midst of the Great Depression, the Chicago Title and Trust Company ran a series of full-page ads illustrating the research conducted by the economist and former realtor Homer Hoyt for *One Hundred Years of Land Values in Chicago*. The Title and Trust Company published "The Curve That Says I WILL" in the *Chicago Daily News, Chicago Daily Tribune, Chicago Evening American, Chicago Herald and Examiner, Chicago Illustrated Times*, and many suburban newspapers. It features a graph with a dark curving line tracing the growth in Chicago's total land values, from $168,800 in 1833 up to $5 million in 1926, and down again to just over $2 million in 1933. Illustrations of Chicago's growing skyscrapers echo the upward force of the graph, although their shadows slope ominously downward. An inset shows a smooth, exponential curve labeled as Chicago's population increase, implying that land values must also increase exponentially. The text explains, "Real estate throughout Greater Chicago has recently passed through its fifth great deflation. A hundred-year perspective upon Chicago land values is the tonic needed in these times. In it there is courage and inspiration for real estate ownership. . . . After every depression, the aggregate land value of Chicago has recovered and gone ahead." The title proclaims that this curve "says I WILL," one of the slogans of turn-of-the-century Chicago, implying that readers will dare to invest in Chicago real estate.[8]

This message is clearly meant to reassure potential real estate investors, and yet the line of land values is strikingly wobbly. Each precipitous decline on "The Curve That Says I WILL" represents many individual fortunes lost. In the book whose data had provided the information for this graph, Hoyt was explicit about the foreclosures and bankruptcies that each real estate recession had brought, along with the shoddy subdivisions of each boom. He concluded that the "great social cost" of unrestrained laissez-faire capitalism meant that America might soon turn to a socialist-style planned economy.[9] His was a very different conclusion from the one his sponsors trumpeted in their advertisement. Even the more optimistic, investment-encouraging advertisement version of "The Curve That Says I WILL" shows that Chicago had severe depressions approximately every twenty years in the nineteenth century.

Chicago's vacant suburban land was a particularly dangerous investment. The *Land Owner* complained in 1875 of three recent "fraudulent subdivisions," including Scott's Boulevard Addition to Chicago, which offered "7x9 swamp lots" in the town of Worth, with no streets in between the lots, all "under two feet of water," at a location fourteen miles from Chicago's center and six miles from the nearest railroad. "The inhabitants in the vicinity are composed mostly of bull frogs and mud turtles," the *Land Owner* reported. This is laughable but

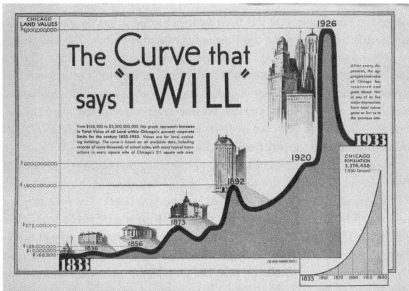

After sponsoring Homer Hoyt's PhD dissertation, the Chicago Title and Trust Company created advertisements illustrating his research into Chicago's first century of property values, graphing the upward trajectory of property values with visual cues to distract attention from the precipitous dips. Titling their graph with Chicago's municipal slogan "I Will," the Company reached a far more optimistic conclusion than Hoyt's dissertation did. Chicago Title and Trust Company, *One Hundred Years of Chicago Land Values* (1933), in Miscellaneous Pamphlets, Chicago History Museum. Image courtesy of the Chicago History Museum, LR-ICHi-64845, as well as the Chicago Title and Trust Company and Fidelity National Financial, Inc.

also tragic for people who put their savings into such poorly planned land, apparently without having had the means to visit the site or the knowledge to judge its suitability. In *The Life and Adventures of Martin Chuzzlewit*, Charles Dickens wrote an entire novel about the risks of investing in isolated and swampy Illinois land. "We are obliged to say that, so far as expert opinion on real estate values in these sections is concerned, there practically is none," Chicago economists reflected in 1931, trying to assess "land whose highest value may range all the way from a pickle patch to a sky-scraper."[10]

Even real estate ads reveal some of the dangers between the lines of their boasts. Consider the *Catalogue of 200 Residence Lots in Bates' New Re-Subdivision of Part of the Celebrated Normal Park* (1881). The first attempt to subdivide this area apparently flopped, warranting this second "re-subdivision." There are only two pages of text describing this area at Sixty-seventh Street near Halsted in present-day Englewood, and a significant portion of that text dwells on possible illegalities in the paperwork: "The title has been examined by some of the best attorneys in the city, and a written certificate given that it is good beyond question. A full warranty deed will be given all purchasers, and a certified copy of a full and complete abstract of title from the U.S. Government down to date, goes with each building lot." These precautions inadvertently reveal all the ways a land purchase might fall through due to inadequate paperwork, a particular risk for immigrants unfamiliar with the American legal system or even the English language. The ad went on to explain that no one would be permitted to buy more than eight lots, because the sellers wanted "actual occupants" who would build houses, not land speculators who would simply drive up prices and then dump the land. The ad also promised that no one could smell the stockyards from this point, and all lots were for "first-class suburban residences," perhaps reminding careful readers that not all suburbs were first-class, residential, or free of the stench of the stockyards. The ad assured readers, "So many railroads make cheap fares a certainty," but it did not specify what those fares would be—as many other ads did—nor did it indicate if the railroads even had stations near this subdivision. The usual suburban advertising tactics of free lunches and band music at a festive picnic "have been omitted," the ad explained, because the place's merits were so clear that a picnic would be unnecessary. But this omission makes one wonder about the solvency of the sellers, especially since, instead of the usual "canal terms" spreading payments equally over four years, these sellers wanted 10 percent cash, 40 percent within thirty days, and the balance in only two years.[11] Buying a home in this re-subdivision was a risk.

For African Americans, homes were a particularly risky investment. Racist ideas about neighborhood succession, a racist property market that charged blacks disproportionately for homes, and racist government policies that drove vice into black neighborhoods meant that blacks' homes tended to depreciate in value in the twentieth century. In 1903 a University of Chicago sociology student noted that because blacks recognized the racist reality of Chicago's property market, few bought land as an investment. Homes were not better than a bank for a poor man if that poor man was black.[12]

Nevertheless Chicago's blacks bought homes. "Some were buying that they might become more respected and influential in the community. The larger number, however, were buying in order to avoid paying excessive rents, and especially to get into desirable neighborhoods." For blacks who wanted to avoid the limited, crowded, overpriced, and vice-filled neighborhoods where they were permitted to rent apartments, one of the few ways out of the Black Belt was to buy a suburban home. They knew that their real estate investments would probably depreciate, but they also knew that a home was more than just an investment strategy: it was a sign of respectability and a comfort. Although they could not control racist conceptions about property values, black homeowners could hope to control some other finances: avoiding unexpected rent increases, profiting by taking in boarders, and economizing through self-provisioning such as garden-grown food and owner-built houses. Homeownership could allow them to live near jobs in suburban factories or in domestic employment. Homes were not an investment for blacks, as they were for whites, but homeownership did offer some freedom and some chance at control. By 1920 Chicago's suburbs of Evanston, Morgan Park, Chicago Heights, Robbins, Lilydale, and Dixmoor all had substantial black neighborhoods. These African American suburbs reveal that homes were bought even by people who did not expect them to be "better than a bank."[13]

Chicago's white ethnics did buy homes and suburban lots as investments. A Swedish immigrant who became a Chicago bricklayer recalled that like "many another bricklayer" in the mid-nineteenth century, he spent weekends visiting the suburb of Lake View, buying a lot on Saturday and occasionally reselling it on Sunday for a $25 profit. He also recalled that in the depression of the 1870s, "many if not most of the affluent bricklayers had lost their homes."[14]

FIFTY CENTS PER MONTH

How could all these workers afford to buy homes? The average annual wage for Chicago's factory workers in 1890 was $590.23, while the cost of a small house was about $1,500. To buy a house, most workers had to borrow money. Chicago's banks began to offer real estate loans to larger customers in 1869, although, until the amortized mortgage became widespread in the 1920s, banks' mortgages generally followed the risky balloon plan: borrowers paid off the interest at regular intervals, while paying off the principal in a lump sum at the end of five or six years. Modified balloon plans—collecting final lump sums of $15,000 on a $17,000 loan, and $67,000 on a $100,000 loan—are featured in "typical" examples of mortgage plans in an economics dissertation written at the University of Chicago in 1920. Chicago's working-class immigrants rarely qualified for such bank loans, often distrusted banks anyway, and usually could find better deals outside of formal banks, so, as a social worker explained in 1924, "the bank is practically never resorted to." Chicago's workers preferred to borrow from friends or relatives, from realtors and real estate developers, or from a building and loan society.[15]

In the late nineteenth century many of Chicago's subdivision developers offered installment payments, usually due annually in four equal payments over four years at 8 to 10 percent interest. B. F. Clarke and Company's typical advertisement from 1873 declared, "FINE RESIDENCE LOTS AT HUMBOLDT PARK, Free of City and Park Taxes, and at IRVING PARK AND NORWOOD PARK, in the most pleasant parts of these suburbs, at very low prices. Terms, one-fourth cash; balance in one, two and three years, with interest at 8 percent, payable annually." These were known as "canal terms," since they were the terms under which the government had first sold Chicago lots to cash-strapped pioneers in the 1830s, using the proceeds to finance the building of the Illinois and Michigan Canal.[16]

These canal terms evolved so that by the 1890s, Chicago developers offered to sell houses for only 10 percent down and monthly payments at 6 percent interest. Buyers then paid the dealers weekly or monthly, in an arrangement that dealers promoted as just like rent. Significantly, dealers usually kept the title in their own name until the purchaser made the final payment, so that one missed payment could mean forfeiting the entire house. This is the story that underlies *The Jungle*. After the institution of federal home mortgage programs in the 1930s, Chicago's white ethnics were no longer subject to that risky home-financing system. Blacks were generally not eligible for those programs, though, so Chicago's African Americans were forced to rely on "contract sellers." Blacks not only paid more for housing than whites; they also had to pay much more for borrowing money and faced disproportionate foreclosures because contract sellers kept the housing title in their own name. Contract buyers, like *The Jungle*'s Rudkus family at the turn of the century and Chicago's African Americans in midcentury, risked losing their entire down payment and all their investments in household improvements after only one month's missed mortgage payment, with little recourse.[17]

Partly to avoid that risk, working-class Chicagoans developed alternative methods of home financing earlier in the nineteenth and twentieth century, before more thorough banking laws made such alternatives impossible for African Americans who arrived after the 1930s. In the early 1920s the Chicago social worker Mary Bruton visited eighty-four homeowners who were receiving charity. She found that 51 percent had financed through contracts with developers; 13 percent financed their homes by borrowing from friends, 6 percent from building and loan associations, and 6 percent from their own savings. Another 16 percent refused to answer her questions, suspecting that she had come to raise their taxes, condemn their houses, or otherwise threaten their investments.[18] Such suspicions indicate how frightened these poor homeowners felt.

The most secure of these charity-receiving homeowners, Bruton concluded, were the 6 percent who had financed through building and loan associations. Unlike banks, these associations offered a plan allowing monthly payments on both interest and principal. And unlike developers' contracts, building and loan associations allowed their members to hold title to the property they were paying for. During the year of reconstruction after Chicago's Great Fire, the Illinois State Legislature passed an act permitting the formation of building and loan societies. Eight new societies incorporated that year. With names like the Workingmen's Savings and Homestead Association, they declared that they would help poor people buy houses. They were known as "poor men's banks."[19]

These associations shared a similar general plan. Members invested in shares, worth $100 each, paid for in monthly installments of 50 cents. After eight years each member would have paid in $48, and after ten years, $60. After about a decade, the association hoped to pay out the par value of $100 for each share. They could afford to pay out so much more than members had paid in because, at twice-monthly meetings, any member who wished to borrow from the group's collective savings was invited to bid on a loan. Someone might bid on twenty shares, worth $2,000, by offering a premium of 25 percent, or $500. The highest premium offered each month won the bid. This particular bidder would then receive the total share value minus the premium (thus $1,500 cash), to be paid back in monthly installments on each share (50 cents each for twenty shares, so $10 monthly), plus 8 percent interest on the $2,000 borrowed (another $13.33 monthly), plus minor fines for late fees, until after eight years with no fines this bidder would have paid $2,239.60 for the $1,500 cash borrowed. The system evolved so that shares could be bought at any time, not only when a new stock was issued. In the early twentieth century, building associations ceased charging premiums, only membership dues and interest. They also insisted that borrowers pay one-third of the house purchase price as a down payment.[20] Still, the basic system was remarkably stable over time.

The associations' promotional literature explained that their complex system was cheaper than borrowing $1,500 from a "capitalist" at simple 7 percent interest for eight years. The regular monthly payments meant that borrowers didn't "feel the burden as much" as in annual payment plans or balloon schemes. In addition to "the benefit of monthly payments," members gained "the stability" of an institution limited by stricter rules than nineteenth-century banks. The building and loan associations also claimed that members gained a feeling of equality from working with a mutual association run by its own members. *The Working Man's Way to Wealth: A Practical Treatise on Building Associations* explained that banks had "a tendency to aristocracy" in which a "preferred class" of capitalist stockholders made decisions and money, "skim[ming] off the cream of profits" that workers had invested. Unlike banks, building and loan associations offered "the only plan by which the working man can become his own capitalist, and create a source of wealth from which he can supply all reasonable demands." It was a mutual plan "of the people, by the people, and for the people." This system of "mutual help for self-help" began in Scotland in 1815, spread to Philadelphia in the 1850s, and reached Illinois by 1872, most likely imported by immigrants familiar with building and loan associations in Europe. It was a collective, immigrant-organized effort of workers striving to become their own capitalists.[21]

"The person who can lay away or invest fifty (50) cents per month, can own one share of stock, thus bringing it within reach of the humblest," one Chicago building and loan association explained. "To the mechanic, laborer, salesman, clerk and tradesman, and all persons of small means, anxious to relieve themselves of the burden of rent, this Association offers the easiest and cheapest mode by which they can, in a few years, become independent of the landlord," declared three other associations. Building and loan associations emphasized that they were ideal for any person who already owned a lot and wished to buy a house, or for anyone who wished to combine financing plans, using a loan from the association to pay off an existing mortgage with a developer.[22]

"Begin at once with this systematic plan of saving and borrowing money," advised another building association. "Loans on small houses for working men especially favored." These associations also offered to serve working women. Surprisingly, many of Chicago's building and loan associations announced, "Married women may become stockholders in this

Association and their shares will not become liable for the debts of their husbands." Their by-laws used unusually modern gender-neutral language: "Each stockholder or trustee, receiving his or her certificate of stock, shall be considered as binding him or herself in all respects to comply with the Charter." At the first annual convention of the U.S. League of Building and Loan Associations, held in Chicago in April 1893, Mrs. Mary B. Murrell of Little Rock, Arkansas, read a paper entitled "Women's Place in the Building Association Movement." One association's surviving list of 194 members included twenty-six married women and five single women, thus lending more credence to the *Tribune*'s assertion that even Chicago's working-class women invested in real estate.[23]

American banks faced an "avalanche of failures" in 1873, with another "purge" in the fall of 1877, when Chicago's two largest banks failed, due partly to too many "highly speculative suburban real estate developments." These were years of strikes and labor strife, when Chicago land lost 50 percent of its total value. Few of Chicago's building and loan associations survived the depression of the mid-1870s, but they mushroomed after a revised banking law in 1879, until by 1899 Chicago had 241 building and loan associations and Illinois had 599, with aggregate assets worth $54,104,602. Chicagoans could choose, for instance, between the Austin Building and Loan; Bohemian National Building, Loan and Homestead; or Clerks and Mechanics Building, Loan and Investment Association, depending on whether they identified by neighborhood, nationality, or occupation.[24]

Many of Chicago's building and loan associations had names like Plzen, Pravdo, Towazystwo Pazyczkow, or Vypomocrey Spoleck, emphasizing these organizations' appeal to immigrant workers. In the early twentieth century, Chicago's hundreds of building and loan associations organized themselves into the American-Czecho-Slovak Building and Loan League, the Polish-American Building and Loan League, the Swedish Building and Loan League, and the Lithuanian Building and Loan League, each holding meetings "in their own language" and, according to an official history, "contribut[ing] in no small measure to Americanize the thousands of aliens who have come from different parts of the world to make Chicago their home." They "Americanized" themselves using a savings structure they had imported from Europe.[25]

"The Building and Loan Associations, the poor man's device for financing home-buying, is in Chicago essentially an immigrant institution," a 1931 history asserted. "It is said by Czechs that a girl of that nationality will scarcely consider a marriage proposal of a suitor who has not a 'book,' a membership in such an institution." A half-century earlier, Frank Fucik, a leader of Chicago's Czechs (then known as Bohemians), boasted to the

Chicago Tribune that Bohemians already owned about $16 million worth of Chicago property. "It is a mistake to think that the Bohemians are only common laborers and wood-shovers. They are blacksmiths, watchmakers, and wood-turners, et cetera," he said; they were the skilled blue-collar laborers whom nineteenth-century Chicagoans called mechanics, and for them, homeownership was possible, aided by the twelve Bohemian building and loan societies that existed in 1886, each of which collected an average of $1 a week from their seven hundred members, according to Fucik.[26]

When the *Chicago Tribune* reported on these societies in 1883, the newspaper felt the need to explain to its native-born readers how Czech, German, Irish, and Polish immigrants pooled their savings to purchase a house or lot. More than one social worker noted, "Each of the foreign building and loan representatives visited described his own particular nationality as having the largest proportion of homeowners," further emphasizing the way that immigrant groups used homeownership to strive for middle-class respectability. Italians appeared to prefer private "debts of honor" without paperwork or firm deadlines, and African Americans tended to borrow directly from contract sellers, but all other racial and ethnic groups among Chicago's workers relied on building and loan associations.[27]

The "craze" for building and loan associations "seems to have taken possession principally of the poorer and lower order of our foreign-born element," a letter-writer wrote to the *Real Estate and Building News* in 1888. Calling himself "Caution," the writer warned that building and loan associations were "overdone" and would face an eventual "smash-up." Bookkeeping was too informal, real estate titles were insufficiently investigated, and loans were sometimes given in amounts greater than the value of the property offered as security, he alleged. "The poor people in these institutions know nothing about them," the *Chicago Tribune* declared with patronizing pity in an 1889 article headlined "Nearly Twenty-five Million of Dollars Now in the Hands of Men over Whom There Is No State Governing Power." Other critics complained that some building and loan associations, especially those known as "nationals," bilked their investors in pyramid schemes. In response to articles like these, in 1891 Illinois passed an act requiring an annual audit of the state's building and loan associations.[28]

The first audit, performed in 1892, could locate only 482 of Illinois's 1,006 officially chartered associations but found that all of those were quite sound. The next year Illinois's auditor declared that only five of the state's 563 building and loan associations had failed, a remarkably small number during a year when 360 traditional banks had failed nationwide in what was generally called a panic. In "that terrible winter" of 1893–94, more than 100,000 people were unemployed in Chicago, holding daily mass rallies on the lake front. With each bank failure, many depositors' savings were forfeited in this time before federally insured bank deposits. The state auditor concluded that building and loan associations were "useful and popular institutions" offering "strength in storms."[29]

In 1915 a building and loan leader boasted that these societies were "a cure for poverty." By 1924 building and loan leaders claimed they went to great lengths to support their borrowers: "If a man is temporarily unable to meet his payments, arrangements are made to divert the amount he has already paid on the principal to cover the current interest until he is again able to meet payments on the principal." But the extant auditors' records of Chicago's turn-of-the-century building and loan associations portray numerous foreclosures. In 1894, as depression deepened after the panic, fourteen of Illinois's building and loans went bankrupt, while secretaries of two others attempted to embezzle $47,442.25. The attorney general of Illinois closed down twelve other building and loans, eleven of which were in Chicago, generally for irresponsibly making "loans on worthless real estate," which cost their shareholders $928,050. These are huge sums to lose, representing many people's 50 cents a month.[30]

Illinois's building and loan associations had to foreclose on so many mortgages that foreclosure costs were $496,873.07 in 1898, nearly one-fifth of their total disbursements. That year their assets included $6,141,723.06 worth of real estate, almost all of which they had gained through foreclosed mortgages. More than half of these real estate assets belonged to Chicago building and loan associations, which were less stable than associations in the rest of the state. By 1902 the country was recovering from the depression of the late 1890s, and Illinois's building and loan associations had whittled their real estate holdings down to $2,768,651, of which only $1,715,956 were in Chicago, but by this time Chicago had only 183 building and loan associations remaining. Even the smaller numbers of the first few years of the twentieth century represent a great deal of suffering for people who borrowed only $1,000 or $2,000 at a time.[31]

Using the associations' own estimate of $1,500 per house, the $6,141,723.06 in real estate assets that the state auditor found in Chicago's building and loan societies in 1898 represented at least 4,094 lost homes. The developers, neighbors, and family members who also loaned money did not leave auditor's accounts revealing how many other mortgages were foreclosed, but knowing that building and loans financed 6 percent of homes allows for some speculative calculations. If 6 percent lost 4,094 homes, then 100 percent lost at least 68,233 homes—or more, since building and loan debt was generally recognized as the most stable of all debt options. In 1900 Chicago's total population was 1.7 million people, or approximately 340,000 households, so that conservative estimate amounts to a foreclosure rate of approximately 20 percent. When Homer Hoyt researched Chicago real estate history in the 1930s, he asserted that the foreclosure rate for Chicago's "working people" at the turn of the twentieth century was closer to 50 percent.[32]

One building and loan officer warned especially against making loans in working-class suburbs, because the poorest people were exposed to the greatest real estate risks. Land values could vary chaotically, especially in the cheaper outlying suburbs. A worker might want a home near work in a factory but might have trouble selling such a home to anyone else, especially during times of factory layoffs. A worker might choose to buy cheaper land in unincorporated areas without water, sewers, gas, paved streets, or sidewalks, but that land could become suddenly expensive when governments attempted to install such infrastructure retroactively, after homes had been built there. All homeowners were subject to "special assessment" property taxes to fund municipal improvements near their property in a suddenly imposed tax that, building and loan officials noted, could "become in the near future a burden to our borrower." Another building and loan director admitted that even workers' cash savings were particularly precarious; apparently 75 percent of the stock in building associations "is earlier withdrawn, lapsed or forfeited" instead of being carried to dividend-yielding maturity.[33]

WHY LUCY BECAME HER OWN LANDLORD

Why did Chicago's poor struggle so much to own their own homes if they were such risky investments? One answer is that, because rents could be as high as 25 to 40 percent of a property's value, it took only two to four years' worth of rent to buy a house, so buying was a better long-term economic strategy. Yet rental rates varied over time and neighborhoods, while the impulse for homeownership endured. An 1886 ad for a Chicago subdivision articulated some of what the advertisers understood as the inducements to homeownership:

> A suburban home means no *rent* to pay, no *moving* to do; it means trees, lawn, shrubbery, flower garden, vegetable garden if you want it, *pure air*, room for your children to play away from the street and its evil influences, better *health*, especially for the children; fewer doctor's bills, lower taxes, better citizenship, neighbors who will take a more sincere interest in your welfare, a warm seat in a *comfortable car*. Every payment on your home is a *deposit* in a *savings bank* that

cannot break—something to leave to your family, safe from ordinary disaster, that will increase in value as the years go by. Everything you to do to improve or beautify it adds to its market value.[34]

Thus homeownership might be better than a bank for a poor man because it could produce money from home improvements, while also saving money on city taxes, doctor's bills, moving bills, and even grocery bills. Suburban homes provided comfort: the "warm seat" of this advertisement is a reference to the enclosed suburban rail cars, in contrast to open, crowded, urban street cars. But more than comfort, suburban homes offered potential profit, "safe from ordinary disaster." Unlike an intangible investment in a bank or corporation, homeownership was an investment that owners could touch, hope to understand, "beautify," and improve, and hope to protect from disaster, as they spent their sweat equity to increase their real estate profit.

"In the products of the soil all wealth has its origins," a reporter for the *Land Owner* wrote, recommending real estate investments around Chicago. "A good farm, or suburban garden, with rich soil, judiciously managed, whether its commercial gold value may go up or down, is still the source of a good and comfortable living."[35] Workers might not always reap real estate profits, but they could reap produce from their gardens. Homeownership was better than a bank when it meant garden ownership and truck farming, a useful resource during strikes and depressions, especially to those newly arrived from rural areas.

The promise of pure air, better health, and fewer doctor's bills would have had traction in the late nineteenth century, when Chicago's streets were frequently described as "fetid" and coal pollution left layers of black soot on clothes worn only a few hours. One early ad recommended buying a suburban lot before the summer cholera season began, while others suggested that fresh suburban air could cure yellow fever and "bronchial complaints." It might indeed have improved health. As late as 1930 an eastern European immigrant explained that he moved near the Western Electric Works in the suburb of Hawthorne because of his children's health. "When I first came to Chicago I lived out in a pretty bad district. I lost two children there, so my wife and I decided that we would get out of Chicago and move to a better place where the air would be fresher and we would be more independent." He bought a bungalow in Hawthorne, paying off a long-term mortgage and achieving not only independence but also the health of his other children.[36]

"But pure air, et ceteras, would not retain these sensible people here; nor residence lots at a moiety of city prices, nor low taxes, if they could not have first-class schools," Chicago's real estate press intoned. Along with health, suburban homeownership promised better class status for children. Schools were not the draw everywhere—many working-class suburbs skimped on school services in order to reduce onerous property taxes—but suburbs like Evanston in the north and Morgan Park in the south both developed explicitly as "school villages." Other Chicago suburbs touted the educational value of their open space. "Our children enjoy pure air and abundance of room for sports and exercise, without having to herd with the vicious and vulgar children who haunt city streets and alleys," declared a booster account of Ravenswood. Class segregation was seen as beneficial for child rearing, so homeownership was connected with both production of property values and reproduction of class values.[37]

In one of his intriguing advertising booklets, Samuel Eberly Gross vividly illustrated the multifaceted advantages that he believed workers would gain from homeownership. The pamphlet begins with a scene of Charley and Lucy Graham eating breakfast, worried about how much their $20 monthly rent cuts into Charley's $65 monthly salary as a clerk. Readers learn from the conversation that groceries and fuel cost them $24 a month, a servant is $12 a month, and carfare and lunch for Charley is another $8, leaving only $1 per month for clothing, furniture, and incidentals, while leaving no money in the family budget for a child. After her young husband leaves for work, Lucy says to herself, "I can't and won't sit, year after year, and see Charley look every rent day as he did this morning—blue as indigo and solemn as an owl. Besides when we get old whatever are we to do?" Just then she notices a newspaper advertisement for Gross Park. She visits Samuel Gross, returns "laden with circulars and pamphlets" of his ubiquitous advertisements, and holds a brief consultation with her Irish maid, Maggie.[38]

That evening Lucy Graham takes financial control of her family, transgressing some traditional gender roles while coquettishly observing others. This advertising pamphlet offers a fascinating picture of indirect feminine power, presumably as a model for readers to emulate. "Mrs Lucy rolled her lord's easy chair before the fire, and when he had comfortably seated himself therein[,] coolly perched her wee, little self upon his knee, and began: 'Now, sir, I want to know right away, quick, if you are willing to let me have the financial management of this institution for a term of years, and no questions asked, please?'" Of course he asks questions, but she refuses to respond. Gross's advertisement playfully combines the language of masculine military maneuvers and feminine domesticity:

"Yes or no? Your last chance," demanded the usually gentle Mrs.
    Graham with unwonted vigor.

"Y-e-s."

"An unconditional surrender!" cried Lucy, triumphantly. ["]Now to
    pay you for your great magnanimity, you shall have some music,"
    and going to the piano she sang "Home Sweet Home" with such
    power and pathos as brought tears to her husband's eyes.[39]

The next morning, Lucy takes Charley's wallet and desk keys from him,
"very demurely." Soon she moves them to "a cozy cottage not a minute[']s
further ride from his business than before," a statement that obliquely
implies that some Chicagoans were already beginning to worry about the
burden of long commutes.

Charley is surprised that "rent" is the same as in the old place, especially
when the neighborhood property values increase and when Lucy keeps
adding home improvements. "Gradually, as the years went on, the house
took on a new aspect, looking less and less like a *tenement*, and if Charley
thought about it at all he must have concluded that Lucy had either an angel for a landlord or a new way of managing one." He does not notice laundry drying almost every day in his backyard, but he does notice that Lucy is
more cheerful, buys more new dresses, and also stays home more often in
their "perfect bird's nest of a home—a tiny Eden in which there was no
serpent's trail." Lucy's home improvements include a genteel veranda, an
ivy-covered fence in front of their flower-filled yard, and even a "tiny conservatory" off the dining room. With street improvements and new neighbors, their house's location has become "one of the most desirable
residential portions of the city," but still their generous landlord does not
raise the rent. Charley "was in the habit of saying to his friends that his
wife could do more with $65 than he could do with a $100."[40]

After four years Charley has the chance to start his own business, but he
does not have the necessary $2,500. He tells his wife that this is fine with
him, because she has made their home so pleasant that he is perfectly con-
tent, although he would eventually like to be a better provider for his family.
The next day Lucy hands him $2,500 and reveals her secret: she is her own
landlord and she's just remortgaged their home. She explains that she made
a down payment on this house by mortgaging her old furniture and has
paid for it by taking in laundry. Her husband is shocked. Laundry was de-
meaning work in the nineteenth century. Collecting and distributing heavy
bundles of clothes, toting hundreds of gallons of water along with the fuel
to heat it, then boiling, scrubbing, rinsing, starching, wringing, hanging,
and finally ironing with six-pound irons was difficult and strenuous labor,

often racialized as the task of nonwhite women. Nineteenth-century laundresses usually worked six days a week for meager wages.[41]

Spending so many hours bent over a washtub, washing other people's filth, does not fit this family that also has a piano and a conservatory in their suburban-like home on the edge of the city. But Lucy explains, "You see the moment I saw this place and noticed how clear and free from smoke and dust the air out here was, and what a lovely yard for drying, I conceived the idea of starting a laundry. I knew just how ladies would appreciate a place where they could send their fine linen and have it properly whitened and cared for."[42] Suburban fresh air undergirds Lucy's home business. She has been taking in laundry "by proxy" really, since their Irish maid has been doing almost all the work (with a slight raise in her wages), while another immigrant woman came once a week to iron, freeing Lucy to manage the business and perform only "fine ironing." Lucy explains that her laundry has brought in so much money that she has been paying double the $20 monthly mortgage, so the house was paid off in just three and a half years, and now she's remortgaged it to raise capital for Charley's new business venture. Explaining this, she also explains that she will now return household financial management to her husband and turns the laundry business over to Maggie, because, she says, she's tired.[43]

The story concludes that the Grahams are now wealthy. "None of their fashionable friends would ever have known that the elegant Mrs. Graham had ever taken in washing had she not herself told the story of how she became her own landlord." Mrs. Lucy Graham advises her young friends:

> Now my dears, take my advice and do not throw any money away paying for other people's property; but own your own castle first, and then adorn it as much as you please. It will not cost a cent more. Mr. Graham dates all his success in life from the day we ceased to pay rent, and every hour of our lives we render mute thanks to that large-minded, public-spirited man—S. E. Gross—who has rendered it possible for every man or *woman* to own his or her own home.[44]

This is a remarkable advertisement. It crosses class lines as Lucy becomes a laundress in order to own a home in a fashionable neighborhood. It plays with gender roles as she makes the financial decisions and opens her own business, all so that she can later become a more traditional and prestigious housewife.[45] It portrays real estate as a speculative investment whose property value increases with Lucy's improvements, while it also portrays real estate as a productive space. Suburban fresh air enables Lucy's laundry to prosper, and remortgaging their home provides collateral for Charley's business loan. Homeownership launches them into middle-class roles.

Gross's pamphlet invites all Chicagoans to follow Lucy's example and achieve economic mobility through homeownership. In this ad, Gross is explicitly selling real estate to people who might see a home as a site for work, especially women's waged work.

Gross's sense that his customers wanted homes for both consumption and production was confirmed by Chicago academics a generation later. For his sociology dissertation at the University of Chicago, Julius John Ozog interviewed Chicago's Polish homeowners in the 1930s. Forty-eight percent said they had bought homes because they wanted more space for a growing family; 20 percent were dissatisfied with their old neighborhood and wanted to move away; 10 percent wanted to "escape from the necessity of frequently moving" when landlords arbitrarily raised their rents; and 70 percent agreed that homeownership brought security. Poverty-stricken homeowners gave similar reasons to social worker Mary Frances Bruton, who wrote her dissertation in 1924. Overall, "economic ambition" was their prime motive for homeownership, Ozog concluded, intertwined with "a vague desire" for "social benefits and prestige."[46]

Ozog explained that land meant economic, social, and political capital to many of the Poles he interviewed, because in the peasant societies from which Chicago's workers had immigrated, land had been a crucial tool of production and also, often, a prerequisite for political power. Other Chicago observers also commented on the "peasant" land hunger of Chicago's immigrants. Yet this was not naïve peasant nostalgia. American urban land could be a tool of production for people who ran small shops from their homes—like Lucy's laundry—and for the many people who took in boarders. American property ownership also brought political power in a government based on property taxes, while homes owned in ethnic neighborhoods brought political power in Chicago's ward system. The "peasant attachment to land" that Chicagoans observed in many immigrant homeowners had a material basis in Chicago's economics and politics.[47]

Ironically, producing elite property values requires maintaining the illusion of a production-free zone. Lucy Graham eventually relinquishes her home laundry business. In prestigious neighborhoods productive vegetable gardens had to be hidden from public view, while more decorative flower gardens were proudly displayed. In 1913 a Chicago architect offered plans for a "suburban flat building" that "can be made to look like a private residence," which was, apparently, desirable for the neighborhood. In the post-Victorian separation of home and work, revealing too much of the overlap between home and work could undermine the respectability of a home.[48] This question of respectability and domesticity was an especially vexing question for Chicago's foreigners.

FOREIGN AND DOMESTIC

Chicago social workers' clients told them that owning a home made them "real Americans." Yet homeownership did not always bring recognition of Americanization. A writer for Chicago's Czech-language newspaper *Svornost* complained in 1885 that some Chicagoans insulted Czechs by declaring they "generally dwell in the worst of holes," lived less well than Chicago's Germans, and took in too many boarders. The *Daily Jewish Courier* decried the reputation of Chicago's Jews as building houses only "for incendiarism, in order to collect insurance." Jews were accused of too much production, hoping to profit from insurance, just as Czechs were accused of too much production, hoping to profit from boarders. Both were accused of not adequately shifting to the consumerist ideology of the American family home.[49]

Still, Chicago's immigrant groups hoped to reap the benefits of respectable domesticity. An advertisement in Chicago's Lithuanian paper *Lietuva* proclaimed, "The ownership of real estate insures future security. When a Lithuanian insures his future security by purchasing good income-producing property, he not only profits personally, but brings honor upon his nationality; it is a patriotic as well as a profitable practice." Articles agreed that homes might produce respect as well as income: "All Lithuanians who have saved up some money should purchase buildings and lots. . . . This would not only improve the general welfare of our people, but it would also increase Lithuanian prestige." These same newspapers complained about high property taxes and occasional crooked land sales, but they also bragged about the number of their countrymen who owned Chicago property, and they compared their group's homeownership practices to other nationalities' "cheap and neglected . . . shanties." Such interethnic rivalries are reminders that immigrants could be denied the status usually associated with homeownership, even as they hoped that homeownership would bring status to their own ethnic group.[50]

Respect could prove elusive. When Chicago's immigrants strove to have a middle-class home, they were aiming at a tricky moving target, partly because the word *domestic* has a double meaning: domestic contrasts with both things outside the home and things outside the nation.[51] While Chicago's social workers encouraged immigrants to become domestic and respectable, they also rarely recognized their domesticity. Foreigners' domesticity was, to them, an almost unimaginable oxymoron.

One of Chicago's settlement house workers observed, "The ambition of the immigrant to own property in America is one of his most striking characteristics. For it he will make almost unbelievable sacrifices both of his own comfort and of that of his wife and children, since the heavily mort-gaged house too often calls for the united wage-earning power of the entire family." This could not be middle-class "American" domesticity, she argued, because it involved women's waged work, child labor, and extreme under-consumption in order to afford a home. Chicago's immigrant workers were not really homeowners, according to this social worker; they were heavily indebted tenement landlords who rented out apartments and took in boarders as they struggled to pay off the mortgage. They used what should have been a space of leisure as a space of production.[52]

"Many foreigners have a fear of banks" and prefer to invest their money in real estate, another social worker reported, but then added that such an idea implied they were choosing between a mortgage payment and a bank deposit, when their actual choices were between a mortgage payment and the grocery bill. "It is not unusual when a case has been referred to the United Charities because children are underfed or underclothed that a visit will disclose that the family is making regular monthly payments on a house."[53] Social workers were appalled at the gap between working-class domesticity and middle-class sentimental discourse:

> The old idea of the prosperous workman owning a house of his own—usually a small cottage with a cheerful garden—fails of illustration in the immigrant ten-ement neighborhoods found in all large cities.... In these cases ownership is far from being a sign of prosperity which indicates comfort. The owner of the tene-ment frequently lives in the smallest and poorest apartment . . . an attic or a cellar . . . in order that the more desirable apartments may be used to make the house bring in the largest possible return.[54]

Statistics from a house-to-house canvass by these same social workers re-vealed that half of immigrant homeowners actually lived in single-family houses without other apartments, and the remainder were in two- or three-family houses, not large apartment buildings. Among the home-owners, 42 percent had lived there more than eight years, which was long enough to pay off most nineteenth-century mortgages.[55] Thus their own statistics show that workers' "stringent economies" were probably not as dreadful as the portrait that social workers drew. Still, there was real suf-fering when homes were used as banks.

Reformers asserted that the "land-hunger of the European peasant" in Chicago caused problems of "not simple poverty, but undue frugality." Re-formers worried about two related problems: underconsumption and over-work, especially the overworking of women and children. Middle-class observers declared that immigrants' desire to own homes "means in some cases the sacrifice of the children's education, the crowding of the home with lodgers, or the mother's going out to work," or all three, transgressing middle-class domesticity in order to achieve it. Social workers were less impressed by this strategy than was Gross's Lucy Graham. "The foreign worker wants to own his own home as soon as possible and often before he ought to," complained the settlement house leader Mary Eliza McDowell. "This thrift is not a blessing but too often a curse to the family and not good for the community." Bruton reported that when she interviewed other social workers, they unanimously declared, "There is absolutely nothing a family will not sacrifice to keep up its payments on property, they starve their children and go in rags, they live in dark basement flats which will not rent, they ruin their health by overwork, and they take their children out of school at fourteen to go to work." She also interviewed immigrant leaders and building and loan association officers who "admitted all but the last of these items," insisting "that the day of exploiting the child is past." While denying child labor, these immigrant leaders were proud of the other sacrifices that their countrymen made for homeownership.[56]

Despite skimping on food, crowding in boarders, sometimes collecting the wages of child labor, and requiring mothers to work double shifts at home and in outside waged work, many families lost their houses and savings. Sympathy for the poor slipped into blaming "the cupidity of parents who preferred the purchase of a house to the education of their children." Social workers believed that too many children lost opportunities for class mobility because "at all times the need of keeping up the payments on a house outweighs the need of keeping a child in school." Children also reputedly engaged in petty theft of coal, wood, or chickens in order to help their family economize to meet the mortgage payments. One minister defended these families whose children worked to pay off mortgages: "Surely it is a commendable thing that a family should desire to own its own home. The condemnation is rather upon that system which permits the attainment of that desire only by the demoralization of life."[57]

Such demoralization included taking in lodgers. According to reformers, homeowners were "constantly tempted" to take in lodgers, who were usually single males and who might encourage a husband or wife to drink alcohol, might engage in illicit sex with family members, or might simply bring more crowding, less privacy, and "a great deal of additional work for the overburdened wife and mother who has a constant excuse for not maintaining a satisfactory standard of cleanliness." Social workers believed that offering bigger houses might encourage immigrants to take in still more lodgers, so they advocated building small houses for working people or model houses carefully designed "so that each room can serve one and only one purpose. . . . That is, the living room, dining room, and kitchen are either combined or so open into each other that no temptation is offered to close off part for sleeping purposes." They sought to architecturally incite the poor to a middle-class separation of room uses.[58]

Housing reformers found other extreme economizing strategies among working-class homeowners. In a Polish neighborhood on Chicago's northwest side in the 1920s, people who owned lots but not houses lived in portable garages for years, while they waited to save enough money to build a house, in a strategy known as "garage dwelling." In the Town of Lake 51 percent of sleeping rooms had less than the legal minimum of four hundred cubic feet of air per sleeper, that is, less than a five-by-ten-foot space with eight-foot ceilings. "Sometimes the crowding is unnecessary: the family prefer, especially in the winter, to huddle into the rooms which are near the kitchen and in this way save the expense of extra fuel and an extra stove. . . . The secret of the overcrowding which prevails here is to be explained in part by the un-American standard of living." Foreigners' domesticity did not achieve American middle-class standards of consumption.[59]

One rare social worker admired immigrants' thrifty and productive uses of their domestic space: "Bohemians, who love nature, pure air, and gardens," continually moved to the suburban fringe of Chicago, Josefa Humpal Zeman asserted.

> Often good artisans were compelled to work for low wages, even $1.25 a day; still, out of this meager remuneration they managed to lay a little aside for that longed-for possession,—a house and lot that they could call their own. When that was paid for, then the house received an additional story, and that was rented, so that it began earning money. When more was saved, the house was pushed in the rear, the garden sacrificed, and in its place an imposing brick or stone building was erected, containing frequently a store, or more rooms for tenants. The landlord, who had till then lived in some unpleasant rear rooms, moved into the best part of the house; the bare but well-scrubbed floors were covered with Brussels carpets, the wooden chairs replaced by upholstered ones, and the best room received the added luxury of a piano or violin.[60]

It is a charming story of upward mobility, similar to Gross's tale of Lucy and Charley Graham, with tenant-keeping substituting for laundry as the work of the home. But just like laundry, tenant-keeping could be arduous. Houses pushed into the rear of lots were dark spaces bordering on open sewers and festering garbage piles, in districts congested with others who shared these strategies.[61]

Chicago social workers found that in one small house on Paulina Street, a family of seven lived in a single attic room while renting out the other four rooms. Such small-scale apartments were especially dismaying to Chicago housing reformers, who reported, "These resident landlords make the reform of housing conditions very difficult. . . . Not only are the landlords very poor, but their entire margin of saving for years is mortgaged to pay for the house. There is not only no hope of their making improvements, but they will not even make needed repairs until they are compelled to do so."[62] While avoiding reproducing the elitism of the social workers, it is fair to say that Chicago's immigrants made heroic sacrifices in order to achieve homeownership.

The historical record contains few glimpses of how Chicago's immigrant working class viewed their own extreme thrift. It is clear that many immigrant families chose this route, but there are a few traces showing that others criticized it. "Mr Dooley," the Irish bartender in a popular column in the *Chicago Journal*, asks a client, "Did ye iver know a man be th' name iv Ahearn? Ye did not? Well, maybe he was before yer time. He was a cobbler be thrade; but he picked up money be livin off iv leather findings an' wooden pegs, an' bought pieces iv the prairie, and starved an' bought more, an' starved an' starved till his heart was shriveled up like a washerwoman's hand. But he made money."[63] Dooley's monologue was humorous to Chicago readers because it was a model they would have found familiar. The image of a washerwoman's shriveled hands might even have made them think of Lucy Graham. Actual Chicagoans may not have starved or eaten spare shoe leather like Ahearn, but they did sacrifice for a homeownership that brought a limited upward mobility at great cost. Their sacrifices were so common they could be a subject of humor.

Even advertisers admitted that homeownership could require extreme sacrifices. Gross quoted the Reverend T. DeWitt Talmage:

> In this great country there is room enough for every man and woman to have a home. Morals and civilization demand it. . . . The much-abused mortgage, which is ruin to a reckless man, to one prudent and provident is the beginning of a competency and a fortune, for the reason that he will not be satisfied until he has paid it off, and all the household are put on stringent economies until then. *Deny yourself all superfluities and all luxuries until you can say: "Everything in this house is mine, every timber, every brick, every foot of plumbing, every doorsill."*[64]

The repetition of "every" is ominous, and so is investigating what were the "superfluities" that homeowners had to forgo. In addition to the food, clothing, children's education, heat, and privacy sacrificed for homeownership, there were also sacrifices of municipal services.

Sewers, water, gas, electricity, good roads, sidewalks, garbage removal, police, fire department, and schools: all cost money that many working-class suburbanites did not have. To keep property taxes low, some of Chicago's suburbanizers moved into unincorporated spaces lacking such services. When towns incorporated and sought to provide a bare minimum of municipal services, some of them chose creative financing tactics that were not signs of middle-class respectability. Chicago's suburb of West Hammond developed a saloon and vice district to lure tourists from nearby dry counties, even after Prohibition began in 1920 Cicero allowed the building of the Hawthorne race track, which it then found too expensive to police. Cicero had incorporated in 1867 with a charter "very liberal in its provisions for self-government, and very strict in its clauses against exorbitant taxation." It had no public water system until 1901, and, because of its lack of clout, it had higher gas and electricity rates than in the city of Chicago. But it did have low taxes. It also had nearly twice the illiteracy rate as Chicago and deep problems with police corruption. These trenchant problems were exacerbated when, by 1930, one-fourth of all the property taxes levied in Cicero were delinquent.[65]

In addition to stringently economizing on municipal budgets, there was also economizing within homes. West Hammond's homeowners lacked "amenities" like private toilets and bathtubs as late as 1939. Building homes without bathrooms in cities without sewers led to especially high costs later, when cities and homeowners decided to retroactively add services. This raises the question of whether, instead of an upwardly mobile American dream, such homeownership might have been a nightmare of misplaced resources. Would a better strategy have been to commit resources to educating their children instead of owning their homes? Chicago's social workers thought so.[66]

The policy of Chicago's charities was to insist that clients sell their homes because renting appeared cheaper and seemed to call for less extreme sacrifices. The poor knew of this policy and apparently disagreed. They strategically resisted social workers' attempts to get them to give up homeownership. Social workers complained that poor homeowners pretended their mortgage payments were rent, in a ruse to get charities to help them.[67]

Mary Bruton interviewed Mr. and Mrs. B, an elderly Italian couple who told her they had bought a house in 1912 quite conscious of the fact that they could never pay for it, yet hoping they would die before the balloon payment came due. They used all their savings for a down payment, moved into the basement, let their son move into the attic, and rented the first floor for $30 a month, which, they hoped, would be enough to pay interest and taxes and keep a roof over their heads until death. This was not a bad strategy, since the rent might allow them some income during retirement. But it was not an ideal strategy. Questions of homeownership are never simple financial transactions; they are also questions of shelter, health, and comfort. Mr. and Mrs. B discovered, after they moved in, that the dampness of the basement caused them to suffer from rheumatism, so much so that Mr. B was confined to his bed, unable to work, for twelve years. They had to spend a portion of their small rental income on medicine while they suffered in this dank basement until death.[68]

What alternatives did they have? There were few other options for workers to try to fund retirement, claim middle-class status, or invest their meager surplus earnings. Few immigrants could access quality education for their children, but many encountered Chicago's numerous subdividers, building and loan associations, and others in the business of encouraging homeownership. Advertisements told them:

> A home of your own is your greatest asset, it dispels the fear of old age, it is the secret of contented living, an unfaltering devotion to duty. Prove yourself worthy of the confidence imposed in you, command the entire respect of the community and your family, have a fixed determination, where there is a will there is a way, be invincible in your determination, you are up against hard facts that chafe you, the goal is not as far away as you might suppose it to be.[69]

This is a great deal of exhortation, suggesting that the message required reiteration. Some clearly resisted the pressures for homeownership, while many others were convinced by the advertisement's message. Defending Chicago's Polish homeowners in his dissertation for the University of Chicago's Department of Sociology, Ozog wrote that what might appear to be a "sacrifice" to native-born elites might be, for immigrants, "an advance, socially and economically."[70] A home was better than a bank for a poor man. It was, nevertheless, a great risk.

CHAPTER 5

cɴɔ

Mapping Chicago, Imagining Metropolises

Reconsidering the Zonal Model of Urban Growth

Swedish-born Henry Ericsson arrived in Chicago on March 31, 1882. He spent his first evening in the city looking at a map spread out on the kitchen table of his Uncle Lind's home, near Prairie Avenue and Twenty-ninth Street. Lind first used the map to ask what Ericsson would like to see the next day, the one day he planned to explore the city before beginning work. Then Lind used the map to shift his nephew from the position of tourist to that of real estate speculator. "He slyly asked me where I would buy if given my choice," Ericsson recalled when writing his memoir sixty years later. "Pronto, I put my finger down on what was to become the Midway Plaisance!"[1]

Ericsson chose to imagine buying a house next to what looked like a picturesque park on the edge of the city. Yet in 1882 the park shown on the map was not actually there on the ground. Ericsson recalled, "Uncle explained that the parks and boulevards marked by broad red lines merely outlined the speculative trend just after the Civil War and that my guess was as wild as the guesses of the promoters of those days before the fire."[2] Chicago's extensive system of parks encircling the city had been proposed in 1869 partly to boost the value of land on the periphery. The city had purchased most of the land for these parks during the 1870s, but in the 1880s much of the park system had not been built. When Ericsson looked at the map on his uncle's kitchen table, the park he pointed to was actually a "sandy waste of unredeemed and desert land" on Chicago's South Side.[3]

A decade later, during the World's Fair Columbian Exposition of 1893, it would become the famous Midway, and nearby land prices would balloon up to 1,000 percent.

Ericsson did not actually have the money to buy any land in 1882, when he looked at the map on his uncle's kitchen table. Instead of investing in semi-suburban space by the embryonic park on Chicago's South Side, he moved into a downtown tenement, then eventually invested in property north of Chicago, near other Swedes. Still, he was proud to remember that if he had bought in 1882, he might have made a great profit, especially if he had sold precisely in 1893 during the World's Fair boom, before the depression that began in 1894.

Ericsson's story reveals the tenuous balance between cartographic maps on paper, cognitive maps in people's minds, and actual conditions on the ground in Chicago. It reveals much about Chicago's early suburbanization. Ericsson's uncle encouraged him to imagine himself as a homeowner as soon as he arrived in Chicago, even before he had any money to buy a house. Ericsson himself imagined his own homeownership on the city's periphery, on the nearly suburban border that Chicago's real estate press often described as "outside the circle of the parks and boulevards."[4] Ericsson's imaginary home was next to a park on the map, but not on the ground. His story shows that the projections of Chicago's early maps were often a projection into the future.

Maps helped people imagine their burgeoning metropolis by making projections about urban growth. Chicago's mapmakers began by commodifying land into a grid, then superimposed circles in order to structure that grid. From the circles on the nineteenth-century boosters' maps advertising speculative real estate, to the development of Chicago's inner loop of elevated trains and outer loop of parks and boulevards, to the bird's-eye views illustrating Daniel Burnham's *Plan of Chicago* (1909), Chicagoans frequently imagined their city as a series of circles. It was the circle of parks and boulevards that Ericsson used to orient himself as he sat at his uncle's kitchen table, looking at a map.

In 1924 University of Chicago sociologist Ernest Burgess codified the preceding half-century of mapmakers' circles by publishing a famous bull's-eye diagram, hypothesizing that every city would grow outward in circles. In the decades since Burgess's diagram, many have questioned his hypothesis, but it remains a powerful tool for Americans who seek to understand urban growth by imagining a central commercial core balanced by an expanding suburban ring. Despite the long-lasting power of this model, even Burgess recognized that on-the-ground politics resisted his efforts at abstraction. In less famous research projects, Burgess's students and colleagues mapped a complex, multinucleated city, including suburban industries, vice districts, retail centers, and working-class residential areas alongside the middle-class suburban bungalows that Burgess's zonal theory had predicted. Their maps offer intriguing alternative ways to image Chicago's cultural landscape and America's suburbanization.

Like Henry Ericsson and the academics in the Chicago School of sociology, many Chicagoans used maps to envision their metropolitan region. Maps are not simply representations of natural geography; they are powerful constructions of culture, politics, and economics. Mapped images of circles and metaphors of nature attempt to hide regional conflict, while they help support the creation of regionally based identities. Maps help sell real estate, entice tourists, encourage philanthropy, guide investors, plan construction, and assert control. Maps made predictions about how the city would grow. Reexamining these maps illuminates Chicago's growth, including the complex relationship between city and suburbs.[5]

ENCIRCLING CHICAGO

The seminal urban map of Chicago, James Thompson's "Map of the Town of Chicago" (1830), was a "dream" in which muddy paths and scattered houses appeared as ordered roads and neat city blocks. Thompson's plat laid the foundation for the geometrical grid that would dominate Chicago. After the Land Ordinance of 1785, surveyors had divided the American West into gridded townships that would identify abstract land boundaries, orient bureaucrats, facilitate real estate transactions, and suggest a future urbanity. The grid does not help a traveler seeking a topographically efficient route or a farmer seeking a fertile field, but it does conveniently convert land into a commodity. The names of early maps reflect this commodification, as in Edward Benton Talcott's "Chicago with the several additions compiled from the recorded plats in the Clerk's office, Cook County, Illinois. The lots in the original town . . . will be offered for sale . . . on the 20th of June 1836," a map published in New York for out-of-town real estate investors. Even without such explicit titles, the implied reader of Chicago's earliest urban maps is a land buyer.[6]

The mapped grid eventually influenced the aesthetic assumptions of many Chicagoans. In 1869, when Frederick Law Olmsted rejected the grid by designing picturesquely curving streets in his model suburb of Riverside, Chicago's commentators did not universally admire his plan. As late as 1891 a guidebook complained that Riverside's roads "run only in curves, and hence the view of the place is somewhat obstructed."[7] Some real estate journalists defended Olmsted's curves, explaining that Riverside "differs from most suburban neighborhoods in avoiding the angles, which, though desirable for every plan that looks forward to a city in the future, are too stiff and formal for such adornment and rusticity as should be combined in a model suburb."[8] Riverside was self-consciously a model suburb, but it was an exception. Morgan Park, Pullman, and a few other nineteenth-century Chicago suburbs imitated its curving roads, but most Chicago suburbs chose a gridded street plan instead, following the model laid out in the maps of the 1830s. A grid was cheaper to design and easier to sell. A grid facilitated potential annexation into the city, at a time when the line between city and suburb continually shifted. A grid fostered fungibility.

Popular bird's-eye-view prints of early Chicago—including an 1854 lithograph by Ed Mandel that exaggerated the extent to which Chicago had spread over the prairie, an 1857 lithograph by Christian Inger, an 1871 illustration by Theodore Davis in *Harper's Weekly*, and a famous 1898 print by Currier and Ives—emphasized the orderly grid of the city's public streets, extending out across the flat prairie in a semicircle. In order to distinguish land from the interchangeable grid, Chicagoans gradually added a series of circles superimposed on the grid. Mapmakers appointed the courthouse near the intersection of Randolph and Clark Streets as the center of the city, then drew concentric circles around that administrative center, marking all points one mile from the courthouse, two miles, three, four, and on up to eight miles in a classic Rand McNally map of 1884—a map similar to the one that Henry Ericsson looked at on his uncle's kitchen table. A few Chicago realtors' maps recentered these circles on their own subdivisions, clarifying where potential buyers could go if they traveled a mile or two in any direction from that subdivision, but these were an exception. Most frequently the center of the circles was the Chicago courthouse. In 1871 the *Map Showing the Burnt District in Chicago*, published in Saint Louis "for the benefit of the Relief Fund," portrayed the irregular red wound of the area burned by Chicago's Great Fire superimposed on neat black circles centered on the courthouse. Apparently the non-Chicagoans who were being asked to send donations for the relief of fire sufferers wanted to know how the burned area related to Chicago's center and periphery, which they perceived as circles structuring the grid.[9]

In 1874, in his book promoting investment in Chicago's suburban real estate, Everett Chamberlin included a large foldout map showing a circle every mile for twenty-two miles around Chicago, much farther than the metropolitan area at the time. In Chamberlin's map, even the ripples in Lake Michigan reinforce these many concentric circles, subtly suggesting further centrifugal expansion. The circles are transected by

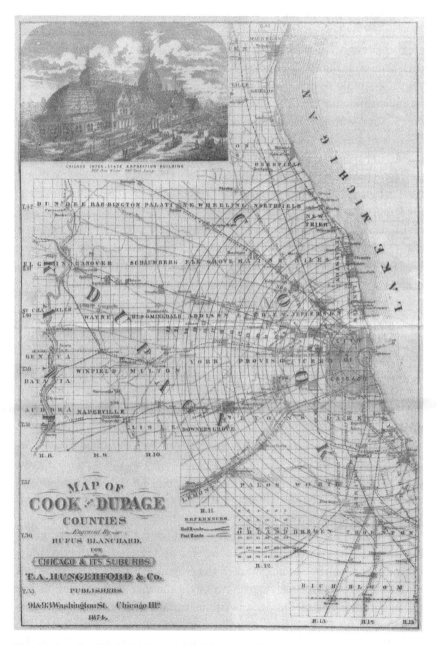

Like the map that Henry Ericsson recalled viewing on his first night in Chicago, this 1874 map of Chicago emphasized concentric circles superimposed onto the grid of administrative lines. From Rufus Blanchard, "Map of Cook and Dupage Counties," in Everett Chamberlin, *Chicago and Its Suburbs* (Chicago: T. A. Hungerford & Co., 1874).

railroad lines that help structure Chamberlin's text and further emphasize Chicago's expansion.[10]

Mapped circles are not unique to Chicago. In 1847 J. C. Sidney had created a popular map of Philadelphia that enclosed the city in a single circle
with a ten-mile radius. Even some early maps of Los Angeles include circles.
They are simple to draw and encouraging to boosters selling visions of a
steadily expanding city. They were particularly predominant in Chicago after the Civil War. Earlier regional maps of Chicago tend to place the city to
the side of the frame, emphasizing the city's relationship with its western
hinterland or eastern markets, not yet evincing the confidence that led
Chicago's post–Civil War mapmakers to place their city at the regional center. From an 1875 advertisement for Lawndale to an 1889 advertisement
for Auburn Park, Chicago real estate ads frequently showed suburban subdivisions situated within concentric circles. These mapped circles imply a
reader who was relatively unfamiliar with Chicago and wanted to know
how far a street or subdivision was from the center of town. This implied
reader believed the center of town was the courthouse and judged land
values by their distance from that civic center.[11]

Such mapped circles were so ubiquitous that they may seem natural, but
many American cities lack a single unassailable center that remains the
same for all residents over time. When Olmsted first proposed Central Park
in Manhattan, some feared it was dangerously north of the community's
"true" center. Chicagoans probably imagined various centers to their city,
but—perhaps because so many map readers were so new to the city—
mapmakers seem to have collectively agreed on setting up a single set of
concentric circles around their city, centered on the government headquarters. Chicago's official center shifted in 1911, when the modern street-
numbering system placed the coordinates 0,0 at State and Madison Streets,
a few blocks from the courthouse, at the southeast corner of the original
1830 plat of the town yet still quite close to an agreed-upon center.

The consistent circles on Chicago's maps offered a guide to newcomers,
but it was left to the discretion of viewers to decide whether the two-mile,
four-mile, or ten-mile radius marked the beginning of the suburbs. It was
also up to viewers to translate the circles on the map to actual conditions
on the ground—until Chicagoans began to build the circles their maps
projected.

In 1869 Chicago's proposed parks and boulevards began to clarify the
question of where the suburbs began, while also transforming the mapped
circles into a physical reality. A proposed system of parks connected by boulevards circled the city just beyond the four-mile radius line on the map,
increasing to the six-mile line on the South Side. This oval of parks was the

red line on the map that Ericsson had observed at his uncle's kitchen table. "Within the circle of the parks and the lake, land will never recede in value," Chicago's monthly real estate newspaper the *Land Owner* declared in 1872. "Without the circle, men who load up must be cautious. . . . Such an explanation becomes necessary in view of the constant attempts to palm off remote and worthless lands upon a non-resident public who have over-confidence in anything that any scalawag plats out and calls a Chicago 'Addition.'" In their prose description of this circle of parks, the *Land Owner* offered a mental map of the city, using the parks circle to help real estate investors who were not familiar with Chicago. In 1872 this parks circle was still outside the municipal limits, yet, according to the *Land Owner*, all the land inside the circle was the "heart" of Chicago. Outside that parks circle, in the farther suburbs, "the surplus population, the overflowings of the seething cauldrons, will seek homes. Large manufactories that require room will [also] go there." This is a suburbia of working-class homes near factories, a place where real estate investment is far riskier than in the center of the city.[12]

The *Land Owner* continued, "We have made this explanation of the real estate topography of this city, not for residents, for all our people know this fact, or ought to, but for strangers." Strangers did rely on these imagined circles, as Ericsson's experience shows. Like other American cities, Chicago developed its park system partly to cultivate the taste of the masses and partly to provide healthy breathing spaces for the urban population, but also because parks enhanced the value of property in their vicinity: "In a purely economical point of view, parks are necessary. They always produce more wealth than they cost." Even before the World's Fair was built in Jackson Park in 1893, Chicago had spent an estimated $24 million on its system of eight large and twenty-nine small parks, connected by thirty-five miles of broad boulevards circling the city. Many asserted it was money well spent because it enhanced the value of real estate by clarifying the map of Chicago.[13]

By making the maps' circles visible on the ground, Chicago's parks and boulevards guided people around the city, especially after the annexations of 1889 enlarged the city to what seemed to many to be an unwieldy size. Many visitors spent a day riding in carriages around the circle of park boulevards and looked forward to the time when an outer beltway would add another, wider circle to the map. As a British tourist exclaimed in 1897, "Chicago, straggling over a hundred and eighty-six square miles was rather a tract of houses than an organic city until somebody conceived the idea of coupling her up with a ring of parks connected by planted boulevards."[14]

Yet that same tourist described Chicago as the "most beautiful and the most squalid, girdled with a twofold zone of parks and slums."[15] This paradox of picturesque parks next to poor slums was made even more complex by the barrenness of some of the parks, along with the almost pastoral homeownership of some of the slums. The same *Land Owner* that had described working-class housing near large factories in Chicago's suburbs also boasted about the elegant country homes in other Chicago suburbs. The seemingly simple circles on the map held a confusing conglomeration of classes and uses on the ground.

The next of the map's imagined circles to be physically manifest was a smaller, inner circle: the Loop, which was a group of cable cars circling downtown after 1882, then electric streetcars after 1887, and then, after 1897, the current system of elevated streetcars.[16] These transit cars needed space to turn around, hence the loop, which also provided access to what came to be known as the Central Business District. In the blocks around the courthouse, businesses had clustered and land values had escalated, boosted by Potter Palmer's shrewd maneuverings after the Great Fire, when he built the Palmer House hotel slightly south of the most fashionable area, reaping real estate profits by shifting the downtown district southward to the area he owned. Retail stores, offices, and banks eventually found it worthwhile to pay high rents for this central district where, they hoped, proximity to each other would bring in enough money to offset the high land costs and increasing congestion.

In the innermost circle of Chicago's business district, speculators agreed that land had become so valuable that it was worthwhile to build vertically. After the Great Fire, Chicago's architects experimented with fireproofing, wind bracing, hydraulic elevators, iron framing, and, in 1883, steel-beam construction, leading to the development of the modern American skyscraper, emphasizing commercial utility in massive and relatively unadorned buildings, in what has come to be admired as the Chicago School of architecture.[17] With America's first skyscrapers soaring in the carefully delimited circle of the Loop, Chicago's downtown became a model for all of America's downtowns.

As early as 1876 an Australian visitor had declared, "The business part of the city probably surpasses in the even regularity and magnificence of its shops, stores, and warehouses any other in the world."[18] Twenty years later the warehouses had mostly moved out of the Loop, but the magnificent regularity remained. "You feel the hot breath of speculation quivering behind these windows," a French visitor wrote in 1895. "The invariability of natural laws gives to the most unbridled daring the calmness of geometric figures."[19] The economics of land values, the technological progress of elevators and steel beams, a seemingly natural desire among elite men to separate their businesses from their residences, and a seemingly natural desire of businesses to concentrate together in one dense area: all made downtown seem inevitable. The circle had been on Chicago maps for decades. The skyscrapers contained by the elevated Loop of trains made that imaginary circle visible on the ground.

Yet downtown was always more complex than the imagined circle on the map or the actual circle of the Loop. When a University of Chicago sociology student wrote a dissertation titled "The Natural History of the Central Business District," he carefully mapped the land use patterns of Chicago's central area in 1884 and 1935, ironically revealing a nearly countless mix of uses. His maps are dizzy with typed labels for the numerous downtown habitats he identified. Areas for commission merchants, wholesale businesses, the garment industry, train depots, storage, slum housing, vice businesses, printing presses, cheap hotels, and what he labeled "residence changing to business" all crowd in overlapping wedges alongside the more prestigious offices and first-class retail of Chicago's 1885 downtown. Homes existed downtown, this sociologist admitted, but they did not fit early sociological theories about urban growth, so they must be "changing to business." But in 1935 the sociologist's map reveals that residential lodging houses remained downtown, tenaciously defying the sociological theory. Trains took up more room on the 1935 map of downtown, while automobile shops, motels, publishing houses, the paper industry, and clubs had been added to the mix in an only slightly simplified jagged array. The downtown loop was never homogeneous.[20]

Combining business and civic functions, the privatized public space of downtown at the turn of the century sought to entice middle-class white female shoppers and white male office workers. This development was justified with allusions to the "natural ecology" of cities and to neutral market forces, but it was never free from human decisions and politics. The seemingly natural development of downtown has long required extensive promotion, including institutional buttressing by private companies and public planners. Associations of downtown businessmen, government officials, cultural institutions, and transportation engineers have had to wage campaigns to keep downtowns viable despite congestion, competition from outlying business centers, and a fluctuating tax base.[21]

In 1912 another British tourist explained Chicago's downtown Loop to visitors who did not yet know what a downtown "ought" to look like:

> The loop is a belt-lined terminal, slightly less than a mile in diameter, designed to serve the elevated railroads that stretch their caterpillar-like structures over three directions of the widespread town. Within it are the theaters, the hotels, the department stores, the retail district, and the wholesale and the railroad

terminals. Just without it is an arid belt and then somewhere to the north, the west and south, the great residential districts. So it is a mistake. For, with the exception of a little way along Michigan avenue to the south, the loop has acted against the growth of the city, has kept it tightly girdled within itself.[22]

Where that visitor saw a mistake and a constrictive girdle, others saw a natural downtown that simply needed more institutional support to buttress this "natural" area. "The Chicago loop is the most efficient natural organization to do business possessed by any city in the world," the *Chicago Tribune* declared in 1915, while at nearly the same time a lawyer for the outlying business districts called it "a vast monopoly," not a natural development.[23]

Downtown Chicago had been doubted since its beginnings in the 1880s, partly because many were uncomfortable with Chicagoans' rapid embrace of "cliffdwelling." Chicago's downtown was initially quite dark, both because of the dense soot from coal pollution and because Chicagoans had developed skyscrapers before developing adequate artificial light. Even after gaining electric light and reliable elevators, downtown merchants found they faced threats. In the first decades of the twentieth century, downtown merchants advocated for a subway to relieve congestion, while outlying business leaders opposed the proposal. "You cannot wipe out this great center," a downtown business leader told the outlying business associations in 1911, but his declaration reveals a fear that someone could do just that: wipe out downtown, or at least leave it to choke in its own congestion. Observers had begun to call the downtown Loop a constrictive "noose." In 1911 fully two-thirds of the passengers on surface transit lines never entered the central business district. By the 1920s some downtown merchants, including the trendsetting Sears, Roebuck Corporation, had started building new retail stores in the suburbs.[24]

Through the twentieth century the center of Chicago's downtown has migrated north of the loop, while other department stores and offices have leaped outward to new suburban locations in spaces like Schaumberg. Despite being buttressed by modern zoning, extensive urban planning, and a vast increase in the roles of government, America's downtowns declined between 1920 and 1950.[25] Chicago's circles did not offer as much clarity as they seemed to promise.

Paralleling the development of downtown, the inner circle of the Loop seemed to create a need for an outer circle of prestigious suburbs. "It is absolutely essential that the men and women who are crowded together during the day time in very congested business districts, have the opportunity to enjoy a complete change of environment after the strenuous working hours," declared the Chicago School of Correspondence's 1913 booklet *Modern American Homes.* Reprinting plans from the *Ladies' Home Journal, House Beautiful, American Homes and Gardens, Country Life in America, National Builder,* and other popular journals, this booklet communicated the consensus that "not even the nicest flat can take the place of a home with a garden around it. The latter will mean somewhat more work but is amply compensated for . . . physically and mentally."[26] Suburbs were portrayed as a respite from modern methods of production, yet they also meant "somewhat more work" in the cost of housing, the effort of commuting, and the labor of caring for a suburban estate. Despite that work, the outer circle of housing seemed an important balance to the inner circle of business.

Mapped circles suggested suburbanization. "Residences cannot compete with businesses for sites at the center," one University of Chicago sociologist explained confidently in 1928. Residences "are not so much locations for production as for consumption, and consequently they cannot afford to pay the high rents that the accessibility at the center commands."[27] Like many of Chicago's sociologists, he believed that natural economic laws led residences to cluster in a suburban ring around the commercial center: close enough to access it but far enough away to increase the supply of land and thus make land cheaper. This was an oversimplification. Residences were not for consumption only; many workers moved out to be closer to the factories and also did waged work within homes. Even elites did not move out to suburbs simply for nonproductive purposes. They were often willing to pay high prices for homes in prestigious suburbs, homes that enabled them to reap financial rewards through rising property values, access to business networks, and the opportunity to reproduce class status in their children. Also, businesses were not in the center only; many factories selected the less expensive land of suburbia. As Chicago realtor Homer Hoyt recognized, "Outlying settlements within and without the city limits of Chicago ran the entire gamut of the social scale from the squalid quarters in South Chicago . . . to the spacious estates of the millionaires of Lake Forest."[28] The factories and the homes of the factory workers complicated any neat home/work binary of suburb and city. Eight miles northwest of the city was the working-class suburb of Dunning, eventually annexed into the city of Chicago, while eight miles west was the wealthy suburb of Riverside, defying any model of simple rings. Yet the rings, first created by mapmakers selling real estate to out-of-town investors, then reinforced by the physical circle of the parks and the Loop, continued to structure Chicagoans' view of their city.

A French tourist described the street-level chaos that defied any easily mapped rings:

Close beside the preposterous, Babel-like [downtown] building extends a shape-
less bit of ground, undefined, bristling, green with a scanty turf, on which a lean
cow is feeding. Then follows a succession of little wooden houses, hardly large
enough for a single family. Next comes a Gothic church, transformed into a
shop, with a sign in great metal characters. . . . Vacant lots, shanties, churches,
ruins,—speculation will sweep over it all to-morrow, this evening perhaps, and
other "buildings" will spring up. But time is needed, and these people have none.
These two years past, instead of completing their half-finished city, they have
been amusing themselves in building another over yonder, under pretext of
their exhibition. It is entirely white, a dream city, with domes like those of
Ravenna, colonnades like those at Rome, lagoons like Venice, a fair of the world
like Paris.[29]

That visitor was referring, of course, to the World's Fair and Columbian
Exposition of 1893. After vigorous lobbying to be the city to host the fair,
and then more lobbying to determine which section of Chicago would reap
the benefits of the fair's boost to land values and business traffic, after
more than $5 million spent on construction, after a delay of a year past the
actual anniversary of Columbus's landing in America, and despite the deep-
ening depression in America, an astonishing 27,529,400 people passed
through the gates of the Chicago's World's Fair and Columbian Exposition.

One of the most famous photographs of the fair shows a woman dressed
in white, observing the monumental White City from far above. Others
enjoyed viewing the fair from the top of the Ferris Wheel, which had been
invented for this event. Paradoxically celebrating America's modern progress with neoclassical Greek-style architecture, attempting to assert both
old-fashioned art and new-fashioned technology, all while prohibiting African Americans from exhibiting in the White City (except in the Haitian
building), Chicago's World's Fair was fascinatingly conflicted. The neoclassical White City was counterbalanced by the more carnivalesque Midway
Plaisance, which featured the world's first Cracker Jacks alongside recon-
structed "native villages" that were organized by museum anthropologists
in order to display a perceived racial evolutionary hierarchy, subtly justi-
fying American imperialism. Eskimos, forced to wear their traditional cos-
tumes while displaying themselves in Chicago's hot summer heat, went on
strike and then quit to work in Chicago's factories. As Americans tried to
picture their place in the world at this fair, they communicated ideas about
race, work, leisure, imperialism, and modernity. They also communicated
ideas about urban planning.[30]

Instead of a two-dimensional map, the White City part of the World's
Fair was a three-dimensional model city. John Wellborn Root, one of the

architects of the White City, announced that it led people "out of the wilderness of the commonplace to new ideas of architectural beauty and nobility." Architectural historians concur that it was "a high point in the history of the American architectural profession . . . a crystallization of a new civic image" of harmoniously planned designs by professional architects. It was a temporary city, designed to inspire actual cities elsewhere. It was built all at once in a setting carefully constructed to appear older and more organic, foreshadowing the neotraditional designs of late twentieth-century elite suburbs. In its time its largest impact was on central cities. The White City popularized the Beaux Arts style that came to characterize many downtown government buildings and cultural institutions of the Progressive era.[31]

"The inception of great planning of public buildings and grounds in the United States was in the World's Fair in Chicago," Daniel Burnham declared, immodestly telescoping from his own work to all "great planning" in America. After his celebrated design of the White City, Burnham was invited to lead urban planning efforts in Washington, D.C., Cleveland, San Francisco, Manila, and then back to Chicago, at the behest of the civic-minded businessmen of Chicago's Merchants' Club and Commercial Club. Despite Burnham's boasting, his was not the first plan of Chicago: the Federal Land Ordinance of 1785, the canal building that was begun in the 1830s, the sewerage and grade raising of the 1850s, and the parks planned in the late 1860s were all long-term plans before Burnham ever arrived. Still, his plan, inspired by the 1893 White City, was a particularly comprehensive document, backed by powerful elites and promoted extensively. It helped to inaugurate professional Progressive-era City Beautiful planning in America.[32]

In 1907, when Burnham began working on his plan, he first instructed his staff to collect every map of the city they could find, installing them in an office on the top floor of the Railway Exchange Building, where they could look out at the city from above, with a view similar to the bird's-eye view maps.[33] The document they collectively produced, Daniel Burnham and Edward Bennett's *Plan of Chicago* (1909), was visually impressive and would become a classic. It opens with a watercolor by Jules Guerin showing a view of Chicago from high above the lake, southeast of the city. With impressionistic fuzziness, the painting almost resembles abstract art. It clings to specificity in the sphere of Lake Michigan. The curve of the roads around Chicago echoes the curve of the lake. The concentric circles on the nineteenth-century maps could hardly seem more natural than in Guerin's watercolor frontispiece. The *Plan* then displays photographs of the White City, with text explaining that Chicago should learn from the fair's monumental, controlled, and homogeneous model. "Chicago, in common with other great cities, realizes that the time has come to bring order out of the chaos incident to rapid growth, and especially to the influx of people of many nationalities without common traditions or habits of life."[34] To make immigrants Americans, to make workers bourgeois, to make the city more prosperous, and to make the map of Chicago more orderly: that was the goal of this plan.[35]

A series of maps in the *Plan* depict Chicago as the center of radiating circles. In addition to the frontispiece watercolor, one image portrays Chicago literally in the center of a circular frame, the center of seven states.[36] Another shows Chicago as the focal point of shipping routes and land routes, the capital of a commercial empire.[37] Burnham and his coauthors proposed a monumental pentagonal civic plaza and cultural center west of the existing courthouse, with grand boulevards extending outward in a star pattern, encircled by a series of beltways. Proposing to consolidate rail transit, insert new diagonal avenues, broaden streets, extend Chicago's system of boulevards, and beautify the harbor with piers and parks, it was an ambitious plan. Although this monumental and expensive vision, "so grand it was grandiose," has not been fully realized, it continues to inspire many city planners.[38]

Chicago's elites, who privately financed the *Plan*, recognized that they needed to persuade the general public to support it. After spending $80,000 producing the *Plan*, these civic-minded businessmen then spent more than $20,000 promoting it. As one speaker explained at the banquet introducing the *Plan*, "Public confidence must be secured ward by ward, street by street. The people must be shown what the *Plan of Chicago* means to them, so that there may be had an irresistible public opinion behind this great movement." To win over public opinion, they held more than five hundred public talks accompanied by two hundred lantern-slide images, displayed the sumptuous illustrations in the *Plan* at the Art Institute, carefully cultivated media support, and even produced a two-reel promotional film. Many of the *Plan*'s backers formed political advisory teams and eventually joined the Chicago Plan Commission. Much of the publicity was coordinated by Walter Dwight Moody, whose full-time job was to make Chicagoans "plan conscious."[39]

To encourage plan consciousness, Walter Moody wrote primers about the plan, including a textbook distributed to every eighth-grader in Chicago throughout the 1910s and 1920s.[40] He explained that recent urbanization posed new challenges to social science, which he defined, fascinatingly, as "the science of maintaining health and good order among people of different families and different races when brought closely in contact." To maintain order among Chicago's diverse population, "every Chicagoan, neighbor to neighbor, should catch the Chicago Plan spirit and talk about it. It is the one Chicago issue that all Chicago can and should unite on—a non-partisan, non-political business plan to harmonize some of the loveliness and unloveliness of physical Chicago, an idea to make a practical, beautiful piece of finished fabric out of Chicago's crazy quilt." According to Moody, the *Plan* would not only clarify the disordered map of Chicago; it would lure business and tourists, improve the economy, relieve congestion, improve health, and add beauty.[41] The textbook began with a progression of images of Chicago's urbanization, from a view of Fort Dearborn's few houses to a bird's-eye view of nineteenth-century Chicago, through the White City, and then to maps of the *Plan*'s proposed civic center and beltways. A large map of the Midwest, showing circles up to a five-hundred-mile radius around Chicago, enlarged upon the concentric circles of nineteenth-century maps. Chicago's potential hinterland was vast, this map implied, but only if Chicago improved her physical facilities by voting for the proposals in Burnham's *Plan*.[42] Review questions at the end of each chapter capture the textbook's tone:

> In what way is the spirit of Chicago like that which made Rome the greatest city of all time? Why are Chicago's opportunities to become great and famous so much better than those of ancient Rome? . . . State five advantages Chicago has over Paris in carrying out a city plan. . . . State the reasons why London is an ill-planned city. What lessons may Chicago learn from London's history? . . . Why can the policies of the Chicago Plan Commission be relied upon as the right ones? . . . Why may we be sure that our citizens will accomplish the beneficial improvements suggested in the Plan of Chicago?[43]

Encouraging comparisons to other illustrious cities while also working to instill trust in administrative government agencies, this didactic extension of Burnham's *Plan* was Mayor Richard Daley's favorite book.[44]

Moody also wrote a ninety-three-page booklet touting Burnham's plan for the "owners of Chicago," distributed to every property owner in the city and to anyone who paid more than $25 a month in rent. Extending the discourse of domesticity and respectability, linking property ownership and citizenship, this booklet declared that city-owned property, including the parks, sanitary district, and land in Cook County, if sold all at once, would bring $1,000 to "every voter in Cook County. . . . When we think of these things, and remember all that property is ours—a great fortune we are to leave to our children—we begin to feel a new responsibility and a new pride in being citizens of Chicago. We feel that we ought to handle that property well, don't we, and increase its value if we can?"[45] The way to increase its value, according to this booklet, was to support the *Plan of Chicago*. Moody was convinced that private profit would overlap with public good and create a clearer, more orderly map.

Despite this extensive exhortation, Chicagoans were not persuaded. They resisted much of the expense and grandiosity of the *Plan*, although between 1912 and 1934 Chicago voters did approve eighty-six *Plan*-related municipal bond issues, covering seventeen separate projects and costing a combined $234 million.[46] The lakefront parks and the wide expanse of Michigan Avenue north of the Loop are two results of the *Plan*, along with the bilevel Wacker Drive. The Civic Center by Daley Plaza is a much-changed version of the *Plan*'s proposed civic center, along with some beltway highways, suburban forest preserves, and the Beaux Arts architecture of many Chicago institutions, but most of the *Plan* remains unbuilt. The "problem" of a disorderly map remains.

It is tempting to conclude that the authors of the *Chicago Plan of 1909* overreached by creating a grand plan from the top down, ignoring the citizens except as subjects of propaganda after the plan had been decided upon. Recent urban planners have shifted to small-scale planning with deep community input, yet this can result in repetitive meetings leading to tepid compromises. "Make no little plans," Burnham is rumored to have said. "They have no power to stir men's souls."[47] Without Burnham's grand plans, Chicago might now lack its splendid lakefront park system and valuable boulevarding of Michigan Avenue. Chicago voters had the wisdom to turn down the less splendid parts of the *Plan*, including the soulless civic center and the disruptive diagonals. The limitations of the 1909 *Plan* are not simply grandiosity or elitism; the main limitation is the underlying assumption that "ordering" a city means sorting it into mappable parts.

The most influential maps of all were not actually in the *Plan*. Without needing to exhort every Chicago eighth-grader or property owner, it was the maps and assumptions of zoners, sociologists, and real estate appraisers that quietly entered bureaucratic policies and bankers' calculations, deeply affecting Chicago's—and America's—built environment of the twentieth century.

CODIFYING RINGS

When Chicago city officials developed their first zoning ordinances in 1922, they created closely detailed block-by-block maps resembling those made earlier by the residents of Hull House and by the Sanborn Fire Insurance

Agency. Adapting policies of private subdivisions and elite suburbs, Chicago's zoning proponents advocated making the city "harmonious." Their color-coded maps illustrated whether each lot held single-family homes, duplexes, apartments, retail business, light industry, heavy industry, noxious industry ("emitting considerable odor, noise, or toxic or corrosive fumes"), railroads, parks, or unclassifiable other uses. Their maps revealed a mixture of uses and helped make the case for new laws to separate each mapped color. Zoners hoped to keep neighborhoods "orderly" by limiting building height, establishing front yards, and separating districts into five categories: private residences, apartments and hotels, "high class shopping," and "general retail" along with light manufacturing. The color-coded map would be simplified. Chicago neighborhoods would become less diverse, and the value of property—they hoped—would be more secure.[48]

University of Chicago political science professor Charles Merriam had been encouraging Chicago to enact zoning rules since 1914, when he was an alderman. The Chicago Real Estate Board promoted Merriam's plan and in 1917 especially urged racialized zoning to prevent property depreciation. Legal wrangling kept zoning from becoming official until 1922, when the city was motivated to keep pace with its newly incorporating suburbs, including Winnetka, Evanston, and Glencoe.[49]

Mortgage lenders agreed with zoners and sociologists that mixed-use or mixed-class areas were naturally deteriorating. In 1924 Chicago realtor Frederick Morrison Babcock wrote the first standard textbook on real estate appraisal, which became required reading in the Standard Course in Real Estate, a two-year curriculum endorsed by the National Association of Real Estate Boards and offered at business colleges, YMCAs, and four-year colleges. Babcock analyzed property values as a series of rings. In the central business district of Chicago, he explained, real estate values were well established, so he could assess values with an accuracy of plus or minus 10 percent. In the "apartment district," moving outward from the central business district, he believed an appraiser's accuracy was only within 20 percent. And in the "residential district," the largest zone, "on the borders of cities where rapid changes are taking place," the accuracy of any appraisal was only within 33 percent. The problem of a large suburban zone undergoing complex changes was compounded by the difficulty of ever definitively assessing residential values. Babcock wrote in 1924 that neighborhood values were so difficult to assess that appraisers should simply compare a house with any other houses recently sold in the same district, adjusting for street improvements, distance to stores, and distance to transportation. Beyond that, the outer ring was too complex. Still, Babcock's widely used textbook helped spread the idea of urban rings far beyond Chicago.[50]

While Babcock's practical experience led him to conclude that he could not adequately assess neighborhood values, University of Chicago sociologists did attempt to determine how neighborhoods would change over time. Just after Babcock's textbook, Ernest Burgess published his zonal theory of concentric circles in 1924 in the *Publications of the American Sociological Society*, then in 1925 in an anthology called simply *The City*. Burgess adapted a half-century of Chicago maps and codified them in a model of abstraction and urban theory that has been called—with some hyperbole—"the most famous diagram in social science."[51]

Like many American social scientists of the early twentieth century, Burgess sought to identify archetypal patterns and technical rules that he thought were scientific, not historical. He strove for universal abstraction. Every city would have a "loop," Burgess assumed, using the name for Chicago's downtown to describe all downtowns. "In all cities there is the natural tendency for local and outside transportation to converge in the central business district," he asserted. "Quite naturally, almost inevitably, the economic, cultural, and political life centers here."[52] Burgess was writing long after railroads had developed beltway spurs around Chicago, after the stockyards and steel plants had pioneered industrial suburbs, and during the years when trucking was permitting less fixed-path industrial transport, spurring even more decentralization of industries outside of downtown areas. He was aware that retail stores had begun building suburban branches, but he believed these "satellite loops" were actually examples of smaller business areas centralizing themselves, while still subordinate to the grand business center of Chicago's Loop.

In Burgess's theory, every city expanded in a series of concentric circles, like smooth ripples emanating from a pebble dropped in a lake. Outside the Loop would be the "slums," which included vice districts, "immigrant colonies," and rooming houses with their "purgatory of lost souls." Burgess explained that this "area of decay" was leavened by forces of "regeneration," including "the mission, the settlement, the artists' colony, [and] radical centers—all obsessed with the vision of a new and better world." It was a futile obsession, he implied, because the natural pattern of the city would always have the equilibrium of a slum zone encircling a downtown zone, in an ongoing ecological process of "differentiation, reorganization, and increasing differentiation."[53]

Outside the slums, Burgess wrote, "The next zone is also inhabited predominatingly by factory and shop workers, but skilled and thrifty. This is an area of second immigrant settlement, generally of the second generation. . . . The inhabitant of this area in turn looks to the 'Promised Land' beyond, to its residential hotels, its apartment-house region, its 'satellite

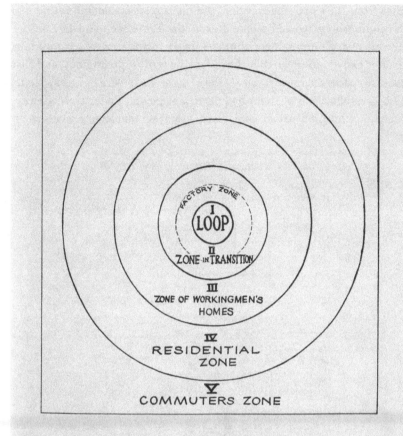

CHART I. The Growth of the City

In his seminal work on the growth of cities, sociologist Ernest Burgess abstracted from a half-century of Chicago maps, asserting that all cities would expand in a bull's-eye pattern of concentric circles, with each zone moving outward in what he thought was a natural, ecological pattern. From Ernest Burgess, "The Growth of the City: An Introduction to a Research Project," in Ernest Burgess, Robert Park, and Roderick McKenzie, eds., *The City* (Chicago: University of Chicago Press, 1925), 52. Reproduction courtesy of the University of Chicago Library Preservation Department.

loops,' and its 'bright light' areas."[54] He was writing in the 1920s, when apartments and residential hotels were considered prestigious, so he complicated his description of the "Promised Land" of outer-ring elite residences with what now seem to be incongruously urban architectural structures. Like earlier realtors, Burgess let his viewers decide which circle defined suburbia. Still, he implied suburbanization by declaring that the farther from the Loop one traveled, the more respectable and residential each neighborhood would become. It was "the 'Promised Land' beyond."

The effects of Burgess's zonal model linger in widespread assumptions that cities expand in rings, that the outer ring is most prestigious, and that single-use spaces are most stable. None of these ideas were Burgess's alone, but his crystallization of them had particular power. Roderick McKenzie, another of Chicago's urban ecologists, asserted that every city has an

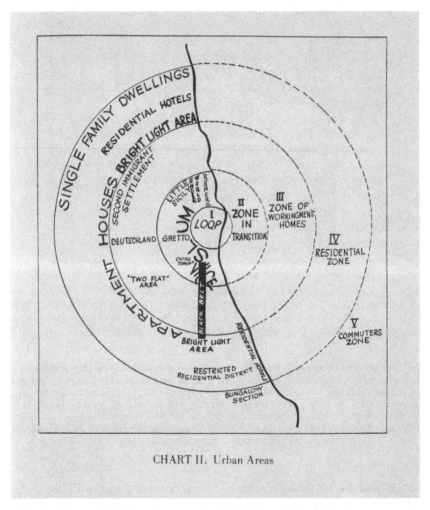

CHART II. Urban Areas

Applying his abstract circles to Chicago, Burgess recognized that both the physical geography of Lake Michigan as well as the cultural geography of racialized neighborhoods cut through his circles. From Ernest Burgess, "The Growth of the City: An Introduction to a Research Project," in Ernest Burgess, Robert Park, and Roderick McKenzie, eds., *The City* (Chicago: University of Chicago Press, 1925), 55. Reproduction courtesy of the University of Chicago Library Preservation Department.

"organic structure" that "serves as a selective or magnetic force attracting to itself appropriate population elements and repelling incongruous units, thus making for biological and cultural subdivisions of a city's population." It was as useless to resist this segregation as to resist magnetism. Seemingly naturally, "racial and linguistic colonies," along with "age and sex segregations," developed in every large city. The higher stages of development, Chicago's urban ecologists believed, were the most homogeneous areas of the city. As Burgess explained, "In the expansion of the city a process of distribution takes place which sifts and sorts and relocates individuals and groups by residence and occupation," and this sorting offered the group "a place and a role," as if segregation were positive.[55]

To explain this process of sorting, Burgess and his colleagues borrowed metaphors from biology, evolution, ecology, and warfare. They described an "urban metabolism" in which one zone "invaded" another in a "process of displacement and selection" that resembled ecological plant successions. These multiple metaphors all share the idea of systems undergoing a process of invasion and incorporation, whether of food into a body, armies into another country, species into a habitat, or weeds into the crabgrass frontier of suburbia. In the sociologists' desire to identify archetypal, general patterns, they used the language of nature, a language that evaded politics, obscured market forces, and minimized individual choice.[56]

Burgess published an early version of his zonal model in the *Annals of the American Academy of Political and Social Science* in a special issue on "the American Negro," in which he explained that blacks would move out in the same expanding circles as had Chicago's earlier European immigrants, in a segregation that was "not the product of race prejudice alone but the result of the interplay of factors in urban growth."[57] Burgess hoped that his description would keep people from resisting the expansion of Chicago's black neighborhoods, since he believed violent resistance was futile when faced with the inevitable ecology of cities. Despite his hope to avoid racial violence, his assertion that inner zones "invaded" outer zones and that neighborhoods might tip downward after "invasions" of different classes or races eventually added fuel for Chicago's racist bomb-throwers, blockbusting realtors, and exclusionary groups of property owners.

Burgess's zonal maps became an enormously influential tool with which sociologists sought to understand cities. To take just one example: starting in the late 1920s, University of Chicago sociologists gathered the admission statistics to the Cook County Psychopathic Hospital, plotted the residences of diagnosed psychopaths onto a map of Burgess's zonal circles, and concluded that insanity was "ecological." In what they called "Zone I," the Central Business District, a one-mile circle around Chicago's courthouse, the rate of insanity was 362 per 100,000 adults over age thirteen. In "Zone II," the circle one to three miles from the courthouse, rates of insanity decreased from 191 to 131 per 100,000. Rates of insanity continued decreasing with distance from the center city, so that by "Zone IV," five to seven miles from the loop, the rate of insanity was only 71 per 100,000. Moving to the suburbs seemed to foster mental health. To their credit, when Robert E. L. Faris and H. Warren Dunham published this research as *Mental Disorders in Urban Areas: An Ecological Study*, they did acknowledge that race, class, and variations among psychological diagnoses meant that urban zones alone were not necessarily the sole cause of the variation in insanity rates that they had mapped onto Burgess's zonal hypothesis. Still, they concluded that "disordered" areas might lead to disordered minds and that the inner zones of Burgess's theory were more disordered than the outer zones.[58]

Just as Burgess had extrapolated from land sellers' maps of Chicago, his academic theory continued to work in tandem with market theories. By 1932, when Chicago's leading real estate appraiser, Frederick Babcock, wrote his second textbook for realtors, he had adapted Burgess's zonal theory. By then Babcock was chief appraiser for the Federal Housing Administration, further helping to make Chicago ideas national. Babcock taught America's assessors that all real estate values depended on predicting fifteen to thirty years in the future, since "values are a reflection of probable future utilization of properties." Thus "the data required have much to do with the general city pattern as well as with the actual property. The setting as well as the jewel is considered in marking the price tag." Babcock believed that this general city pattern was a sort of "natural zoning" created by the natural selection processes of competitive capitalism. Traveling in from the outskirts of a city was like watching an embryo develop, he explained, recapitulating the whole evolution of a species in the succession of land uses. His ideas of ecology and evolution were a clear echo of Chicago School sociologists, but he added that actual conditions were not quite as clear as theory might imply. He warned appraisers, "The actual sections separately described are frequently overlapping. The sections are not homogeneous and are not uniformly improved with structures of the type the descriptions would lead one to expect."[59]

Babcock used Burgess's theories, but he saw far more variation, contingencies, and exceptions. He advocated combining both "the 'radial' school and the 'ring' school" of city growth, since he believed that cities grew both along radial transportation lines and in rings of concentric circles. Babcock imagined a city as a large and somewhat supernatural necklace: "Districts are comparable to beads on a string, if we assume the string to be fastened at the city center and the beads to be plastic, expandable, and compressible."

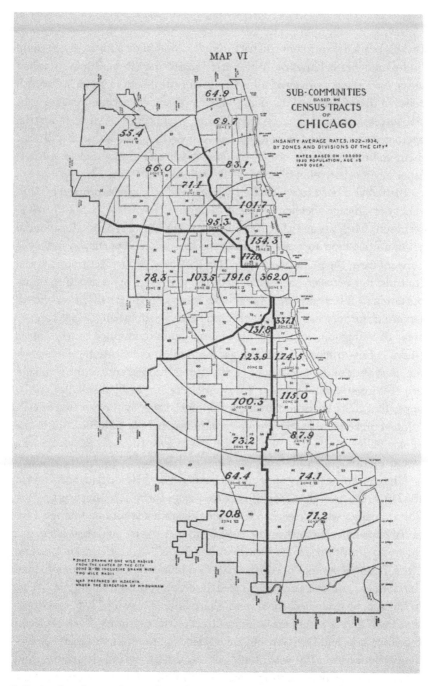

MAP VI

SUB-COMMUNITIES
BASED ON
CENSUS TRACTS
OF
CHICAGO

INSANITY AVERAGE RATES, 1922–1934,
BY ZONES AND DIVISIONS OF THE CITY*

RATES BASED ON 100000
1930 POPULATION, AGE 15
AND OVER.

Reflecting the influence of Burgess's zonal hypotheses, Robert E. L. Faris and H. Warren Dunham mapped the addresses of people admitted to the Cook County Psychopathic Hospital between 1922 and 1934, calculating "rates of insanity" for every 100,000 residents. Their map included circles superimposed at radii of one, three, five, seven, and nine miles and seemed to show that, with the exception of what they called the "disordered" southwest side, rates of insanity steadily decreased as residents moved to the suburban periphery. "This presentation definitely establishes the fact that insanity, like other social problems, fits into the ecological structure of the city," they wrote. From Robert E. L. Faris and H. Warren Dunham, *Mental Disorders in Urban Areas: An Ecological Study of Schizophrenia and Other Psychoses* (Chicago: University of Chicago Press, 1939), 36. Reproduction courtesy of the University of Chicago Library Preservation Department.

On this beaded string some districts didn't simply slide outward: they could "jump" along radial lines or even "burst," scattering into multiple suburban areas. Also, the outer ring of suburbs was not the most prestigious. Babcock believed that residential districts would all "gradually decline in value." Racial succession could quicken this decline, while commercial or industrial encroachment might temporarily halt the decline, but he predicted that many suburbs would eventually become "obsolescent," blighted semislums, especially if urban renewal lured residents back downtown.[60]

The radial theory to which Babcock referred was first expressed by University of Chicago sociology student Clarence Elmer Glick. In his 1928 dissertation, Glick argued that cities expand like wheel spokes: "Residential communities tend to grow up along the lines of transportation radiating outward from the modern cities. In these we may also expect to find social controls. But between these 'spokes of the wheel' are areas awaiting transportation facilities and development. Such areas are in transition and vice in its various forms seeks such areas." He called these suburban "twilight areas," areas of ambiguous legal jurisdiction and light community control, areas where "vice—drinking, gambling, gang activities, prostitution—finds shelter." Just west of the prestigious North Shore, the residents of the elite suburb of Winnetka established a "forest preserve" in the Skokie Valley, in the hopes that this park would bring greater official oversight to an area of vice. A forest preserve may appear to be a natural aspect of suburbia, but in the Skokie Valley it was part of a political battle over the class of people who would use this space and the types of leisure that would be permitted there.[61]

"The concentric theory of city growth is defective," Homer Hoyt declared in 1937 in an article in the *Chicago Insured Mortgage Portfolio*.[62] Hoyt was another Chicago realtor who, like Babcock, became an academic author and then a national housing economist in the New Deal. In 1939 he published his sector theory in *The Structure and Growth of Residential Neighborhoods in American Cities*. Taking advantage of Works Progress Administration data for more than thirty American cities, Hoyt recognized the diversity of each ring around a city. In Chicago, he explained, there were "sharp lines of cleavage" between "high-rent areas" and "low-rent areas." State Street on the south side, Wells Street on the north side, and Harrison and Lake Streets on the west side marked community boundaries. The wealthy and poor areas both expanded outward, Hoyt believed, leaving "deteriorating" areas in their wake, with the exception of the urban improvements on the near north side and the impediment of the stockyards in the south to interrupt these straight "lines of march."[63]

Although Hoyt begins with the triangular wedges between the spokes of a wheel instead of the simple circles of a bull's-eye, his theory of ever-outward growth eventually resembles Burgess's theory. Hoyt asserted:

FIGURE 28

THEORETICAL PATTERN OF DISTRIBUTION OF RENT AREAS
IN 30 AMERICAN CITIES

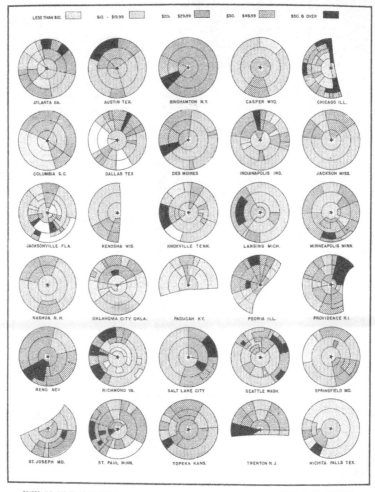

This map of Chicago's historical population densities illustrates radial growth along spokes of transportation instead of centrifugal growth in even circles. From Homer Hoyt, *According to Hoyt: Fifty Years of Homer Hoyt* (Chicago: Homer Hoyt Associates, 1967), 376. Reproduction courtesy of the University of Chicago Library Preservation Department.

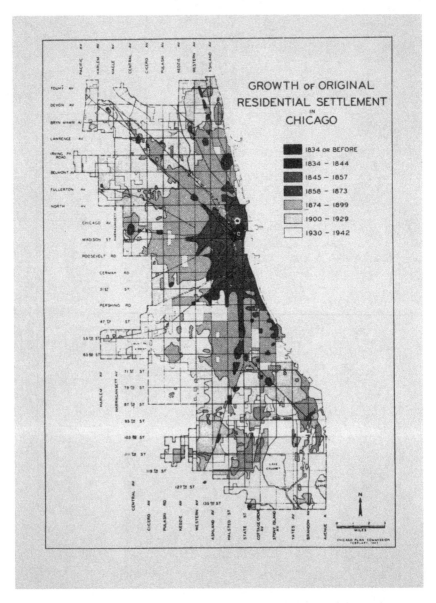

As a federal housing department official, Homer Hoyt collected national data to document that instead of simple bull's-eyes, most cities expanded in class-based pie slices. From Homer Hoyt, *According to Hoyt: Fifty Years of Homer Hoyt* (Chicago: Homer Hoyt Associates, 1967), 587. Reproduction courtesy of the University of Chicago Library Preservation Department.

The growth of high-rent residential areas in Chicago proceeded outward from the center of the city to the periphery, and save for the exceptions noted and accounted for, in generally straight lines. Meanwhile, low-rent areas expanded southwest and northwest in the sectors in which this type of growth originally commenced. Out beyond these low-rent areas intermediate-rent areas developed as a result of the outward movement of the more ambitious members of the immigrant races, and the quality of these graded upward as the distance from the city increased.[64]

Hoyt's sector of ambitious immigrants resembles Burgess's "zone of second immigrant settlement," and in his assertion of outward growth, Hoyt echoes Burgess's "Promised Land." Still, Hoyt theorized with more specificity than Burgess that cities grew not just outward in concentric circles but linearly in radial wedges: growth "tends to proceed along established lines of travel; along the fastest existing transportation lines; toward higher ground; toward the homes of community leaders; in the direction of free, open country; and in the same general direction as the trend of movement of the chief retail and office buildings."[65]

In 1947, in his doctoral dissertation at Harvard's Department of Sociology, Walter Firey noted the similarities of the underlying assumptions of both Burgess's concentric theory and Hoyt's sector theory. In both theories the only role of people is to comply with the "inevitable pattern." According to these theories, people compete for space "on a biotic, subconscious level." Other Chicago School sociologists of urban ecology, including Robert Park and Roderick McKenzie, gave humans a slightly more active role, yet it was generally limited to minimizing cost. Tradition, politics, and cultural values were recognized only as "complicating" factors, not primary causes: "interesting minor variations" to Burgess, "certain extraordinary factors" to Hoyt.[66]

Burgess and Hoyt took a half-century of realtors' maps and republished them in schematic diagrams that were particularly powerful. The ecological theories of Burgess and other Chicago sociologists were part of a forceful feedback loop, drawing on the wider culture, adding a patina of scientific academic authority, and quickly becoming part of Chicago's culture. The zonal theory even appears in James T. Farrell's *Studs Lonigan* trilogy. This trilogy depicts a young Irish tough whose family reluctantly moves from Burgess's inner "zone of workingmen's homes" further outward when that inner zone becomes part of a widening "zone in transition." At the center of the story, Farrell portrays Studs Lonigan listening to a soapbox speaker who paraphrases Burgess's zonal theory:

He explained that the City of Chicago could be divided into three concentric circles. The innermost of these circles was the business or downtown district, the Loop. . . . The second circle housed manufacturing and wholesale houses, slums, tenements, can houses and other haunts of vice. The outer circle made up the residential districts. . . . Some of the Negro booboisie had gotten into the big gypping process, and like their white brothers, they did not like to live in stench, and sandwiched in between a whore house and the junk shop of Isadore Goldberg. . . . [This] produced a pressure stronger than individual wills, and resulted in a minor racial migration of Negroes into the white residential districts of the south side. Blather couldn't halt the process. Neither could violence and race riots. It was an inevitable outgrowth of social and economic forces.[67]

The speaker almost footnotes Burgess: "These factors also were not mere hearsay, but plausible ideas presented by members of the Department of Sociology at the University of Chicago, and developed from the work they had already done on a community research programme." Unimpressed by that research, Studs and his friends reject this analysis of unavoidable natural expansion: "Studs supposed that the guy would let a nigger jazz his sister."[68]

Although the speaker, like Burgess, believed that it was futile to resist the natural forces of urban ecology, it was possible to reach a different conclusion from the sociological metaphor of plant invasions. Weeds, after all, require weeding. Throughout the first half of Farrell's story, Studs and his friends beat up blacks and Jews who "invade" their neighborhood or merely cross their paths.[69] Nevertheless Farrell's plot reinforces the sociologists' message that resistance is eventually futile.

Farrell attended the University of Chicago, took sociology classes, and even wrote a term paper saved by Burgess. Farrell drew upon Burgess's work in his attention to the spatial dimensions of the city and was also inspired by Frederick Thrasher, who studied the culture of youth gangs with ethnographic street-level methods.[70] This combination of sociological approaches meant that Farrell's portrayal of the "natural" expansion of the zonal city was complicated by his characters' deep sense of loss for their old neighborhood, parish, and gang territory. The suburbs, in this story, are not the "Promised Land" that Burgess described. The ethnographic street-level view subtly contradicted the Burgessian view from far above the city.

KNIVES, WHEELS, AND AMOEBAS

Burgess published his zonal theory in an article called "An Introduction to a Research Project," but when many University of Chicago students actually undertook that research, they found an on-the-ground complexity that—though they never expressed it so combatively—significantly undermined his theory.

Burgess recognized that in the specific example of Chicago, the natural landscape of the lakefront cut through his circles, while the personal and coerced choices of Chicago's ethnic and racial groups created not only the Black Belt but also a "wedge" of Germans and floating areas of Sicilian and Chinese neighborhoods interrupting his abstractions. His colleagues and students added even more complexity to his circles. In 1915 Graham Taylor's *Satellite Cities* identified suburban industries that Burgess ignored. Others tried, in vain, to fit the prestigious residential district of Chicago's Gold Coast into Burgess's theory of concentric circles, mostly by explaining that it must be a "disordered" area destined to change.[71] In 1925, working concurrently with Burgess, Walter Reckless wrote his dissertation, "The Natural History of Vice Areas in Chicago," revealing extensive suburban vice that required even more modification of Burgess's zones.[72]

Reckless explained that Chicagoans had visited outlying beer gardens and suburban cafés throughout the nineteenth century, but it was especially after 1911 that Progressive-era reformers successfully pressured the city to tighten surveillance of vice within municipal boundaries, so that more and more gambling, prostitution, and illegal alcohol sales moved to the Chicago suburbs, creating "dives on the fringe."[73] Some working-class suburbs found that liquor-licensing fees helped fund their local government, while resort owners found that police control was often weaker in border areas near state or county lines. Administrative exigencies, not natural ecology, accounted for suburban vice alongside suburban residences. Striving to stay within the conventions of urban ecology, Reckless wrote:

> The first zone in the metropolitan area beyond the city limits has all the characteristics of a frontier. . . . Here industries that were crowded out of the city are finding new locations; residential suburbs are growing up along the lines of transportation. On the other hand, the original inhabitants are moving out, or preparing to. Everything is new and unsettled. Like the area about the central business area in which the city slums are usually located, it is an "area of transition," an area of demoralization, also. In both cases an older type of community organization has disintegrated; both areas await the advance of a new type of urban organization, but in the meantime they have become the rendezvous of those who practice vice and crime.[74]

Despite Reckless's efforts to explain this as simply another "zone in transition," like the zone that Burgess had identified around the Loop, he significantly shifted the "transition" zone to the outermost, supposedly prestigious circle. Reckless also considered issues of governance—from the city's vigilant vice squad to the poorer suburbs' underfunded governments—that complicated Burgess's belief in a neutral, natural urban ecology.

The basic zonal theory had no explanation for the vice industries in what Burgess had called a zone of commuters, although he must have been aware of Reckless's dissertation or common newspaper headlines of the time trumpeting "West Suburbs in Turmoil over Vice War," "Vice Activity Shifts from West to North Suburbs," and state's attorney raids on south suburbs, along with articles about the exploits of the notorious gangster Al Capone, who was based in Chicago's West Side suburb of Cicero.[75] Chicago's suburban vice districts eluded Burgess's ecological explanations as well as later stereotypes of the homogeneity of suburbs.

Other Burgess students revealed additional complexities as they attempted to map Chicago's growth. By 1930 fully two-thirds of Chicago's retail trade was transacted outside of the central business district, in "satellite" business districts, according to Malcolm Proudfoot's dissertation, "The Major Outlying Business Centers of Chicago."[76] Proudfoot relied predominantly on the observations of Chicago businessmen, especially a marketing analysis written in 1929 by the Chicago General Outdoor Advertising Company. Proudfoot tried to fit this patchwork pattern into a bull's-eye framework. "The [outlying] centers form an irregular, widely spaced, and yet evenly balanced semicircle about the midpoint of the central business district," he wrote, though no such semicircle appears on Burgess's diagram, and in fact it is difficult to perceive any semicircle on Proudfoot's map of Chicago's twenty major outlying business districts, widely dispersed among the major intersections of the city's grid.[77]

Proudfoot's careful work notes that many neighborhoods have a "marked heterogeneity," and 15 percent of the street frontage in each "business" area was actually residential. He concluded that many of these spaces were "transitional in character," in a statement that reflects the monoculture bias of many Chicago School sociologists: if a space was not easy to label, it must be transitioning to a space that would be easier to map. Proudfoot's dissertation includes a wonderful map of population density in one swath of Chicago, extending westward from the Loop. Instead of the neat semicircles that Burgess's theory would have predicted, this illustration shows an amoeboid swirling, interrupted only by the large landholdings of corporations and government groups.[78]

Amoeboid swirling also appears in Robert Charles Klove's master's thesis, in which he traces the "life cycle" of buildings, an idea that grew out of the economics of the mortgage industry as well as the sociologists' idea that cities function like biological organisms. Klove mapped a corridor along Chicago's northwest suburbs, labeling each neighborhood on a scale from birth to maturity to something close to death, but his careful map of "residential land patterns" actually portrayed very few patterns.[79]

In the proliferation of images of wheels, spokes, satellites, grids, and amoebas, it is clear that Chicago never did urbanize in Burgess's zonal rings. The specific, grounded evidence in all these dissertations reveals not natural circular zones but contested corridors, radiating outward with deep complexity. As students used street-level investigations inspired by businessmen as well as academic theories, they complicated Burgess's bull's-eye schema so much as to suggest it should be overturned. But instead of overturning the zonal theory, these students labeled the many heterogeneous areas they found "transitional." Perhaps they recognized that overly chaotic amoebas do not actually offer a more useful guide to understanding urban growth than overly simplified circles. It is only Lewis Copeland's fascinating 1937 dissertation that offers a nuanced and useful alternative between those two poles.

PIXELATED STARFISH

Lewis Copeland recognized that Chicago's region resulted from the interaction of physical, technical, legal, and economic forces. Foreshadowing the insights of modern environmentalists, Copeland noted that there is not a clear difference between "natural" physical landscapes and "cultural" landscapes. He explained that Chicago's media had a vested interest in encouraging a wide range or people to imagine themselves as members of "Chicagoland," because the larger the idea of Chicagoland, the larger the audience for Chicago's papers.[80]

Copeland investigated the contours of Chicagoland by asking where the golf courses are for which the *Chicago Tribune* reported golf scores. Which communities send contestants to Chicago's Golden Gloves Boxing contest? How far from Chicago are the Chicago daily newspapers the main source of people's news? In which non-Chicago papers do Loop merchants place ads, soliciting customers for downtown Chicago? This led to many more questions about Chicago's market geography: Where do Chicago department stores offer same-day delivery, next-day delivery, or thrice-weekly delivery? How about bakeries and groceries: to where do they deliver? These questions, of course, are related to issues of infrastructure and transportation. How far from Chicago in every direction can a person travel on a train journey of thirty minutes? What if people measure by price instead of time: how far can a commuter get for a 25-cent train ride? What are the telephone calling rates for the regions around Chicago, encouraging connections among people? And where are the homes of people who have unpaid traffic tickets in the city of Chicago? These questions of shared media, sports, markets, transportation, and infrastructure led to other questions about group affiliations. Where are the residences of the students at the University of Chicago? How about the students at the less elite Chicago School of Cookery? Where are the 850 churches that are members of the Chicago Church Federation? Where are the homes of people listed in the Chicago *Social Register*? Which towns sent firemen to help in the great stockyards fire of 1934? Which towns adopted Eastern Standard Time when Chicago did, in 1933?

Copeland mapped all this and more on one hundred maps and fifty-three tables. He also mapped population density, the percentage of nonnative whites, the number of subdivided lots available, and the location of farms and factories, but mostly he mapped a market-influenced geography of community allegiances. His maps show decisions made by individual people, reinforced by business policies, and strongly reinscribed by media creating an imagined community who follow the same sports, shop at the same stores, and adjust their clocks at the same time.

Some of Copeland's maps resemble squiggly versions of Burgess's bull's eye, but many more contain no simple spheres. Some are quite linear, such as the map of members of the Social Register, which extends in a long tentacle beside the lake breezes of the North Shore, away from Chicago's more industrial south shore, where canals and railroads had long encouraged industry that the city's elites generally preferred to avoid. This was an environment simultaneously reinforced by nature, infrastructure, economics, and fashion. Copeland asserted that his maps "illustrate the ecological basis underlying the distribution of functions in the metropolitan community," but they actually offered important complications to Burgess's ecological approach and Hoyt's sector theory.[81] Economic forces are what are most influential to Copeland's "ecology," and it is behavioral economics more than any classic profit-maximizing theory. Copeland's maps show the influence of human decisions on spatial organization.

Copeland's maps were never as popular as Burgess's or Hoyt's. They were complex and contingent on local issues. Copeland resisted simplification, explaining that regional boundaries "are not fixed, but indefinite . . . gradient lines."[82] His dissertation was never published, but his ideas remain worth pursuing.

Copeland identified a large "metropolitan economy," covering the states surrounding Chicago, distinguished by the federal reserve bank district, demarcated by the places that read Chicago's large morning papers and listened to Chicago radio stations, places within an overnight ride of Chicago. These were places that sent livestock and milk to Chicago, students to Northwestern University, contestants to the regional Golden Gloves boxing

Fig. 91

The distribution of the names listed in The Social Register is very similar to that of the Chicago leaders and the membership of the clubs. All but 1 per cent reside within the metropolitan district. Here again we find the concentration in the popular suburbs and the conspicuous absence of the social elite in the middle class and industrial suburbs.

In Lewis Copeland's hand-drawn map, each dot represented five addresses in the 1926 *Social Register of Chicago*, revealing that Chicago's elite clustered in the North Side suburbs, not in an evenly spaced circle. "Distribution of the Addresses Given in the Social Registry of Chicago 1926," in Lewis Copeland, "The Limits and Characteristics of Metropolitan Chicago," master's thesis, University of Chicago, 1937, figure 91. Reproduction courtesy of the University of Chicago Library Preservation Department.

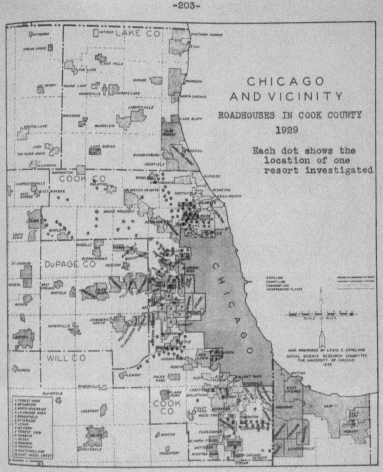

CHICAGO
AND VICINITY

ROADHOUSES IN COOK COUNTY

1929

Each dot shows the
location of one
resort investigated

Fig. 83

Roadhouses seek locations in the "twilight" zone around
the city limits where police control is relaxed. Here restrictions are not as rigid or are lacking due to the conflict between
the city, county, and state governments, and the absence of organized public opinion and community agencies. With the coming of
the automobile such resorts are even more attractive because of
the greater degree of anonymity they permit. The map shows only
the houses most frequently patronized by people from Chicago
investigated by Reckless. Others are located out as far as 50 to
60 miles from the city. Adapted from Reckless, op. cit., p. 124.

This map, which Lewis Copeland adapted from Walter Reckless's 1925 dissertation, "The Natural History of Vice Areas in Chicago," shows that resorts and roadhouses clustered in the interstitial area between the spokes of the wheel of radial settlement. From Lewis Copeland, "The Limits and Characteristics of Metropolitan Chicago," master's thesis, University of Chicago, 1937, figure 83. Reproduction courtesy of the University of Chicago Library Preservation Department.

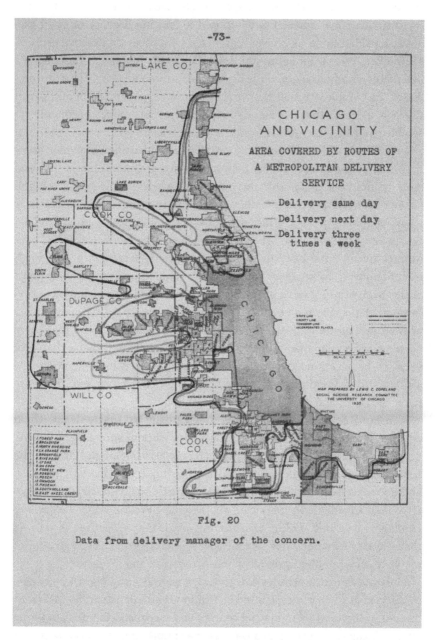

Fig. 20

Data from delivery manager of the concern.

Lewis Copeland's hand-drawn map of the delivery schedule of a Chicago retailer reveals the modified radial lines of Chicago's market geography, based on transportation infrastructure and reinforced by population density. From Lewis Copeland, "The Limits and Characteristics of Metropolitan Chicago," master's thesis, University of Chicago, 1937, figure 20. Reproduction courtesy of the University of Chicago Library Preservation Department.

tournament, and merchandise buyers to Chicago's wholesalers.[83] This area was a circle with a radius of two hundred to four hundred miles, yet it was a very lopsided circle, as Chicago competed with other commercial centers. Milwaukee, Peoria, Bloomington, Danville, South Bend, and Indianapolis had their own wholesalers, while Evanston, Hammond, Gary, Elgin, Aurora, Joliet, and Waukegan had their own major newspapers, competing with Chicago so much that Copeland's circle of the metropolitan economy resembled an elongated outline of the state of Texas.[84]

Within this wider economic region, Copeland identified a smaller "metropolitan community" that he believed shared a common social life and daily economic activity. This was the space where people read Chicago's smaller afternoon papers, not just the larger morning editions. This was where people shopped at Chicago's department stores or commuted daily into the city. It was the suburban space within thirty-five miles of the Loop, or forty-five minutes by train, or less than 20 cents in train fare—although each definition, by space or time or cost, mapped onto slightly different circles in the careful work of Copeland. Even if space, time, and price corresponded, they did not necessarily reflect everyone's personal geographies of work and leisure. Copeland noted that traffic data indicated that more people traveled daily from homes in Chicago to jobs in Indiana than vice versa, so he questioned whether the area around Gary, Indiana, was really a suburb to Chicago or even a satellite.[85] The closer he looked, the more fuzzy Burgess's bull's-eye circles became.

Copeland defined suburbs fairly traditionally as spaces from which people commuted almost daily to Chicago for work or shopping or leisure. Yet other suburbs were visible on his maps: industrial satellite cities in the southeast and south, along with farms, roadhouses, failed subdivisions, and not yet subdivided land. Chicago was part of a "tri-nucleated" industrial area, Copeland wrote, citing the Census Bureau's study *Location of Manufacturers, 1890–1929*.[86] Considering all his maps together, it appears that the city expanded not like a bull's eye of circles or the segments of sector theory, but like a gridded starfish, complex and contested.

Growing along the arteries of waterways, railways, and highways, guided by the grid of county lines, shifted by fashions and a penchant for lakefront breezes, punctured by industrial centers and vice districts and competing cities, Chicago's suburban area was never a simple sphere or even sector. It contained the houses of many subscribers to the Chicago Symphony Orchestra, but it also held roadhouse saloons. It was contingent on local issues, yet the pixelated starfish that Copeland's many maps imply actually matches more American cities than Burgess's less political, seemingly universal spheres.

Despite the institutionalization of Burgess's zonal model, Chicago never had simple rings. Burgess's theories failed to adequately describe the Chicago of his time, let alone all American cities. The factories were farther out and more scattered in suburbia, and so was vice. Some elite residential districts remained stubbornly close to downtown. Nevertheless many geographers and historians concerned with explaining American urban decline have uncritically adopted and simplified Burgess's model, overemphasizing the divide between city and country while underemphasizing suburban diversity. More recent studies of the "industrial garden" of urban regions as well as the brownstoners who gentrify urban areas have only begun to reconceptualize urban expansion beyond Burgess's zonal model.[87]

The effects of Burgess's theories linger in assumptions that "downtown" is natural, that separate uses are stable and admirable, that cities expand in rings, and that the outer ring is prestigious and predominantly residential. The longest-lasting of his theories is the idea that the most differentiated, most easily labeled areas on a map must be the most stable areas. Although few Americans speak of racial "invasions" anymore, many still believe in "blight," the fear that one incongruent use might spoil the property values of an entire neighborhood. The flip side of this idea is a belief in "gentrification," as if one upper-class resident could tilt the class status of a whole neighborhood. Long-term mixed-class and mixed-use spaces do exist in America, in a dynamic that deserves more attention.

In the most clear-eyed challenge to the Chicago School of urban ecology, Walter Firey's 1947 dissertation at Harvard insisted that culture was intrinsic to understanding urban growth. Land promoters, fashion trends, local values, historic symbols, and community networks all affect spatial decisions. Chicago sociologists' theories did not fit Boston's wealthy and poor sections of Beacon Hill, both close to downtown; the economically inefficient use of space in Boston Common, urban churches, and urban cemeteries; or the "localized social solidarity" of the Italian North End. Firey concluded that mixed-use downtowns could be stable. He believed urban planners should consider historic sites not only for tourism but also for fostering a sense of community and should attempt only slow redevelopment in order to protect the cultural character of neighborhoods.[88] One wonders what American cities would look like if more midcentury planners had taken Firey's suggestions instead of Burgess's.

For most of the twentieth century, mortgage lenders used sociological models to establish criteria for allocating loans for home repairs or purchases, favoring loans for new buildings in single-use spaces segregated from other classes and uses. Such policies became self-fulfilling prophecies.[89] Since mixed-class areas could not qualify for loans, new owners could not move in easily and old owners had difficulty raising capital for building repairs. As mixed-class areas declined, they seemed to validate the bankers' reluctance to lend there. These self-fulfilling prophecies came to be known as redlining and became national policy in the 1930s, when New Deal programs such as the Home Owners Loan Corporation and the Federal Housing Administration—led by the Chicagoans Frederick Babcock and Homer Hoyt—made these local practices national. Through the New Deal, theories based on sociologists' abstractions of turn-of-the-century Chicago influenced twentieth-century America.

Realtors wondering where to build their next subdivision, bankers deciding where to safely make mortgage loans, tourists trying to orient themselves in the sprawling city, officials trying to improve that city, media aiming to create an imagined community of greater Chicagoland, and residents selecting spaces for homes and businesses, all relied on mental projections based on maps like Burgess's inaccurate zonal diagram. These maps had consequences in programs of urban renewal and policies of mortgage lending, as well as overlooked suburban vice districts.

There were other powerful maps that Chicago residents used to explain the city to themselves, including parish maps, political ward maps, and a mental map of where black people were permitted to live, work, or play. Studying all these maps reveals how deeply mixed actual land uses were on the ground. Space was contested, and it is those contests that merit further investigation, along with the many heterogeneous areas that defied administrative assumptions of homogeneity.

CHAPTER 6

⌒√⌒

The Mortgages of Whiteness

Chicago's Race Riots of 1919

Thirty-eight people died in Chicago's race riots of July 1919; 537 were hospitalized and about one thousand were left homeless by arsonists. "For four days this old city has been rocked in a quake of racial antagonism, seared in a blaze of red hate," the *Chicago Defender*, the city's black newspaper, reported.[1] The riots affected the entire city, but their locus was the former Town of Lake, where the working man's reward was proving elusive.

The riots had many causes, but above all Chicagoans rioted over spatial politics. Neighborhood parks, Catholic parishes, commutes to work, and developing myths about property values were the issues that led thousands to fight each other. Chicago's race riots of 1919 reflect the hardening geography of racial boundaries in twentieth-century America and reveal what had changed since the Town of Lake had first been settled as a diverse working-class suburb after the Civil War. By 1919 the area had become a famous white slum even while "preserving property values" was becoming shorthand for preserving white privilege.

Lake had become a crowded urban village where each house contained an average of three families, interspersed with small businesses, all in the shadow and stench of the stockyards. About one-third of the buildings were owner-occupied. There were numerous social service agencies, churches, and parochial schools in this neighborhood of immigrants. Carl Sandburg called it a space of "gaunt involuntary poverty from which issues the hoodlum." The state attorney of Cook County informed Sandburg that "more bank robbers, payroll bandits, automobile bandits, highwaymen and strong-arm crooks come from this district than any other." Investigators from the University of Chicago declared that infant mortality rates were five times higher than in the lakeshore district one mile to the east.[2]

It was a polluted environment and a poor one, but it was also a place where people had struggled to own their own homes and fought to preserve their fragile investments in their homes and churches and schools. They fought to be able to live less than a block's walk to the nearest local grocer or saloon. They fought to preserve their former suburb and to resist moving to newer suburbs, and in this fight they consolidated ideas about whiteness and property values.

CHICAGO'S RACIAL GEOGRAPHY

In 1790 Jean Baptiste Point du Sable was the first to purchase land in the space that would become Chicago. He built a "hut" on the near North Side, by what is now Michigan Avenue's Golden Mile. Point du Sable was a mix of African, French, Native American, and Santo Domingan. By the early twentieth century, when rumors spread that the presence of blacks decreased property values, several observers pointed out that Point du Sable's race had not adversely affected the value of early Chicago real estate. They repeated a supposed Potawatomie saying: "The first white man to settle at Chickagou was a Negro."[3]

By 1870 Chicago's five thousand black residents lived in every ward of the city as well as numerous suburbs. Chicago had instituted some progressive policies during Reconstruction, including a civil rights law and, in 1874, an officially desegregated school system. After the collapse of Reconstruction, many blacks who had held political office in southern states relocated to Chicago in what observers called "the Migration of the Talented Tenth." By 1893 Chicago's black population was fifteen thousand, still just a small fraction of the more than million Chicagoans. Some blacks settled north of Chicago, near domestic service jobs in the suburb of Evanston, as well as on the near West Side. Many gathered in a neighborhood around Clark and Harrison Streets, on the south fringe of Chicago's business district, an area that escaped the Great Fire of 1871 but was completely burned in 1874.[4]

During the 1880s and 1890s, pushed by racism and pulled by their own preferences for living near black-led institutions, new black migrants were increasingly limited to Chicago's Black Belt on the South Side. Extending just two blocks west and east of State Street, stretching south to Thirty-fifth Street and eventually Fifty-fifth, this narrow strip contained 56 percent of Chicago's blacks in 1900, 78 percent in 1910, and 90 percent by

1930. The structures that kept blacks within the ghetto were hardening in the early twentieth century.[5]

In 1904 ten thousand African Americans began working in Chicago's stockyards, replacing striking whites. They slept in bunk beds inside the yards, suffering not only the stench and lack of personal space but also a fire and an outbreak of smallpox. They considered those unhealthy bunks safer than commuting through the former Town of Lake during the strike, where black strikebreakers suffered knifings, beatings, and eye-gougings. Most blacks were laid off when white strikers returned to work, but during World War I many more blacks entered packinghouse employment. By 1919 half of all black males who held manufacturing jobs worked in the meat industry, totaling about one-quarter of the employees in the larger meatpacking plants.[6] The majority of adult black males in Chicago in 1919 had worked in meatpacking at some point in their lives, most commuting to Lake from the Black Belt.

The boundaries of the Black Belt solidified just as Chicago's black population exploded. When World War I disrupted European immigration, Chicago's factories turned to African American southerners to fulfill their need for what they called "greenhorns," newcomers who would do arduous labor relatively cheaply, without joining unions. Factories did not usually need to recruit directly. Instead blacks themselves told family and friends that in Chicago after 1915, African Americans had a rare opportunity to enter industrial employment. Pulled by Chicago's relatively high wages and the visions of freedom reported in the widely circulated *Chicago Defender* as well as letters from friends who had already moved north, pushed by the boll weevil and racial violence in the South, blacks moved to Chicago hoping for a better life, including a fairer legal system, more educational opportunities, and better housing. Almost seventy thousand African Americans streamed into Chicago during World War I, at the beginning of the Great Migration. Exaggerating the number, a headline in one of Chicago's newspapers declared, "Half a Million Darkies from Dixie Swarm to the North to Better Themselves." This headline reveals mixed sentiments on the part of the white newspaper: admiring blacks' hopes for self-betterment, yet criticizing the animal-like "swarming" of "darkies."[7]

Between the census of 1910 and 1920 the black population of Chicago mushroomed from 44,103 to 109,594, an increase of 148 percent, an increase that could not be contained by the newly hardening borders of the Black Belt. In those same years the white population increased only 21 percent.[8] Vacant apartments were available in white neighborhoods, but blacks who moved beyond the Black Belt risked bombings and other vigilante violence. Pioneering blacks did manage to extend the Black Belt's boundaries south from Thirty-fifth Street to Fifty-fifth, but westward they were blocked by Wentworth Avenue (now the Dan Ryan Expressway), a wide avenue whose streetcar lines helped reinforce its status as a territorial boundary. African American "Old Settlers" blamed uncouth newcomers for the hardening of Chicago's racial geography in the 1910s, yet it was mostly sheer numbers that brought blacks to the notice of whites as well as developing ideas about property values.

Many newly arriving blacks had to double- and triple-up in apartments, settling in dark basements and crowded rooms. Chicago offered jobs for blacks and some schools, but no housing, especially after 1917, when the wartime economy halted all new construction. In the summer of 1919 a survey of realtors revealed that 664 African Americans applied for ninety-seven available apartments, and only fifty of them found accommodation. Landlords created "kitchenettes"—generally single-room apartments with a single gas burner—and charged high rents for the tiny places, since demand so far exceeded supply. People lived in frame shanties without plumbing; they put up with leaky ceilings and broken windows, rotting floors and hingeless doors. Between 60 and 76 percent of black households took in boarders, not necessarily because they wanted the extra income and but also out of friendship for fellow migrants who could find no other housing. Living space in the Black Belt was so cramped and unsanitary that Richard Wright called it "our death sentence without a trial."[9]

"Don't make yourself a public nuisance," the *Defender* advised new migrants arriving in Chicago. "Don't live in unsanitary houses, or sleep in rooms without proper ventilation. Don't violate city ordinances relative to health conditions." Yet it was very difficult for many new migrants to heed this advice, given the limited housing options open to them. "Don't encourage gamblers, disreputable women or men to ply their business any time or place," the paper added, but Chicago's police pushed vice into the Black Belt, where blacks could not avoid living near gamblers and brothels—and where careless white observers concluded that blacks neighborhoods must always contain vice and dilapidated housing.[10]

Some black Chicagoans did manage to suburbanize. "The uncomfortable and inadequate dwellings of the black belt could be avoided only by the purchase of property elsewhere," the Chicago Commission on Race Relations explained in 1923, emphasizing black purchases of suburban property. A sociologist writing about black real estate ownership in Chicago noted that as early as 1854, "we see the beginning of what in later times has become a general practice, that is, to buy outlying property." Blacks bought suburban property because it was affordable; it gave them better access to jobs in suburban factories as well as jobs in domestic service; it allowed some self-provisioning; and, especially after 1915, it was one of the few ways they could live outside the Black Belt. At the time of the riots African Americans lived in industrial suburbs such as Maywood and Chicago Heights, domestic service suburbs such as Evanston and Glencoe, rustic owner-built suburbs such as Robbins and Dixmoor, as well as recently annexed suburbs such as Morgan Park and Lilydale. Still, blacks were confined to only a few suburbs that faced small riots of their own throughout the 1910s and 1920s.[11]

Chicago Heights had two years of "minor clashes" between 1918 and 1920 so serious that the sheriff temporarily prohibited gun sales in order to thwart potential race riots. Evanston used restrictive covenants and realtor pressure to push its black residents westward in the 1910s, in a hardening of racial boundaries. The African American owner-built suburb of Lilydale was criticized as a "bad mistake," where uncomfortable houses were isolated from schools or jobs. The multiracial suburb of Specialville was accused of vice and dubious policing, specifically levying large traffic fines on outsiders in the "Specialville speed-trap racket," and became so notorious that Specialville found it necessary to change its name in the 1920s to Dixmoor. Still, these suburbs were spaces where blacks could attempt to avoid the problems of the Black Belt.[12]

In Robbins, the Chicago Commission on Race Relations wrote, "men and women together are living as pioneer families lived—working and sacrificing to feel the independence of owning a bit of ground and their own house." They sacrificed municipal services; like many other working-class suburbs, Robbins had no paved streets and no sidewalks. They sacrificed their time in long commutes and in building their own homes. Robbins was "difficult to reach, unattractive, and uninviting," but it was a space where African Americans could try to create their own community: "There are 380 people all told, men, women, and children, living in something more than seventy houses. It is a long mile down the road to the street car, but daily men and women trudge away to their work, taking with them the feeling of home ownership, of a place for the children to play unmolested, of friends and neighbors."[13]

Despite their rusticity, these were sites where African Americans could escape the Black Belt and expand their access to homeownership, safety, and independence. In the 1940s these areas would become magnets for development of modest mass-produced homes for African Americans because they contained some of the only large parcels of land open to blacks.[14]

Like Chicago's European immigrants, many of Chicago's African American migrants had rural backgrounds and knowledge of how to grow their own food. They used homeownership to cushion the impact of corporate capitalism by cultivating their own gardens and taking in boarders, using homes for self-provisioning and small businesses. "The opportunity for garden patches is an attraction for many Negroes," the Chicago Commission on Race Relations explained.[15] Yet unlike those earlier European immigrants, blacks faced more limited choices about where they could live, more limited access to capital, and increasing assumptions about black people bringing "blight" that would lower property values. Homes had been "better than a bank for a poor man" when that poor man was white, but racist governmental and banking policies meant that blacks' homes tended to depreciate in value from the turn of the century onward. In places like Lilydale, it was difficult for black homeowners to recover the money they had invested.

Even this black suburbanization was limited. Of the 2,440 employees who worked at the suburban Argo Corn Products Refining Company (near the current Midway Airport), almost all the whites lived nearby, in the suburbs of Summit, Brookfield, Lyons, and Riverside, as well as on the southwest fringes of the city. The longest commute for white workers was thirty-two minutes. Blacks, on the other hand, faced an average commute of an hour. At the suburban Argo plant, 96 percent of black workers lived in downtown Chicago, within the Black Belt. They had little choice.[16]

White workers had more chances to suburbanize. The suburbanization of industry that had begun in 1865 with Chicago's stockyards accelerated in the early twentieth century. South of the city, U.S. Steelworks in Gary, Indiana; Wisconsin Steel in South Deering; and the many factories of the Calumet Industrial District attracted workers to live on the fringes of Chicago. West of Chicago, the McCormick Works of International Harvester, the Western Electric Company in Cicero, and numerous smaller companies also attracted workers. Beyond the lure of decentralized industry, working-class suburbs offered more chances at homeownership because of cheaper land and less strict building codes.[17] But not everyone wanted to move there. In 1919 the whites who rioted could have moved out, as Burgess's zonal theory predicted that they would, but instead they chose to stay and fight against the pressure they felt to resuburbanize.

THE RIOTS OF 1919

On July 27, 1919, the temperature in Chicago was 96 degrees, fourteen degrees above average, the third day of a midsummer heat wave. Seventeen-year-old Eugene Williams went to the beach, while other Chicagoans sat on their stoops to escape the heat and their overheated and overcrowded apartments. In the first six months of 1919, blacks attempting to move beyond the borders of the Black Belt had been met with twenty-four bombs. For decades white Chicagoans had used racist violence to keep blacks out of white neighborhoods, but bombing was a new and terrifying tactic that had begun in Chicago in 1917. One six-year-old girl died in those bombings. No one was prosecuted for these bombings, and the police appeared uncooperative. Racial tensions were high. Twice during the summer of 1919 hundreds of police had been sent into neighborhoods near the Black Belt to quell potential riots.[18]

Eugene Williams went to a beach where, "by common consent and custom the two racial groups kept within well-understood limits." An imaginary line extending from Twenty-ninth Street was the "well-understood" dividing line between blacks and whites, a line extending across the sand and into the water. But on this afternoon that customary line was challenged. "On this afternoon, some ugly spirit in the mob seemed to make each section anxious to provoke the other," one white Chicagoan recalled a few years later. "'Daredevils' from each group sallied toward the other, and some of their forays were marked by stone-throwing." Williams may have been one of these "daredevils," or he may have been a bystander. He may have been a poor swimmer who panicked when a white swimmer approached him. He may have been stoned to death. Accounts differ. What is known is that, around 4 p.m. on Sunday, July 27, Eugene Williams drowned.[19]

Other blacks on the beach believed that Williams had been stoned to death, and they asked the policeman on the scene, Daniel Callahan, to arrest a white man whom they accused of throwing the fatal stone. Callahan refused. There may have been gambling going on, and the policeman may have been in league with the gamblers, or he may have simply been a racist who was unconcerned with protecting blacks. Again, accounts differ, but most agree that the blacks on the beach were furious. Eventually Officer Callahan arrested one of the blacks, further angering the crowd, and Callahan called for backup. When other police, including one black officer, gathered around Callahan, another black man, James Crawford, shot into the group of police. The police returned fire, killing Crawford. That evening, as rumors spread and crowds wandered Chicago's South Side, twenty-seven blacks and four whites were beaten, seven blacks and five whites were stabbed, four blacks and one white were shot. The race riot had begun.

Monday morning was mysteriously quiet, but that afternoon, as blacks left work at the stockyards, the violence resumed. Inside the packing-houses, on killing floors that were already slippery with blood, it would have been easy to injure a fellow worker if anyone had wanted to bring the rioting inside work. But no one did. In 1919 they did not seek control over the racial conditions of factory work, but they did hope to maintain control of their homes and neighborhoods.[20]

Many scholars have traced the causes of the riot to conflicts over labor. In the first two decades of the twentieth century, blacks had been recruited to break strikes of Illinois meatpackers, coal miners, building tradesmen, newsboys, steelworkers, garment workers, and hotel workers, a record that led some white Chicagoans to consider blacks a "scab race."[21] During the summer of 1919 Chicagoans faced increasing inflation, growing unemployment, and a new strike almost every day, as the government-arbitrated no-strike period of World War I came to an end. The Stockyards Labor Council was attempting to organize all of Packingtown and was beginning to reach out to black workers when the riots disrupted that tentative interracial union.[22] Although the riots exacerbated racial divisions among workers, they had causes beyond workplace politics. Chicagoans in 1919 explained the riots' causes as issues of housing, parks, and commuting, along with policing, rumors, and gangs. These were politics of space more than politics of labor.

The police were said to have inadequately investigated the house bombings earlier in 1919; the policeman at the Twenty-ninth Street beach refused to arrest any whites after Eugene Williams drowned; and the Chicago Commission on Race Relations declared that the rioting was spurred by blacks' "lost faith" in the police. Four-fifths of all the police officers in Chicago in 1919 were sent to the Black Belt during the riot, not the white area of Back of the Yards, where 41 percent of the violence happened. Police arrested so many more blacks than whites that judges and juries complained about racial bias. "I want to explain to you [police] officers that these colored people could not have been rioting against themselves," one judge reportedly said. "Bring me some white prisoners." Despite this judge's request, police arrested blacks at twice the rate of whites. And it was the police who caused at least five of the deaths of the riot by shooting into crowds of black people.[23]

The issues of policing tactics were magnified by rumors, although not the expected rumors of rape and lynching that inflamed so many other riots in America. This was a riot not about patrolling the sexual boundaries of racial formation but about patrolling the physical boundaries of black living space. It was rumors of police brutality, mob violence, and especially arson that caused more mobs to form in Chicago in the middle of the hot summer of 1919.

On Monday afternoon, July 28, as blacks left work, white mobs gathered at the stockyard gates and the streetcar stops. Chicago's racial geography meant that blacks had to commute to Packingtown from the Black

Belt, more than one mile east. On Monday afternoon, rioting white mobs stopped Packingtown's streetcars by pulling down the overhead wires, parking trucks across the streetcar tracks, and even gathering a group of four- and five-year-old children who milled about on the tracks at Forty-seventh Street so the streetcar could not get through, enabling teenagers and adults to open the streetcar doors and drag out black passengers, chasing them through the backyards of the former suburb of Lake, and beating them brutally. Thirty people were severely injured in these street-car brawls; five were killed, including one white man whom blacks attacked in self-defense.[24]

By Monday night whites had begun driving automobiles through the Black Belt, shooting from car windows. Blacks responded by building barri-cades of trashcans, stopping any cars or streetcars that entered the Black Belt, and, often, shooting back. There was a pitched battle at the Angelus apartment house, a white-occupied building within the Black Belt, at the corner of Thirty-fifth and Wabash, where blacks complained that a white sniper was shooting from a fourth-floor window. The *Chicago Defender* proudly recounted black resistance to this sniper in their neighborhood: "The mob charged the building and the battle was on. Police were shot. Whites were seen to tumble out of automobiles, from doorways and other places, wounded or suffering from bruises inflicted by gunshot, stones or bricks." What the *Defender* did not report, but the Chicago Commission on Race Relations did, was that the one hundred policemen who gathered at the "besieged" Angelus building claimed they could find no sniper. Then, after someone in the crowd threw a brick, the police responded by shooting into the crowd of approximately 1,500 blacks, killing four and injuring many. The *Defender* had reported a story of black empowerment, and this was indeed part of the news of the riot: blacks fought back. The Chicago Commission on Race Relations revealed the incredible odds against which blacks had to fight. The events at the Angelus were the second time in two days in which Chicago police had fired indiscriminately into a crowd of African Americans.[25]

Arson began that night. Numerous black homes in "mixed neighbor-hoods" were burned, leaving 229 injured and eighteen dead. Mobs wan-dered the city, while others retreated to their houses. By Tuesday the "contagion of the race war" had spread to the West Side, the downtown Loop, and a few isolated pockets on the North Side. A streetcar-operator strike, beginning Tuesday morning, added "a new source of terror for those who tried to walk to their places of employment." Many simply did not go to work. White merchants locked up their shops in the Black Belt and black workers stayed away from the white sections of town, despite their need for food or paychecks. By Saturday the Red Cross was delivering food to the besieged Black Belt, while the packing companies arranged for that week's wages to be paid via the Chicago Urban League, the YMCA, and Jesse Binga's State Bank in the Black Belt, so workers would not have to make the risky journey to work.[26]

Between the Black Belt and the Stockyards lay Canaryville. It was a Canaryville gang known as "Ragen's Colts" that was said to be responsible for many of the drive-by shootings in the Black Belt, streetcar beatings near the stockyards, and arson in mixed neighborhoods. Ragen's Colts were an "athletic club" of boys funded by Democratic alderman Frank Ragen, coached by Catholic priest Father Brian, and protected by the Back of the Yards substation of the Chicago police. On Monday Ragen's Colts "stationed" themselves at the gateway to the Yards, using clubs to beat blacks on their way home from work. On Tuesday evening two to three hundred members of Ragen's Colts targeted one block of Shield's Avenue in Canaryville where nine black families lived alongside whites. The gang systematically worked from corner to corner, entering houses, throwing furniture out of windows, and setting fires behind them.[27]

Ragen's Colts Athletic Club did participate in athletics; their baseball scores were reported in Chicago newspapers. They were also a social club, whose dances were regularly described as lewd, drunken, and violent. They once heckled an anti-Catholic speaker and murdered a neighborhood Peeping Tom. The *Chicago Tribune* described their storefront clubhouse at 5142 South Halsted Street as "a hangout for the south side's toughest gangsters" and a space where young men periodically received gunshot wounds. When members were turned over to the Back of the Yards police, they were frequently released on "lack of evidence." They had influence in their neighborhood.[28]

"Every street gang in Chicago aspires to be an athletic club with rooms of its own," sociologist Frederic Thrasher declared. His study of 1,313 Chicago gangs identified 302 "athletic clubs" that had begun as gangs but now gathered in rooms rented by politicians, enjoying that politician's "pull" with police and judges. Gangs repaid their political patrons by performing "various types of 'work' at the polls, such as slugging, intimidation, kidnapping, vandalism (tearing down signs, etc.), ballot-fixing, stealing ballot boxes, miscounting, falsifying returns, etc." In the decade after World War I politician-supported athletic clubs like Ragen's Colts made up the youngest cog in Chicago's political machine.[29]

With the Great Migration, traditionally Republican-voting African Americans had tilted the balance of power in Chicago's politics. The impact of the black vote was particularly apparent in the April 1919 reelection of

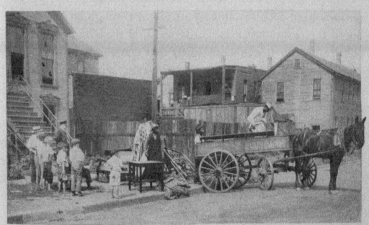

NEGROES UNDER PROTECTION OF POLICE LEAVING WRECKED HOUSE
IN RIOT ZONE

Housing issues were at the root of the riots. In this news photograph, a black family with police protection moves out of their home that has been vandalized by white rioters. From Chicago Commission on Race Relations, *The Negro in Chicago* (Chicago: University of Chicago Press, 1922), 22. Reproduction courtesy of the University of Chicago Library Preservation Department.

Republican mayor "Big Bill" Thompson, who won by a slim margin of only 21,622 votes in this city of 698,920 voters. He had received more than fifteen thousand votes from the Black Belt alone, almost enough to tip the election. Although blacks were less than 4 percent of the population of Chicago, one Democratic newspaper complained, "Negroes elect[ed] Big Bill." In his first term as mayor, Thompson had angered many Chicagoans by closing saloons on Sundays, thus disrupting traditional ethnic leisure customs. He angered others by being profligate with city finances, accumulating a debt of over $4 million. Blacks voted for him because he supported them, but whites charged that the blacks were gamblers and brothel owners. In the election campaign of 1919 Mayor Thompson infuriated many white Chicagoans by courting the black vote so openly that he even hugged black babies. Four months after his election, in the view of some Chicagoans, it was "the condensed venom of political hate and race-hates [that] gave Chicago five of the worst days it had ever known."[30]

Democratic alderman Frank Ragen would have been quite aware that if the mostly Republican blacks had managed to move westward, they would have threatened his hold on power. His job was at stake, but what was at stake for the hundreds of teenagers who had joined Ragen's Colts? Were they really only rioting on his behalf?

The Chicago Commission on Race Relations declared that gangs and athletic clubs were such "an important factor throughout the riot" that they caused the riot to last longer than the first clash on the beach.[31] Beyond political wards, it was gang wards that contributed to Chicagoans' sense of territoriality in 1919. The "typical gang," according to Thrasher's study of 1927, had participated actively in the riots; one gang was even named the Murderers because of "its exploits in the race riots." In the month after the riots, the police temporarily closed clubs that had rioted, clubs whose total membership was reportedly seven thousand youth. Many of their names, such as Our Flag, Mayflowers, and the White Club, emphasized their claims to whiteness and patriotism, while other club names—Aylwards, Hamburgers, Emeralds—suggest a particular pride in white ethnicity.[32]

Gangs banded together around a park, poolroom, street corner, or clubhouse, defending their territory as one of the "valued prerogatives of gangland," Thrasher declared. He identified gangs as an "interstitial" age group between childhood and adulthood, operating in the "interstitial" areas of the city. Their "characteristic habitat" was "that broad twilight zone of railroads and factories, of deteriorating neighborhoods and shifting populations, which borders the city's central business district," thus adding "gangland" into Burgess's zonal hypothesis.[33]

Gangs' neighborhoods were shifting, and the gangs resisted those shifts. Thrasher found relatively few gangs in the rooming houses and apartment districts of Chicago, or in areas that were entirely industrial without any residences. He did find gangs in areas where immigrants owned homes, and especially where Catholic parish boundaries gave a strong sense of place. These youths' families had invested heavily in homes now threatened by declining property values. The gangs were not simply defending politicians; they were also defending their familiar corner, park, and bathing beach, their sense of what space was theirs, their local parish, and their families' mortgages of whiteness.[34]

Ragen's Colts were not only sponsored by the alderman of their ward; they were also coached by the priest of their parish. During the riot they drew their battle line at Wentworth Avenue, a parish boundary for All Saints Church in Bridgeport as well as Corpus Christi Church near Grand Avenue. Catholic parishes are not as portable as Jewish minyans and Protestant congregations. Catholic parishes are structurally rooted geographic spaces.[35]

In Back of the Yards, the area contested during the riots of 1919, 92 percent of families sent their children to parochial schools. They paid $5 a year for this schooling and also donated an average of $11.44 a year to parishes—small but crucial donations that allowed working-class people to erect elaborate, expensive edifices. Festivals, fraternal organizations, charity societies, lending libraries, dramatic societies, and literary and cultural groups were arranged through these parishes. In 1916, in addition to 143 "territorial" parishes for English-speaking Catholics, Chicago had 121 "national" parishes for Catholic immigrants, along with one "Negro" parish, which was listed as if it were for another nationality. The former Town of Lake supported ten national parishes. In this overwhelmingly Catholic area, Irish lived next to Germans, Poles, Czechs, French Canadians, Slovakians, Lithuanians, Ukrainians, and Greeks, who all shared a religion but not a parish.[36]

As early as the 1910s some of these churches struggled with what would later be called "white flight." In 1914 Father Matthew Schmitz of the German parish of St. Augustine—one of the first parishes in the Town of Lake—warned his parishioners against what he called "Wanderlust":

No one has a good reason to move away from St. Augustine's Parish, since there are enough respectable homes to be found here. And our people should not let themselves be edged out, rather they should hold together and remain united, for here in St. Augustine's Parish all the people and all their needs are taken care of in a manner not often possible in many other parishes. I hope that in the future, our people will remain . . . so that the parish may not decrease.[37]

Yet people did leave, as Father Schmitz's warning hints that they were already doing. In 1918 St. Augustine's stopped offering Sunday morning mass in German. In 1925 Father Vincent Schrempp found it necessary to deliver another sermon against moving away: "The attractive religious services of St. Augustine's you will miss elsewhere. And whether it is healthier in other parts of town than in the stockyards district is very questionable. Hence, stay in the parish! Before you sell your home, consult with such as have left the parish. You will hear their regrets and how they deplore their move."[38] Still people left. Second-generation Germans had gained some economic stability and wanted to relocate to what they considered healthier and more respectable suburbs.

Their suburbanization was spurred by multiple trends after World War I. The war, followed by the immigration laws of 1924, limited new European immigration, leading to some decline in attachments to ethnic neighborhoods. The growing popularity of the automobile, coupled with the prosperity of the 1920s, would also encourage a suburban building boom. Perhaps even more than the private automobile, trucks encouraged suburbanization after World War I, because moving materials by truck allows for more flexibility in the location of factories than railroads ever had, and suburban residences followed the suburbanizing factories. Factory location, transportation technology, immigration law, economic prosperity, and ideas about neighborhood succession all combined to make the period after 1918 a period of rapid suburbanization. The Great Depression and World War II slowed this suburban movement by virtually halting new home construction, so that many now associate suburbanization with the 1950s, but it was a movement that began after 1918.[39]

Chicago's Catholic parishes faced difficult choices in these years, especially because racist fears of blacks meant that the gradual and peaceful zonal succession predicted by Burgess's theory could be quite rapid, expedited by realtors who "commercializ[ed] racial antagonism," encouraging panicky whites to sell out. Nuns who had taught schools that faced drastically declining enrollments, priests who had expected to minister to congregants who spoke Croatian or German or Polish, parish members who had donated their scarce savings to build a school and church that was the center of their social as well as religious lives: all were terrified by the arrival of African Americans in their neighborhoods. This explanation does not seek to pardon those who resorted to rioting but to understand the forces that compelled them. Some churches built elaborate structures and advised parishioners against moving away. Others underwent changes in leadership and eventually welcomed blacks.[40]

In Back of the Yards, the leaders of St. Augustine tried to resist white flight by spending $120,000 on a new parish hall and $27,000 on a pipe organ during the 1920s, expensive building projects that strained the finances of the remaining families, eventually making it difficult for the parish to support its own poor during the Great Depression. The changing complexion of urban parishes was a process that lasted decades, from the sermons at St. Augustine in 1914 to the riots around the Trumbull Park Homes in the 1950s to the open housing marches that Martin Luther King led in Chicago in 1966. In the mid-twentieth century many Catholics on the fringes of Chicago, in South Deering and working-class suburbs like Berwyn and Cicero, reported that they had already moved once because of blacks; they did not want to move again, yet they could not envision sharing their parishes with blacks. "We built this church," two elderly couples told the pastor of St. Kevin's. "It's our church and the Niggers can't come here."[41]

In the riots of 1919 in Back of the Yards on Gross Avenue, the residents of the University of Chicago Settlement House "prevented a group of one race [from] driving a team of horses and heavy-laden wagon over the prostrate body of a member of the other race, who had been knocked unconscious." Nearby, in Bubbly Creek, rumors reported that four or fifty-six or a hundred bodies had been hidden among the chemical and animal waste from the packing plants that kept this creek still bubbling. No human bodies were ever found in Bubbly Creek, but the rumors were persistent, highlighting the fears many held of this creek and neighborhood.[42]

On Wednesday, July 30, the heat wave broke, a heavy rain drove people indoors, and the state militia arrived. The militia had begun gathering in armories near Chicago as early as Monday night, but Mayor Thompson told reporters that he resisted inviting them into the city until he was prompted by rumors of further arson. It was housing he sought to protect. The arrival of the militia, along with the cooler weather and soaking rain on Wednesday night, did quell the rioting. The militia stayed a week, and sporadic violence continued, but most of the fighting was over by Wednesday, except for one often overlooked but very revealing convulsion.

Early Sunday morning, at 3:30 on August 2, forty-three houses burned in six square blocks on Hermitage, Wood, Honore, and Lincoln (later Wolcott) Streets, between Forty-third and Forty-fifth Streets, just across Ashland Avenue from Samuel Eberly Gross's subdivision. Michael Mroz, of 4350 South Hermitage Avenue, went door to door, warning his neighbors of the approaching flames. Thanks to his warning, no one died. Although a few people suffered minor burns and one fireman hurt his knee, these nighttime fires injured mostly property, not people. In a week of murders, stabbings, and beatings, this arson may seem relatively minor, but the fires burned property that was not only shelter but also an investment, a community, a parish, and an identity.

SCENE FROM FIRE IN IMMIGRANT NEIGHBORHOOD "BACK OF THE YARDS"

Although little remembered today, the fires in Packingtown were a traumatic part of the riots of 1919. Burning "the working man's reward," the arsonists stirred up anger against African Americans. From Chicago Commission on Race Relations, *The Negro in Chicago* (Chicago: University of Chicago Press, 1922), 16. Reproduction courtesy of the University of Chicago Library Preservation Department.

The community responded collectively to the arson in Back of the Yards. The Catholic convent associated with a nearby Lithuanian parish distributed food that had been donated by the packinghouse of Swift & Co., the field house of Davis Square Park housed the homeless, and a Catholic priest from the neighborhood's Polish parish arranged for furniture, a stove, and a small "purse" to help any of the homeless who lacked fire insurance.[43] This response reveals a dense local safety net, with the local government, private packing company, and both the Lithuanian and Polish parishes cooperatively providing relief. This communal support helps explain why so many people were deeply loyal to their urban neighborhoods.

The houses had burned rapidly, "as if oil or gasoline had been used," leaving behind refugees and rubble in "a scene that might have been a ruined town in France," the *Chicago Tribune* wrote, at a time when memories of World War I were still fresh. Twenty white witnesses claimed they had seen blacks lurking in the vicinity with soaked rags and torches. "Blame Negroes for fire," the *Chicago Tribune* announced on August 5, citing a police bulletin notice seeking "seven or eight colored men . . . wanted in connection with the burning of about 200 houses in the stockyards district." In reality, forty-three houses were burned, not two hundred. It was late at night, in a neighborhood with few streetlights, in darkness that led some to question the witnesses' unanimity about the race of the arsonists. It was also during a week when cordons of police and militia patrolled both the Black Belt and Back of the Yards.[44]

"Do you think a colored man would go into this district back of the yards to set fires when 7,000 colored men have refused to go to the stockyards to get paid even though their families were starving?" asked Louis Anderson, an African American alderman from the Black Belt. "It is preposterous to think that any colored man would go west of Halsted Street without a guard of police or militia in these times. It is impossible that the fires were set by Negroes. The publication of such charges means more ill feeling, more arson, and more murder." Others agreed. "The Negroes weren't back there, they stayed at home after that Monday," settlement house head Mary Mc-Dowell declared. The superintendent of Armour & Company added, "I believe it goes without saying that there isn't a colored man, regardless of how little brains he'd have, who would attempt to go over into the Polish district and set fire to anybody's house over there. He wouldn't get that far." It is a curious alibi: any black person would have been brutally beaten blocks away.[45]

The Commission on Race Relations believed that it was whites with blackened faces who started the fires in order to stir up more rioting. The grand jury investigating the riots agreed, declaring, "The jury believes these fires were started for the purpose of exciting race feeling by blaming same on blacks." Even the *Chicago Tribune*, while emphasizing the theory of black arsonists, mentioned that it could also have been whites in blackface trying to stir up racism, or it might have been radicals from the International Workers of the World, upset that "Poles and Lithuanians are conservative union men [who] repeatedly have refused to listen to the pleas of radicals in the yards." Like the rumors of a Parisian communard in 1871, this rumor charged that irresponsible radicals attempted to stir up strife in the city by starting fires in workers' homes.[46]

Almost all of the homes that burned seem to have been the homes of Lithuanian, a suspicious detail in a neighborhood of mixed ethnicities, where the Polish parish of Sacred Heart Church coexisted uneasily with the Lithuanian parish of Holy Cross just three blocks away. After the arson, the two priests of the Lithuanian and Polish parishes gave a joint speech condemning the house burnings in an extremely rare "token accommodation" between the two parishes. Both official parish histories, written in 1980, blame "gangs of Irish boys" for the arson. The Lithuanian history declares that it was Irish gangs angry at Lithuanians for not having participated in the riots, while the Polish history states that the Irish were angry at Poles for not having rioted. What is apparent in these competing accounts is the underlying ethnic tensions.[47]

Race relations in Chicago were not simply black and white. A superintendent of the Armour Company reported that he had heard "there was as much friction between the Poles and Lithuanians who worked together in the Yards as between the Negroes and the whites." There were tensions between Poles, Lithuanians, and Irish as well as between white ethnic groups and blacks. In 1921 one of Chicago's Polish newspapers would complain of "a band of Lithuanians saturated with mad hatred against Poland." In 1914 one of Chicago's Lithuanian newspapers reported that Poles "have no honor and no character." Old World nationalisms carried over to the New World, sometimes deepened by the experience of immigration and exacerbated by World War I, leading to shouting matches as well as rock throwing between European immigrants who referred to the race riots as a "black pogrom." One of Chicago's Polish newspapers, the *Dziennik Chicagoski*, even printed two articles side by side, one blaming Irish gangs for the arson, the other blaming blacks.[48]

The riots helped move race relations toward a black-white binary. Although it was never proved whether the arsonists were blacks responding to provocations, Poles disputing parish boundaries and Old World politics with Lithuanians, Irish teenage troublemakers from another parish, or simply whites determined to keep other whites angry at blacks, the result of the arson was deep black-white racial animosities that lasted decades.

Black workers had hoped to return to the stockyards on Monday morning, but the Sunday-morning fires kept them away for another week. When blacks did return to work on August 7, the packers arranged for the three thousand returning workers to be accompanied by 1,500 policemen: one policeman for every two black workers. These policemen were ostensibly there to protect blacks, but white union members saw such a heavy police presence as a sign of provocation, arguing that police were traditionally used to escort scabs during strikes and that they had "been used recently to intimidate the workmen." Union spokesmen offered to have union members themselves protect the black workers in the yards. When the police arrived anyway, between seven hundred and five thousand whites walked off their jobs in protest and declared that thirty-two thousand would strike if the police presence continued. The police withdrew. The racial tensions between white and black workers did not subside. These divisions—as well as divisions among branches of white unionists—helped lead to the failure of the next strike, in 1921, and helped keep unions out of Packingtown for another decade.[49]

In that decade the Back of the Yards area healed slowly from the arson of 1919. The careful record made by the 1925 Sanborn Fire Insurance map reveals that, of the twenty-five lots on Lincoln Street between Forty-third and Forty-fourth, seven were still vacant six years after the fire, while two other lots held only small stables. The average of 4.5 vacant lots per block was unusual for this area, implying that poverty-stricken homeowners had difficulty rebuilding after the fires. Beyond those vacant lots, this was a dense neighborhood where shops and flats were interspersed with one- and two-story wooden dwellings, set back from the street with a variety of front yard sizes that created a jagged streetscape and reflected the diverse choices of owner-builders instead of a master builder. Many lots held rear dwellings and sheds. Those rear dwellings and the preponderance of two- and three-family houses help explain why, in 1919, the forty-three burned houses reportedly held nine hundred people, more than twenty people per house.[50]

By 1928 there was only an average of one vacant lot per block. More people had rebuilt by then, but few of the Lithuanians whose homes had burned had managed to return. In R. L. Polk's reverse directory of 1928, which lists the residents of each street, Polish names dominate. There was a Garcia family, a Schultz family, and an O'Connor family all living on Honore Street, suggesting the presence of a few Mexicans, Germans, and Irish in this immigrant district, but the majority of residents were Poles.[51] The rebuilt area was a crowded neighborhood, with each house usually containing three families. The Polk directory gives a wonderfully fine-grained sense of the neighborhood. For example, 1741 Forty-third Street housed Paul and Blanche Wnunkowska, Stanley and Mary Ternowska, Joseph and Stella Kiecin, Walter and Mary Kuruc, and Christopher and Blanche Brazulis, along with the unnamed children of those five families and the Wnunkowskas' grocery store. The Wnunkowskas owned this building, probably paying the mortgage with income from their grocery and tenants, using an investment strategy that was common among many immigrant homeowners. Their grocery would have faced competition from the seven groceries around the corner from them on the 4300 block of Hermitage, as well as the seven additional groceries around the other corner, on the 4300 block of Wood. Altogether the nine blocks of this district held forty-five groceries, interspersed with single-family houses, many multi-family dwellings, and small shops of barbers, butchers, confectioners, dry goods sellers, shoe repairers, and tailors. About one-third of the houses in this neighborhood were owner-occupied, yet many owners, like the Wnunkowskas, shared their homes with renters and sometimes small businesses. This was a mixed-use neighborhood, and not all the uses were odor-free; in 1928 there was one livery stable, two garages, one coal company, and one cigar manufacturer interspersed among the homes. Every block had at least one "soft drink" seller; this neighborhood of nine square blocks held thirty-nine "soft drink" shops that before Prohibition would have been called saloons.[52]

The riot of 1919 was an attempt to preserve this community of corner stores and saloons, Catholic churches and small businesses. The arson in Back of the Yards was an affront to this neighborhood, an affront that was featured in white newspapers more than many more violent aspects of the riots. Burning what had been advertised as the working man's reward seemed to embody the threat that many whites assumed African Americans posed to their property values and their neighborhoods. It was a polluted environment and a poor one, but it was also a place where people had fought to preserve their fragile investments in home, church, corner store, saloon, and parochial schools, all a walkable distance to work. As late as 1970 the area of the former Town of Lake remained 95.6 percent white, because whites fiercely protected this neighborhood.[53]

"WHITE PERSON PROPERTY OWNER"

While Chicago's gang areas, Catholic parishes, and ward politics all reinforced a spatialized sense of identity, what exacerbated this territoriality in 1919 was emerging notions about property values. In 1903 in the South Side suburb of Morgan Park, white residents had declared that they could tolerate the thirty black families who owned homes there, but they were concerned about newcomers, "irresponsible young colored men [who] have drifted into the neighborhood, attracted by the apparent prosperity of those who have purchased property." Morgan Park whites were applying an older discourse linking domesticity and respectability; they preferred established property-owning blacks to the seemingly shiftless newcomers. Similarly people in Woodlawn in 1897 had threatened to tar and feather anyone who rented to blacks; there renting was the problem, not homeownership. Morgan Park posted notices "warning all negroes not owners of property to leave at once." Yet black renters kept coming. In 1917 the Morgan Park Businessmen's Association sought an injunction against the owner of a large apartment building who permitted black tenants. Despite such white resistance, blacks continued to move to Morgan Park so that, by 1923, the Chicago Commission on Race Relations lauded Morgan Park as one solution to the riot-inducing conditions in central Chicago.[54]

Unlike the residents of Woodlawn and Morgan Park who preferred black homeowners to renters, in 1919 Chicago realtor L. M. Smith explicitly told a reporter that he could tolerate black neighbors who were renters, not owners. "If they come in as tenants, we can handle the situation fairly easily," Smith declared. "But when they get a deed, that's another matter. Be sure to get us straight on that. We want to be fair and do what's right."⁵⁵ He may have sincerely believed that he was being fair, but the Kenwood and Hyde Park Property Owners Association, which Smith led, also promoted deeply racist ideas, evident in statements such as "Niggers are undesirable neighbors and entirely irresponsible and vicious."⁵⁶ Echoing new zoning policies against nuisance industries, the journal of the Kenwood and Hyde Park Property Owners Association explained:

> Keep the Negro in his place, amongst his people and he is healthy and loyal, [but] remove him, or allow his newly discovered importance to remove him from his proper environment, and the Negro becomes a nuisance. He develops into an overbearing, inflated, irascible individual, overburdening his brain to such an extent about social equality that he becomes dangerous to all with whom he comes in contact.⁵⁷

Despite such egregious comments linking spatial identity and social identity, Smith and his Association were gradually finding it convenient to disavow personal racism and instead cite a supposedly race-neutral argument about property values. They called themselves a Property Owners Association and titled their journal the *Chicago Property Owner's Journal*, implying that all legitimate property owners were white.

In 1917 the Chicago Real Estate Board had campaigned to organize "owners societies in every white block for the purpose of mutual defense," defending white homes from the effects of black neighbors, explaining that this was done as "a financial business proposition and not with white prejudice." The Chicago Real Estate Board led the way for the National Association of Real Estate Boards, which, in 1924, added to its code of ethics that members were forbidden from introducing "members of any race or nationality" into a neighborhood where they "will clearly be detrimental to property values."⁵⁸

The *Chicago Property Owner's Journal* explained a few months after the riots, "To damage a man's property and destroy its value is to rob him. The person who commits that act is a robber. Every owner has the right to defend his property to the utmost of his ability with every means at his disposal." Because African American homeowners were seen as automatically lowering property values, by this logic African Americans who purchased houses outside of the Black Belt could not help but be "robbers." Unlike the older discourse linking domesticity with respectability, in this new "market imperative" discourse, black homeowners were equivalent to thieves. The *Property Owner's Journal* was explicit about reacting to the "robbery" by black homeowners with threats of punishment: "Any property owner who sells property anywhere in our district to undesirables is an enemy of the white race and should be discovered and punished. Protect your property! Property conservatively valued at $50,000,000 owned by some 10,000 individuals is menaced by a possible Negro invasion of Hyde Park."[59] This was the inflammatory language of the mortgages of whiteness.

Since the nineteenth century, working-class whites had received what David Roediger and W. E. B. DuBois have identified as "the wages of whiteness." Whites were often paid more than blacks, but even when they "received a low wage [they were] compensated in part by a . . . public and psychological wage." These wages of whiteness included the reassurance that even the poorest whites were not at the bottom of the social hierarchy: whites could enter any park or theater; they could expect civil treatment from public officials; and their children could attend any public school. They received the psychological wage of believing that they were still better than blacks, and this prevented working-class whites and blacks from allying together to fight for their common interests.[60]

By 1919 in Chicago one significant aspect of the wages of whiteness had become what I call the mortgages of whiteness: an implicit, often unfulfilled promise that white people might profit from homeownership as long as they could keep blacks away from their neighborhoods. The racial and ethnic composition of Chicago's neighborhoods had been shifting ever since Chicago had neighborhoods, but earlier Chicagoans had judged their property's value by criteria broader than the racial makeup of a neighborhood. They judged the comfort of a particular building, its convenience to transportation, and its productive use as a laundry, market garden, boardinghouse, or other small business. In the twentieth century, the idea of property values narrowed to include only the expected retail value of a house, which depended on making assumptions about the opinions of an unknown, supposedly representative buyer. Blacks eager to escape the congestion and vice of the Black Belt certainly did not pay low prices for property, but panicked whites fleeing a supposed black invasion might lower property prices. In this property values discourse, the implied buyer was only white. Preserving property values began to mean preserving single-class, single-use, and single-race areas.[61]

Immediately after the riots, Alderman Terence Moran introduced a resolution calling for fixed zones of white and black residences, explaining, "Each race has certain prejudices arising from social causes, which prejudices are more apparent where the property rights of the races become involved."[62] Moran's resolution did not pass, but he had political allies. Later in 1919 Alderman Schwartz, addressing a meeting of the Grand Boulevard district of the Kenwood and Hyde Park Property Owners Association, declared that the mere threat of black incursion had resulted in $100 million in lost property values. "Now it is not only the loss of money that interests us. It means not only that somebody has lost comfort in living; someone has lost joy in his home; someone has lost the opportunity to give his children the environment that he wanted to give."[63] Earlier a home was seen as more than just a bank: it was shelter, a legacy to one's children, a community, a social status, and a promise of class mobility. Increasingly, though, it was all of those things only because of its presumed resale value.

Kenwood and Hyde Park's L. M. Smith announced, "We can't have these people coming over here. . . . They injure our investments. They hurt our values. We are not making any threats, but we do say something must be done." That "something" included threatening letters, verbal harassment, physical beatings, and, fifty-eight times between 1917 and 1921, bombing the property of blacks or those who sold to blacks. In those years there was one bombing approximately every twenty days, bombings that destroyed more than $100,000 worth of property and killed two African Americans. In 1917 the Chicago Real Estate Board had urged racial zoning to avoid what they claimed was $250 million in property value depreciation. By the mid-1920s Chicago's realtors and property associations developed "something more subtle" to keep blacks out of mostly white neighborhoods: restrictive covenants that barred property owners from selling to restricted races. By 1930 three-quarters of Chicago residential property was bound by restrictive covenants.[64]

"No single factor has complicated the relations of Negroes and whites in Chicago more than the widespread feeling of white people that the presence of Negroes in a neighborhood is a cause of serious depreciation of property values," concluded the Chicago Commission on Race Relations.[65] Poor people had hoped that investing in homes would be better than a bank for them. By 1919 some recognized that these hopes would not be realized. Poorly planned developments, industrial pollution, neighborhood crime, aging buildings, the beginning of Chicago's deindustrialization, a biased housing market, unequal access to credit, and inadequate municipal services were all abstract forces, difficult to fight. Blacks were scapegoats, more easily attacked than those complex, amorphous forces.

Like other newcomers to Chicago, the blacks of the Great Migration often moved into already deteriorating neighborhoods with older buildings requiring significant repairs. Facing a limited supply because of the racist housing market, blacks had to pay higher prices for these less desirable homes, thus leaving little extra cash to pay for needed repairs. The Chicago Commission on Race Relations concluded that "prior depreciation" caused blacks to move into a neighborhood more than blacks caused "present depreciation," but this fine argument held little traction with whites looking at the deteriorating Black Belt and looking for someone to blame for their own teetering property values.[66]

Public and private institutions reinforced the myth that the presence of blacks depreciated property values. City government pushed vice districts into African American neighborhoods and was consistently lax about garbage collection and street cleaning in black neighborhoods. A racist job market often left blacks poorer than whites; this was compounded by a racist credit market. With the twentieth-century institutionalization of banking, Chicago's newest black migrants found it harder to form their own lending institutions than older white ethnic immigrants had. The all-white Mortgage Bankers' Association barred black members until the 1960s, and association membership was required for every student in mortgage banker training courses. Unequal access to housing credit meant that "a dollar in the hands of a black man" was worth less than "a dollar in the hands of a white man."[67]

Like the black marks on Chicago maps showing where African Americans lived, by 1919 many white Chicagoans believed that black people "tainted" a neighborhood and would "blight" property values. Earlier the black residents of Morgan Park had been examples of respectable black homeownership. In the years after World War I, with the influx of the Great Migration, white Chicagoans started to see blacks as slum dwellers, the opposite of homeowners. A broadside for an October 1918 meeting of the Kenwood and Hyde Park Property Owners Association asked, "Shall we sacrifice our property for a third of its value and run like rats from a burning ship, or shall we put up a united front and keep Hyde Park desirable for ourselves?" The broadside exhorted, "Every white person Property Owner in Hyde Park come to this meeting," in a particularly clear instance of the discursive overlap that was developing between whiteness, homeownership, and citizenship. In just a few years this phrasing would come to seem redundant: *homeowner* would become shorthand for *white citizen.*[68]

Unlike the often unspoken wages of whiteness, the mortgages of whiteness were publicly discussed, yet in the putatively race-neutral language of homeownership. Increasingly throughout the twentieth century, opponents of racial liberalism spoke in seemingly color-blind language, urging supporters to "get back your rights," demanding the right to "our jobs," "our schools," and especially "our homes," without ever having to state that they were asking for the right to discriminate on behalf of white privilege.[69]

The idea of homeowner rights to protect property value by discriminating against blacks began in Chicago in the years around the riots,

THE MORTGAGES OF WHITENESS (175)

becoming institutionalized in the next two decades. In the 1920s Chicago's realtors, land-use scientists, and zoning officials all reinforced the idea that property reached higher values in single-race neighborhoods. In the 1930s government housing programs structured both credit and property markets along racial lines, while simultaneously disavowing government's role, pretending it was the free market that set what can aptly be called residential apartheid.[70]

This residential apartheid not only divided whites from blacks; it also helped form twentieth-century whiteness itself. Before World War II many Americans thought of Irish, Italians, Jews, and Czechs as separate races: not quite white, but not entirely nonwhite either. They were probationary whites. As late as 1945 two Chicago sociologists reported, "Such ethnic groups as the English, German, Scotch, Irish, and Scandinavian have little adverse effect on property values. Northern Italians are considered less desirable, followed by Bohemians and Czechs, Poles, Lithuanians, Greeks, and Russian Jews of the lower class." Combining skin tone with class and time since each group first migrated to Chicago, this ethnoracial ladder concluded, "Southern Italians, along with Negroes and Mexicans, are at the bottom of the scale." This scale demonstrates the not-quite-whiteness of many European immigrants, or what David Roediger calls their "inbetweenness," in between the binary of black and white. For some probationary whites, uniting against blacks helped them to become more definitively white. Like nineteenth-century whites performing blackface minstrelsy, twentieth-century white rioters contributed to a popular sense of whiteness by crossing lines of respectable behavior only to further reinscribe those lines.[71]

Ideas about the property value of whites, promoted by realtors and housing economists in the 1910s and 1920s, then inscribed in New Deal housing policies in the 1930s, helped create ideas about whiteness itself, uniting foreign- and native-born, working and upper class. By demarcating a bright line between the property of whites and that of blacks, twentieth-century suburbs solidified twentieth-century notions of whiteness.[72]

Later, observing a riot in the Chicago suburb of Cicero in 1951, a member of the Catholic Interracial Council puzzled over what seemed to be a perversion of domesticity among groups who still sometimes seemed like white ethnics:

> The town is an enviable picture of order and peace. Czech housewives are second to none in the care of their homes. . . . Indeed, what has gone wrong in Cicero is something good. The homemaking virtues of these people have been oversown . . . by national exclusiveness, by middle class materialism, by the

drying up of human compassion and sympathy for other families in need. They have acquired homes, but they have made them the golden calf to be worshipped and possessed at all costs.[73]

Another Cicero clergyman reiterated, "The God worshipped in Cicero is the unencumbered deed and . . . the town's real churches are its savings and loan associations."[74] This false God was the mortgages of whiteness. People had invested in property, hoping to achieve the working man's reward of upward mobility through homeownership. Liberal, integrationist clergy perceived these desires as a false God, yet even the liberal clergy had trouble distinguishing between the "good . . . home making virtues" and the bad "middle class materialism." The people of Cicero, like the people of Lake, were attempting to enter the white middle class through homeownership. Sharing their precarious racial and class status with black neighbors would mean, they feared, losing that status.

City planners assumed that threatened groups would simply move to suburbs farther away; they failed to understand that moving out would be "the end rather than the fulfillment of a dream." The contested neighborhoods of Chicago and its inner suburbs were not where people dreamed of new suburbanization. They were neighborhoods with high levels of homeownership, low levels of residential movement, and tenacious neighborhood ties. Many architects, urbanists, and planners describe a "sense of place" as a positive force, worth nourishing. The residents of Cicero in the 1950s and Back of the Yards in 1919 both had a remarkably strong sense of place. In 1939 Saul Alinsky and Joseph Meegan famously drew on this sense of place to organize the Back of the Yards Neighborhood Council, a democratic activist group, building on church, youth, ethnic, and class ties, working successfully to improve the neighborhood. Yet, to Alinsky's embarrassment, one of the goals of the Back of the Yards Neighborhood Council became to keep the neighborhood white. Alinsky proposed quotas admitting 5 percent blacks, a compromise that satisfied few blacks or whites. Eventually Alinsky moved on to organize elsewhere, distancing himself from the racist policies of the Council. His experience is a reminder that a positive sense of place can have a negative, exclusionary underside.[75]

Even as the rioting continued that hot July in 1919, Illinois governor Frank Lowden "gave a statement in which he urged that the cause of rioting be removed by provision of proper housing and recreation facilities."[76] The riot had multiple causes, but above all it was a riot about the physical spaces of the city. It began at the swimming beach at Twenty-ninth Street as a dispute over park space. It spread to the streetcars, making it a riot about the right to move freely through the city. It culminated in the arson of homes, illuminating developing ideas about the mortgages of whiteness. Access to homes and parks was understood as the primary issue that had caused thirty-eight deaths, 537 severe injuries, and arson that left one thousand homeless.

The riots of 1919, like the riots of 1872, were led by working-class homeowners defending their urban communities from the pressures of suburbanization. The difference was that in 1872, German and Irish homeowners had attacked city hall, identifying government policies as one cause of sprawl. In 1919 the object of attack was black people, human scapegoats and symbols of a complex housing system.

Conclusion

The City of the Twentieth Century

Turn-of-the-century Chicago exposes the variety of American suburbs. Since the 1860s Chicago's suburbs included industries, immigrants, and a range of classes. These diverse suburbs also changed over time, so that the working man's reward of Lake became the fiercely defended slum of Back of the Yards, the locus of the riots of 1919. Those riots, like the protests of 1872, reveal Chicagoans resisting pressures to suburbanize.

Despite this undertow of resistance, suburbanization in Chicago was overdetermined by a combination of material strategies and ideological visions. Hopes for upward mobility through property ownership, strategies for domestic respectability imposed from above as well as created below, the self-provisioning of a working class resisting the vicissitudes of industrial capitalism, factory locations, beliefs about neighborhood succession, and the growth machine of land speculators, realtors, and city boosters all combined to encourage suburbanization in Chicago and America.

The pattern of Chicago was set by the early twentieth century. The spread of automobiles and trucks after 1920, federal housing programs after 1930, and urban renewal after 1940 all reinforced and intensified the patterns set by 1920. This is not to say that later Chicagoans had no choice. As historian Arnold Hirsch points out, Chicagoans who lived after 1920 still hold responsibility for the solidifying segregation of their city: "The real tragedy surrounding the emergence of the modern ghetto is not that it has been inherited but that it has been periodically renewed and strengthened" by vigilante violence, private businesses, and public policies. By 1945

Chicago's Black Belt squeezed in ninety thousand people per square mile, while nearby white areas housed only twenty thousand. Such crowding, coupled with poverty, meant that diseases proliferated. Schools in the Black Belt ran on shifts in the 1930s, educating each child for only half a day. The more that whites pushed blacks into this slum, the more that some whites concluded blacks must naturally be slum-dwellers and blamed blacks for the conditions that whites had created.[1]

Other Chicagoans, concerned over the housing conditions of the poor, started building public housing in the 1920s. The city built towering blocks of public housing, filled with windows and surrounded by open air, reflecting the tenaciousness of nineteenth-century reformers' concerns with light and health. These housing blocks may have delivered health, at least at first, but they did not deliver safety, community, or a sense of pride—so that, in recent years, Chicagoans have been tearing down their unsuccessful megablocks of modern housing and replacing them with more dispersed houses, returning to the original suburban ideal that many working-class Chicagoans had favored during the period of this study. It remains to be seen if this newer, suburban-style public housing will work out better than the megablocks.

In addition to solidifying the Black Belt and building the reformers' public housing, the twentieth century witnesses the institutionalization of the mortgages of whiteness through private banking policies in the 1920s, federal lending policies after the 1930s, and public housing policies after the 1940s, all of which favored homeownership for whites more than non-whites. Others have told the story of the racist lending policies of twentieth-century banks, but the connection between public housing and white homeownership is less well understood. When the Chicago Housing Authority first attempted to clear the near North Side site that would become the Frances Cabrini Rowhouses, they faced long and vehement protests from the many white ethnic working-class homeowners there. The homeowners rebuffed the Housing Authority's purchase offers, hired lawyers, enlisted the aid of politicians, and caused expensive delays that eventually led the Housing Authority to settle for a site half the original size and then to avoid ever again proposing large-scale public housing in a white neighborhood. Chicago's twentieth-century slum clearance focused on black slums, not white slums. Urban renewal became black removal partly because the legacy of a racist housing market had kept blacks lagging behind whites in rates of homeownership, and it was homeowners who fought fiercely against urban renewal. Black homeowners also fought proposed public housing in Lilydale, West Chesterfield, and the South Side Dearborn homes, but there were fewer black homeowners to wage this battle. Instead the structures of public housing became metonyms for minority racial status, further intertwining space, race, and class.[2]

Chicago's 1919 riots were an early example of many twentieth-century American riots about racialized territoriality, in cities from Detroit to Los Angeles. After 1919 Chicago's riots were more isolated, partly because liberals had learned to pressure newspapers to avoid inflaming riots. They were also more intertwined with government programs such as urban renewal and public housing and less concerned with union or ward politics. Still, Chicago's later riots shared a persistent concern with parish boundaries and property values. Vandalism, arson, rock-throwing, and bomb-throwing recurred throughout Chicago in the 1940s and 1950s, especially at moving season. Rioters included many women and children as whole families worried about their local neighborhoods; 90 percent of rioters lived within twelve blocks of each riot scene, where they attempted to defend their mortgages of whiteness.[3]

Chicago's African American suburbs also endured through the twentieth century. The 1990 census reveals that, although the metropolitan region includes hundreds of suburbs, 40 percent of all black suburbanites live in only fourteen suburbs. All fourteen of those suburbs have had significant black populations since the 1920s. Pushed by discrimination, pulled by desires for community and homeownership, and limited by the generally lower overall economic status of African Americans, Chicago's contemporary black suburbanites still live in the suburbs that blacks pioneered at the beginning of the twentieth century. The boundaries established then are boundaries that linger.[4]

Some of the forces that propelled Chicago's factories to suburbanize during the nineteenth century—including the search for cheaper land, lighter regulations, lower taxes, and fewer unionized workers—eventually propelled those same factories to move beyond Chicago or overseas. Suburbanizing industries became globalizing industries. Nevertheless Chicago's suburbanized industry continues in both blue-collar and white-collar work in "edge cities" such as Schaumburg, whose growth was spurred less by the spatial needs of assembly lines than by the advantages of access to airports, expressways, corporate communities, banking networks, and executives' suburban homes. The causes of suburbanized workplaces shifted during the twentieth century, but the fact that suburbs are not solely residential still continues.[5]

Property-owner politics played out throughout the twentieth century in massive movements resisting neighborhood integration, school busing, and property tax increases. Groups of homeowners have been a strong and often strongly conservative force in twentieth-century America. Yet Adam

Rome has argued that suburban homeownership also spurred the current environmentalism. As Chicago's early housing riots of 1872 reveal, an identification as homeowners can lead to liberal as well as conservative ends. Efforts to protect workers' fragile investments in housing have a flexibility and a political power that deserve further study. It may be one of the strongest motivators of grassroots politics in the twentieth century.[6]

In a front-page article in 2008 entitled "Building Flawed American Dreams," *New York Times* reporters wrote that the twenty-first-century housing "debacle . . . has changed homeownership from something that secured a place in the middle class to something that is ejecting people from it." Chicagoans who experienced their own housing downturns after 1837, 1856, 1873, and 1893 might have told the reporters that this ejection is not new. Nineteenth-century Chicagoans were quite familiar with what their real estate press called "years strewn with the wrecks of fortunes and the destruction of hopes."[7] Like Chicago's history, the current housing crisis exposes the fragility of the American dream of homeownership, the importance of credit as an accelerant or hindrance to social mobility, and the arbitrary aspects of assessing property value. Would Chicagoans who lived through their own cyclical housing recessions have avoided the current crisis? Perhaps—but throughout the turbulent time period of this study, many Chicagoans still speculated in real estate. They hoped homes would be "better than a bank for a poor man." They knew that the American dream could turn into a nightmare, but they still dreamed.

By 1920 Chicago was a suburban city, "the city of the twentieth century," as it announced itself in 1893. It was a city that set the pattern for many twentieth-century American cities: a pattern of diverse sprawl, segregated and contested, formed from below as well as above, and expanding. We have inherited that suburbanized form, constructed to produce profits for particular people in nineteenth-century Chicago and then twentieth-century America, a form that must now be adapted for current needs and values.[8]

Chicago's earliest suburbs sometimes challenged inequality and sometimes promoted it. It seems odd that, in 1889, in gratitude for his mass-produced suburban housing, Chicago's United Workingmen's Society nominated developer Samuel Eberly Gross for mayor. That same year, the *Knights of Labor* newspaper named Gross "the most practical philanthropist . . . for he is helping the people to help themselves."[9] Working-class mortgages did not always help the people help themselves, but the Knights of Labor connected their shift to consumerist politics, especially their fight for the eight-hour day, to their appreciation of Gross's subdivisions. That working-class appreciation of suburban housing stretches back at least to the rioters of 1872, who proclaimed that widespread access to single-family housing was what kept Chicago a city without a proletariat. Up to half of Chicago's early working-class homeowners may have faced foreclosures, but those who succeeded at purchasing housing did gain a tenuous upward mobility, as long as they stayed on the upswings of "the curve that says I will." Housing brought profits and respectability to some people, but it also brought schisms, especially after 1919, between blacks and whites.

Understanding suburbs' diverse past may help us to conceive their possible futures. Understanding the complex causes of sprawl is perhaps one way to mitigate some of its results: the unsustainable environmental impact, the cost in long commutes and foreclosed mortgages, and the politics of privatization and segregation. The built environment often lingers for decades past the forces that built it, but the patterns set earlier may be changing now, as gentrification reclaims urban neighborhoods for middle-class residences and as newer migrants refuse to fit into the black/white binary that emerged in Chicago around 1919. The current housing crisis may give us a chance to rethink our notions of property values and our built-up inequalities after a century and a half of suburbanization.

NOTES

INTRODUCTION: FORGING THE SUBURBAN DREAM IN EARLY CHICAGO

1. Terkel, *Chicago*, 13.
2. Fannie Mae slogan from the 1990s. Other examples of this version of the American dream appear in book titles, including Tom Martinson, *American Dreamscapes: The Pursuit of Happiness in Postwar Suburbia* (New York: Carroll & Graf, 2000); Hayden, *Redesigning the American Dream*; Wright, *Building the Dream*; Garb, *City of American Dreams*.
3. For "growth machine," see Hayden, *Building Suburbia*, 4. Gail Radford adds another useful concept, "the housing delivery system," including the designers, financiers, legislators, and builders who together limit what housing choices individual consumers have, especially once housing construction and financing became more standardized in the twentieth century (*Modern Housing for America* 9). For "segregated diversity," see Nicolaides and Weise, *The Suburb Reader*, 4.
4. Samuel Eberly Gross (Firm), *Tenth Annual Illustrated Catalogue*, 62–63.
5. On workers' presumed whiteness, see especially Roediger, *The Wages of Whiteness*, 3–42.
6. See "Broadsides—Real Estate," Chicago History Museum.
7. Kevin Starr analyzes this imagining in his description of Chicagoans who developed Los Angeles. See Kevin Starr, *Material Dreams: Southern California through the 1920s* (New York: Oxford University Press, 1990), 65–89.
8. Richard Wright, introduction to Drake and Cayton, *Black Metropolis*, xviii.
9. Flinn, *Chicago*, 49, 380.
10. Jackson, *Crabgrass Frontier*, 12–14; Carl Sandburg, "To a Contemporary Bunkshooter," in *Chicago Poems* , 64.
11. Classic studies of the growth of suburbia as an elite retreat include Jackson, *Crabgrass Frontier*, 18–20; Stilgoe, *Borderlands*; Fishman, *Bourgeois Utopias*.
12. Patricia Cline Cohen, *The Murder of Helen Jewett: The Life and Death of a Prostitute in Nineteenth-Century New York* (New York: Knopf, 1998), 64; *Oxford English Dictionary*, 2nd ed. (New York: Oxford University Press, 1989), 17: 86; Todd Gardner, "The Slow Wave: The Changing Residential Status of Cities and Suburbs in the United States, 1850–1940," *Journal of Urban History* 27, no. 3 (2001): 293–312. Gardner believes the lower status of suburbs is even more prevalent in small towns than in big cities. For the wide variety of suburbs around Indianapolis, see also Timothy Sehr, "Three Gilded Age Suburbs of Indianapolis: Irvington, Brightwood, and Woodruff Place," *Indiana Magazine of History* 77, no. 4 (1981): 305–33. As Richard Harris asserts, "It is important to take a comprehensive view. . . . Residential and middle-class suburbs have particular qualities. If we wish to argue that they are

in any sense 'quintessentially suburban,' it is necessary to compare them with the full range of places that have grown up at the urban fringe" (*Unplanned Suburbs*, 11). Viewing that full range of fringe spaces is one of the goals of this work. Similarly Robert Lewis points out, "The place of industrial suburbs within the broader dynamics of urban growth has been lost in the historiography of middle-class suburbs." Robert Lewis, "Industry and the Suburbs," in *Manufacturing Suburbs*, 3. Richard Harris in "Chicago's Other Suburbs" has called for further studies of Chicago's diverse suburbs, a challenge that this book takes up. Along with Harris, another inspiration for this study is Paul Groth's study of the Chicago-based pressures for American home ownership: *Living Downtown*, especially 201–33.

13. Runnion, *Out of Town*, 3–4, 22–23, 46. For another example, see Flinn, *Chicago*, 387: "To those of moderate means a town of the size of Englewood Heights offers many inducements; property is much cheaper than it is in an older and better developed place."

14. Jackson, *Crabgrass Frontier*, 4–10. For a similar definition, see Palen, *The Suburbs*, 9. More recently Jackson has noted that his *Crabgrass Frontier* omitted planned chapters on industrial suburbs and working-class suburbs, and that, in the twenty years since publication, suburbs have become "even harder to define." Kenneth Jackson, foreword to Nicolaides and Wiese, *The Suburb Reader*, xxi–xxii. As Elizabeth Blackmar explains, "The language of housing, overlaid by gender prescriptions, class perceptions, and our own contemporary experiences, is . . . slippery" (*Manhattan for Rent*, 8–9). For the high density of twentieth-century suburban gated communities, see McKenzie, *Privatopia*, 80–82.

15. Douglass, *The Suburban Trend*, 34, 89, 119, 113, 121.

16. Hoover is cited in Baxandall and Ewen, *Picture Windows*, 33; Hayden, *Redesigning the Dream*, 34; Jackson, *Crabgrass Frontier*, 193. Groth, *Living Downtown*, 43.

17. For the public costs of suburbs, see Orfield, *Metropolitics*, chapters 1 and 2. See also Duany et al., *Suburban Nation*, 127–29. For the social production of space, see Williams, *The Country and the City*; Lefebvre, *The Production of Space*; Gottdiener, *The Social Production of Urban Space*; Soja, *Postmodern Geographies*; Harvey, *Spaces of Capital*.

18. For the best periodization of American suburbs, see Jackson, *Crabgrass Frontier*; Ryan, *Civic Wars*.

19. McShane, *Down the Asphalt Path*, x; Nye, *Electrifying America*, ix–xi. For delays between streetcar technology and suburbia, see Marsh, *Suburban Lives*, 15. For delays between laws and suburbia, see McKenzie, *Privatopia*, 98.

20. See Boydston, *Home and Work*; Nancy Cott, "Domesticity," in *The Bonds of Womanhood: "Women's Sphere" in New England, 1780–1835* (New Haven, CT: Yale University Press, 1977), 63–100. For further discussion of the public politics of private homes, see Wright, *Moralism and the Model Home*. For another classic discussion of household economies, see Jones, *Labor of Love, Labor of Sorrow*.

21. For working-class owner-building, see Harris, *Unplanned Suburbs*; Nicolaides, *My Blue Heaven*. For industrial suburbs, see Lewis, *Manufacturing Suburbs*. For minority suburbs, see Wiese, *Places of Their Own*; Davis, *Magical Urbanism*. For precarious urban centers, see Fogelson, *Downtown*; Rae, *City*; Isenberg, *Downtown America*. Anthologies of the new suburban history are Nicolaides and Weise, *The Suburb Reader*; Kruse and Sugrue, *The New Suburban History*.

22. Self, *American Babylon*; Kevin M. Kruse, *White Flight: Atlanta and the Making of Modern Conservatism* (Princeton, NJ: Princeton University Press, 2005); Lipsitz, *The Possessive Investment in Whiteness*; HoSang, *Racial Propositions*.

23. Self, *American Babylon*, 1.
24. For the difference between urban politics before and after the 1940s, see especially Hirsch, *Making the Second Ghetto*; Freund, *Colored Property*. Margaret Garb recently examined Chicago's diverse early suburbs in *City of American Dreams*. Using different sources, I don't see as stark a binary as Garb asserts between a nineteenth-century working-class view of homes as a productive space and a twentieth-century middle-class view of homes as producing only property values, but I do share her conclusion that homeownership "stratified the working class" (8).
25. Discussing the colonial era, Daniel M. Freidenberg has a chapter on "America as a Land Speculation" in *Life, Liberty, and the Pursuit of Land: The Plunder of Early America* (Buffalo, NY: Prometheus Books, 1992). Julian Ralph, "A New York Journalist Visits Chicago," in Pierce, *As Others See Chicago*, 300; *Saturday Review* (London 1874), quoted in Pierce, *A History of Chicago*, 3: 19. See also George A. Birmingham, *From Dublin to Chicago* (1914), reprinted in Quaife, *The Development of Chicago*, 269; d'Eramo, *The Pig and the Skyscraper*, 7–8.
26. Butterworth, *Zig-Zag Journeys in the White City*, 113–14; Isenberg, *Downtown America*, 26–27.
27. Hornstein, *A Nation of Realtors*, especially 18–22, 105–8. For more on realtor's lobbying, see Weiss, *The Rise of the Community Builders*; Freund, *Colored Property*, 15.
28. Isenberg, *Downtown America*, 46, 103. Sears first built suburban stores in the 1920s; the Teich company produced postcards from 1910 to 1940.
29. Nelson Algren, *Chicago: City on the Make* (New York: Doubleday & Co., 1951), 90, 82, and 59.
30. *The Parks and Property Interests of the City of Chicago* (Chicago: Western News Company, 1869), 3–4.

1. "VAST AND SUDDEN MUNICIPALITY": BOOSTING AND LAMENTING CHICAGO'S GROWTH

1. Andreas, *History of Chicago*, 1: 137, quoted in Cronon, *Nature's Metropolis*, 29.
2. Chamberlin, *Chicago and Its Suburbs*, 196; Hoyt, *One Hundred Years of Land Values in Chicago*, 26.
3. Hoyt, calculating the value of land within Chicago's present city limits (*One Hundred Years of Land Values in Chicago*, 33). A. Garrett, *Auction*, in "Broadsides—Real Estate," Chicago History Museum; Henry L. Turner, "Chicago Real Estate," in *Industrial Chicago*, vol. 4: *The Commercial Interests*, 16.
4. Andreas, *History of Chicago*, quoted in Hoyt, *One Hundred Years of Land Values in Chicago*, 31.
5. Turner, "Chicago Real Estate," 19. William B. Ogden letter to H. Moore, January 25, 1841, quoted in Hoyt, *One Hundred Years of Land Values in Chicago*, 42.
6. Hoyt, *One Hundred Years of Land Values in Chicago*; Monchow, *Seventy Years of Real Estate Subdividing*, 1–3; *Land Owner* 7, no. 4 (1875): 57. See also Turner, "Chicago Real Estate," 22; *Real Estate and Building Journal*, (December 30, 1876), quoted in Chicago Title and Trust Company, *One Hundred Years of Chicago Land Values* (1933), in Chicago Title and Trust Company, Miscellaneous Pamphlets, Chicago Historical Society.
7. Robin L. Einhorn, *Property Rules: Political Economy in Chicago, 1833–1872* (Chicago: University of Chicago Press, 1991). Einhorn cites the 70 percent figure from Rima

Lunin Schultz, "The Businessman's Role in Western Settlement: The Entrepre-
neurial Frontier, Chicago, 1833–1872" (PhD dissertation, Boston University,
1985), 402. Hoyt, *Land Values*; Putney, *Real Estate Values*; Chamberlin, *Chicago
and Its Suburbs*; Larson, *The Devil in the White City*, 14.

8. J. W. Foster, "New Chicago," *Lakeside Monthly Magazine* 7, no. 37 (1872): 84.
9. Thompson, *Chicago: A Stranger and Tourists' Guide* (Chicago: Religious Publishing
   Association, 1866), 19. James Parton, "Chicago," *The Atlantic Monthly* 19, no. 113
   (March, 1867), 334–35.
10. Anonymous, "A New Year's Resolution: Boost" (Chicago: circa 1920), in the Chi-
    cago Historical Society's file on "Chicago (Boosterism)."
11. Turner, "Chicago Real Estate," in *Industrial Chicago*, 15.
12. *The Land Owner* 4, no. 9 (September, 1872), 150.
13. The campaign against "curbstoners" is detailed in Marc Weiss, *Rise of the Commu-
    nity Builders: The American Real Estate Industry and Urban Land Planning* (New
    York: Columbia University Press, 1987). 1.79 percent of Chicago's workers were
    real estate executives. For other occupational percentages, see Richard Sennett,
    Families Against the City: Middle Class Homes in Industrial Chicago (Cambridge,
    MA: Harvard University Press, 1970), 88. Anonymous, *Proceedings of the First An-
    nual Meeting of the National Board of Real Estate Agents at the Briggs Houses, Chi-
    cago, October 12–14, 1870* (Chicago: The Land Owner Press, 1870), 13–15. A second
    similar board also failed because it was "too narrow," according to Everett Char-
    ington Hughes, *The Growth of an Institution: The Chicago Real Estate Board* (Chi-
    cago: University of Chicago Society for Social Research, 1931), 18. The third
    attempt to organize a board, in 1883, succeeded. Turner, "Chicago Real Estate" in
    Industrial Chicago, 24. Hughes, *Chicago Real Estate Board*, 32.
14. Jeffrey M. Hornstein, *A Nation of Realtors: A Cultural History of the Twentieth-
    Century American Middle Class* (Durham, NC: Duke University Press, 2005), 21.
    Hughes, *Real Estate Board*, 1 and 33. Membership fees for the Chicago Real Estate
    Board (CREB) were a prohibitive $200 after 1892, in order to limit the organiza-
    tion to the most successful realtors. A few immigrant realtors joined this board in
    the early twentieth century, but the inner circle were white, Anglo-Saxon, and
    educated at prestigious eastern universities. More diverse, smaller-scale agents
    attempted to organize a rival Cook County Real Estate Board in 1908 and the
    Chicago Renting Agents' Association in 1919, yet the CREB remained dominant.
    Female realtors had to join less dominant associations, because CREB refused to
    admit women to membership until 1950. CREB also refused to admit African
    American realtors and, after 1917, promised to expel any realtor guilty of selling
    property to black people in a "white" neighborhood. See Hughes, "The Growth of
    an Institution," 39–47, 163–65; Satter, *Family Properties*, 40, 44, 70.
15. Cronon, *Nature's Metropolis*; Parton, "Chicago," 325.
16. *Land Owner* 3, no. 7 (1871): 331; Wade, *Chicago's Pride*, 267.
17. Population statistics from Spinney, *City of Big Shoulders*, 29, 70. See also Hoyt,
    One Hundred Years of Land Values in Chicago, 280. For annexation, see Pierce, *His-
    tory of Chicago*, 50. Fuller, *With the Procession*, 199; Lady Duffus Hardy, *Through
    Cities and Prairie Lands* (1881), in Pierce, *As Others See Chicago*, 227. For a descrip-
    tion of Potter Palmer's extensive real estate activities, see "Potter Palmer's Chi-
    cago," *Chicago History* 5, no. 10 (1959–60), 289–300.
18. Pierce, *As Others See Chicago*, 214, 370, 377–78.
19. Mary Borden, "Chicago Revisited," (1931), in Pierce, *As Others See Chicago*, 495.
    She added, "One is reminded of a new sort of topsy-turvy colony, a place the exact

opposite of Bombay for instance, or Singapore. If you can imagine that the white men were in Singapore first and that the influx of Malays flowed in on top of them, you'll get a little the feeling I had at moments in Chicago." While ignoring the Native American and French fur trappers who actually were in Chicago first, Borden's image neatly presages Matthew Jacobson's argument in *Barbarian Virtues* that imperialism abroad and immigration at home were flip sides of the same coin. For "probationary whiteness," see Jacobson, *Whiteness of a Different Color*. Modifying this view, Thomas Guglielmo in *White on Arrival* argues that many turn-of-the-century observers distinguished between "race" and "color," so that a Chicagoan might declare himself racially "Southern Italian" while colored "white" and still accessing most of the privileges of whiteness. Einhorn, *Property Rules*, 248–49.

20. For Detroit, see Zunz, *The Changing Face of Inequality*, 152–53. Margaret Marsh confirms this observation for Boston in *Suburban Lives*. Douglas Rae notes this in New Haven in *City*, 95–96, and Stephan Thernstrom confirms it for Newburyport in *Poverty and Progress*. Richard Harris offers the best explanation of this phenomenon in *Unplanned Suburbs*, although Chicago's Progressive-era housing codes meant that it had fewer owner-builders than Toronto. For further comparison between cities, see Roediger, *Working toward Whiteness*, 158–59.

21. *The Parks and Property Interests of the City of Chicago*, 31, 12–13. The last ten pages of this seventy-five-page booklet contain advertisements for Chicago realtors. Abbott, *The Tenements of Chicago*, 170; *Our Suburbs*, 3–4.

22. *Our Suburbs*, 4–5.

23. Chicago shared this shroud with many other coal-burning cities of the time. See Mosley, *The Chimney of the World*; David Stradling, *Smokestacks and Progressives: Environmentalists, Engineers, and Air Quality in America, 1881–1951* (Baltimore: Johns Hopkins University Press, 1999). Rudyard Kipling, *From Sea to Sea: Letters of Travel, Part II* (1899), excerpted in Pierce, *As Others See Chicago*, 251; Giuseppe Giacosa, "Chicago and Her Italian Colony" (1893), excerpted in Pierce, *As Others See Chicago*, 276–77; Waldo Frank, *Our America* (1919), in Pierce, *As Others See Chicago*, 479.

24. John L. Cochran, advertisement for Edgewater, October 8, 1897, reproduced in Chicago Title and Trust Company, *One Hundred Years of Chicago Land Values*, Chicago History Museum; John L. Cochran, advertisement for Edgewater, *Chicago Tribune*, October 5, 1897.

25. See "Cochran's Edgewater," *Edgewater Historical Society Newsletter* 14, no. 2 (2003); "Andersonville and Edgewater," *Edgewater Historical Society Newsletter* 14, no. 3 (2003).

26. Irish landscapers lived in a construction camp in Riverside for many years, while African American domestic servants settled in an enclave in Evanston. For Evanston, see Wiese, *Places of Their Own*, 61–65.

27. Parton, "Chicago," 339.

28. Chamberlin, *Chicago and Its Suburbs*, 167–68, 188.

29. Frank Gilbert, "The Rebuilding of the City," *Lakeside Monthly Magazine* 8, no. 46 (1872): 292.

30. W. R. Hunter, "Chicago's Housing Conditions," *Charities Review: A Journal of Practical Sociology* 10 (1900–1901): 292.

31. Abbott, *The Tenements of Chicago*, 164–65.

32. Borden, "Chicago Revisited," 490. See also George Washington Stevens, *The Land of the Dollar* (1897), in Pierce, *As Others See Chicago*, 399.

33. Dreiser, *Sister Carrie*, 16.
34. See, for instance, the many characters who invest in real estate as "a side-line" in Norris, *The Pit*, 110, 244; Fuller, *The Cliff Dwellers*.
35. Fuller, *With the Procession*, 18.
36. Fuller, *With the Procession*, 21–22.
37. Such pollution may seem to be a novelistic exaggeration, but it was actually not uncommon in coal-burning cities. See Mosley, *The Chimney of the World*; Fuller, *With the Procession*, 166, 243.
38. Fuller, *With the Procession*, 156, 164.
39. Fuller, *With the Procession*, 72.
40. Fuller, *With the Procession*, 206, 267.
41. For the tradition in twentieth-century literature of arrogantly disapproving of suburbia, see Jurca, *White Diaspora*. For its acceleration among intellectuals in the mid-twentieth century, see Becky Nicolaides, "How Hell Moved from the City to the Suburbs: Urban Scholars and Changing Perceptions of Authentic Community," in Kruse and Sugrue, *The New Suburban History*, 80–98.
42. James T. Farrell, *Young Lonigan* (1932), in *Studs Lonigan: A Trilogy*, 14, 17–18; James T. Farrell, *The Young Manhood of Studs Lonigan* (1934), in *Studs Lonigan: A Trilogy*, 269, 375, 412, 422, 433.
43. Farrell, *Young Manhood*, 457, 461–65; James T. Farrell, *Judgment Day* (1935), in *Studs Lonigan: A Trilogy*, 508–9.
44. Carla Cappetti calls this "topographic realism" in *Writing Chicago*, 120–22.
45. Farrell, *Young Lonigan*, 111; Farrell quoted in Cappetti, *Writing Chicago*, 110.

2. "DOMESTIC AND RESPECTABLE": PROPERTY-OWNER POLITICS AFTER THE GREAT CHICAGO FIRE

1. Chamberlin, *Chicago and Its Suburbs*, 87.
2. Chicago Relief and Aid Society, *First Special Report*, 8.
3. Lumber was scarce because whole forests in Michigan and Wisconsin had also burned during that dry and windy year; for descriptions of those fires, see Colbert and Chamberlin, *Chicago and the Great Conflagration*, 475–94. For the best statistics on reconstruction, see *New Chicago*, especially 8.
4. For example, Chicago Relief and Aid Society, *First Special Report*, 9.
5. The legal phrase *proximate cause* comes from Luzerne, *Through the Flames and Beyond*, 91. Statistics about Chicago's other fires of October 1871 are in Colbert and Chamberlin, *Chicago and the Great Conflagration*, 196. For Chicago's recurring fire problems, see Spinney, *City of Big Shoulders*, 80. For the fear of Chicago's growth, see Smith, *Urban Disorder*, 4–8.
6. Colbert and Chamberlin, *Chicago and the Great Conflagration*, 201–2. Colbert and Chamberlin published this book just nineteen days after the fire, according to Bessie Louise Pierce, *A History of Chicago*, 3: 170. Karen Sawislak traces the "anti-Irish, antiworking class, and antiwoman invective" against Mrs. O'Leary, while noting that she was innocent enough that Chicago's fire commission refused to blame her for the great fire (*Smoldering City*, 42–49). For other examples of this moral, see Spinney, *City of Big Shoulders*, 99; Cromie, *The Great Chicago Fire*, 24–30.
7. "A Startling Story," *Chicago Times*, October 23, 1871; Luzerne, *Through the Flames and Beyond*, 186–96.
8. Luzerne, *Through the Flames and Beyond*, 190, 196. See also Sawislak, *Smoldering City*, 46–49. Frederick Law Olmsted refuted these rumors in his article about the

Great Chicago Fire in the *Nation*, November 1871, but a similar story still forms the plot for James Montague's dime novel, *The Fire-Bugs of Chicago* (New York: Frank Tousey, 1897), referred to in Smith, *Urban Disorder*, 25, and cover reprinted at www.chicagohs.org/fire/fanning/pic0471.html.

9. Song lyrics quoted in Smith, *Urban Disorder*, 96.

10. For class segregation, see Blumin, *The Emergence of the Middle Class*, 232, 275. See also nineteenth-century urban chroniclers like George Foster or, later, Jacob Riis, exposing how the other half lives, just a few blocks from the wealthy, but rarely seen by them.

11. Roe, *Barriers Burned Away* http://www.chicagohs.org/fire/fanning/barriers. html. Roe's novel actually concerns a poor but aristocratic Christian hero converting the rich nonbelieving woman he loves, but there are other barriers broached too. When he breaks into her bedroom to rescue her, he is so covered in soot that she mistakes him for a black man, just before she is abandoned by her maids, assaulted by a thief, and jostled by a drunken crowd of mixed classes and ethnicities. In a similar vein, Frank Luzerne described the Washington Street Tunnel: "There rushed into the dark, cavern-like tunnel bankers and thieves, merchants and gamblers, artisans and loafers, clergymen and burglars, matrons and rag-pickers, maidens and prostitutes—representatives of virtue and vice, industry and improvidence, in every grade, and strangely commingling. . . . There were bruises and groans, blows and piercing shrieks, prayers, imprecations, pocket-picking, and indignities unmentionable" (*Through the Flames and Beyond*, 19).

12. In addition to Roe's novel, Horace White, Esq., wrote, "My wife and mother and all the rest were begrimed with dirt and smoke, like blackamoors—everybody was." Quoted in Colbert and Chamberlin, *Chicago and the Great Conflagration*, 251. Andrew Shuman, "The Burnt-Out People, and What Was Done for Them," *Lakeside Monthly Magazine* 7, no. 37 (1872): 43, 45; *New Chicago*, 4; Luzerne, *Through the Flames and Beyond*, 67–68, 101, 119; Colbert and Chamberlin, *Chicago and the Great Conflagration*, 357; letter from Anna E. Higginson, November 10, 1871, reprinted in Angle, *The Great Chicago Fire*, 56. Nineteenth-century men's clothing would have been quicker to put on, less flammable, and more practical for walking long distances, especially for women hoping to avoid sexual harassment in the mixed crowds. Luzerne prints a letter from "Gussie" explaining cross-dressing: "The house was on fire and there was no time to wait. And how terribly careless we girls are about our clothes, we could not lay our hands upon them at the moment. . . . There was an old pair of brother George's trousers, which I had been mending for him, hanging on the hook behind the door, and I pulled them on at once" (*Through the Flames and Beyond*, 150).

13. McDonald, *R. H. McDonald's Illustrated History and Map of Chicago*, 6.

14. "Narrative of Alexander Frear," printed in Colbert and Chamberlin, *Chicago and the Great Conflagration*, 245. For further examples, see Sawislak, *Smoldering City*, 37–42. As Sawislak observes, "Transgressions of the normal spatial and social divisions of the metropolis were subjects that obsessed fire narrators" (40).

15. Shuman, "The Burnt-Out People," 43, 45; Benjamin F. Taylor, "The Chicago of the Poet," *Lakeside Monthly* 10, no. 58 (1873): 256. "I could only think of Sodom or Pompeii, and truly I thought the day of judgement had come," wrote Mrs. Aurelia King, October 21, 1871, reprinted in Angle, *The Great Chicago Fire*, 39. "It is strange that so many thought the day of the final destruction of the world had

come," echoed Mrs. Adeline Rossiter Judd, November 23, 1871, reprinted in Angle, *The Great Chicago Fire*, 69. Nell Irvin Painter argues that rapid urbanization and industrialization left many Americans in the late nineteenth century fearing the end of the world: *Standing at Armageddon: The United States, 1877–1919* (New York: Norton, 1987).

16. Luzerne, *Through the Flames and Beyond*, 70.

17. "Real Estate: No Tendency to Decline in Values," *Chicago Times*, October 22, 1871.

18. Luzerne, *Through the Flames and Beyond*, 181. See also Mrs. Anne E. Higginson, letter to Mrs. Mark Skinner in Europe, November 10, 1871, reprinted in Angle, *The Great Chicago Fire*, 50.

19. For an analysis of the early formation of this domestic ideal, see Nancy Cott, *The Bonds of Womanhood: "Woman's Sphere" in New England, 1780–1835* (New Haven, CT: Yale University Press, 1977); Downing, *The Architecture of Country Houses*, 79. See also Beecher and Stowe, *The American Woman's Home*, 294.

20. Engraving in Luzerne, *Through the Flames and Beyond*, 229; photo in Smith et al., *The Great Chicago Fire and the Web of Memory*.

21. Sydney Howard Gay, "Chicago and the Relief Committee," *Lakeside Monthly Magazine* 7, no. 38 (1872): 173; *Chicago Workingman's Advocate*, October 28, 1871, 1; "Editor's Easy Chair," *Harper's New Monthly Magazine* 44, no. 259 (1871): 133; *New Chicago*, 13. Sawislak, *Smoldering City*, 21, notes that on the same day, another fire in Peshtigo, Wisconsin, left almost ten times as many people dead as Chicago's fire, but garnered far less attention. For the best description of Chicago's economic interrelations in the nineteenth century, see Cronon, *Nature's Metropolis*.

22. *New Chicago*, 7.

23. For the best accounts of the Relief and Aid Society, see Sawislak, *Smoldering City*, chapter 2; Einhorn, *Property Rules*, 233–35. Comparing privatized philanthropy with the privatized military presence in Chicago immediately after the fire, Sawislak points out, "The Great Fire gave a mayor with ordinarily 'weak' powers of office the somewhat ironic ability to exercise substantial authority by *ceding* his right to govern" (*Smoldering City*, 56).

24. *New Chicago*, 7. For another statement of this double goal, see Colbert and Chamberlin, *Chicago and the Great Conflagration*, 425: "No real suffering should go unrelieved, and, if possible, no bounty wasted on the undeserving." See also Sawislak, *Smoldering City*, 5, 60, 82–106, 264–80; Smith, *Urban Disorder*, 64–77. Lori Ginzberg notes that such scientific, professionalized, businesslike charity reflected a post–Civil War hardening of class lines and a masculinization of previously sentimentalized benevolence (*Women and the Work of Benevolence*).

25. See, for example, the characters Miss Pry and Miss Redtape in *Relief: A Humorous Drama* (1872), at www.chicagohs.org/fire/fanning/pic0535.html; Sawislak, *Smoldering City*, chapter 2.

26. Report of a Philadelphia committee, examining relief disbursements, reprinted in Colbert and Chamberlin, *Chicago and the Great Conflagration*, 527. See also "Houses for the Houseless," *Chicago Times*, October 18, 1871.

27. *Chicago Times*, October 22, 1871.

28. Downing, *The Architecture of Country Houses*, 72. As late as 1947 the housing developer William Levitt built a similar small cottage, with room for later expansion, just as the Relief Society had hoped occupants would eventually expand their cottages.

29. Joel Bigelow, letter to his family, October 10, 1871, reprinted at www.chicagohs.org/fire/witnesses/bigelow.html. Expecting real estate prices to rise after the

poor left the fire-ravaged town, Bigelow concludes his letter, "P.S. Don't you think it would be well to take advantage of the present to invest a little money out here?" On endowing charitable institutions, see *New Chicago*, 10–11; Sawislak, *Smoldering City*, 117–19, 268–73. As Einhorn notes in *Property Rules*, 233–34, Chicago's Relief Society "used the huge fund that it accumulated from outside contributions to Chicago's relief as a lever with which to mold and discipline the city's benevolent establishment."

30. *New Chicago*, 8, 13.
31. *Chicago Tribune*, October 12, 1871; General Plan of the Chicago Relief and Aid Society, October 15, 1871, reprinted in Chicago Relief and Aid Society, *First Special Report*, 6.
32. *Chicago Times*, October 18, 1871.
33. Chicago Relief and Aid Society, *First Special Report*, 8.
34. *Chicago Times*, October 19, 1871; Chicago Relief and Aid Society, *First Special Report*, 8–10; Chicago Relief and Aid Society, *Report of the Chicago Relief and Aid Society to the Common Council of the City of Chicago*, 85.
35. Chicago Relief and Aid Society, *First Special Report*, 8, 10. In Chicago Relief and Aid Society, *Report of the Chicago Relief and Aid Society to the Common Council of the City of Chicago*, 83–84, the Society published statistics on who had received food, fuel, and clothing from them, without distinguishing those who had received employment, transportation, or housing. Aid recipients were 36 percent German, 34 percent Irish, and 10 percent "American" at a time when Chicago's population was 33 percent German, 20 percent Irish, and 20 percent native-born American (see also Sawislak, *Smoldering City*, 11); so the Irish were overrepresented and native-born underrepresented among those who asked for relief. One-quarter of families receiving aid were headed by widows, and one-third by elderly or frail people, but of those with occupations, 45 percent were unskilled workers titled only "laborers" or "ragpickers"; 47 percent were skilled manual workers such as a sign painter, sail maker, seamstress, shoemaker, stevedore, sailor, stove maker, and scissors grinder; and 8 percent held skilled positions such as architect, bookkeeper, clerk, engineer, grain inspector, insurance agent, inventor, lawyer, musician, minister, manufacturer, publisher, storekeeper, vessel captain, and veterinary surgeon. The Society helped more blue-collar than white-collar workers, but they did help every class of people as they worked to rebuild Chicago. For rates of property ownership, see Einhorn, *Property Rules*, 249. For the two-tiered class system, see Sawislak, *Smoldering City*, 14. Einhorn reports that the one-fifth of adult males who did own property were slightly older than the average Chicagoan, but otherwise they were a remarkably diverse group, reflecting all classes and ethnicities in proportions close to those of the city as a whole.
36. Chicago Relief and Aid Society, *First Special Report*, 8. Van Sweringen brothers' suburban advertisement (1904), quoted in Stilgoe, *Borderland*, 241. See also Albert Wolfe, *The Lodging House Problem in Boston* (Boston: Houghton Mifflin; Harvard Economic Studies, 1906); Veiller, *The Tenement House Problem*; Albert Beveridge, *The Young Man and the World* -New York: D. Appleton & Co., 1907), 164–66; Deutsch, *Women and the City*, 69, 76; Lees, *Cities Perceived*. For the historical definition of promiscuity, see *Oxford English Dictionary*; Meyerowitz, *Women Adrift*; Odem, *Delinquent Daughters*, 59; Gordon, *Heroes of Their Own Lives*, especially 234.
37. Veiller, *Housing Reform*, 33. Lodger statistics in Hayden, *Redesigning the American Dream*, 20.

38. Harkness, "Real Estate Speculation and Juvenile Delinquency," 14, 28, 18, 23.
39. *New York Times*, February 23, 1894, quoted in Fogelson, *Downtown*, 324.
40. Edith Wharton, *The Age of Innocence* (1920), quoted in Cromley, *Alone Together*, 39.
41. Downing, *The Architecture of Country Houses*, 97.
42. Beecher and Stowe, *The American Woman's Home*, 49. Abbott, *The Tenements of Chicago*, especially 224–36, 342–51. Businessman opposed to tall skyscrapers quoted in *Chicago Tribune*, October 15, 1891, then quoted in Fogelson, *Downtown*, 125; see also Fogelson, *Downtown*, 104, 133, 320–30.
43. Veiller, *Housing Reform*, 5; Harkness, "Real Estate Speculation and Juvenile Delinquency," 47; Embree, "The Housing of the Poor in Chicago," 366.
44. Chicago Relief and Aid Society, *Report of the Chicago Relief and Aid Society to the Common Council of the City of Chicago*, 86.
45. Jacob Riis, *How the Other Half Lives* (1890; New York: Dover, 1971), 1, 216; Henry C. Wright, *Marriage and Parentage* (1855), quoted in Ryan, *The Empire of the Mother*, 97; Edith Elmer Wood, "Report of the Committee on Housing," *Journal of the Association of Collegiate Alumnae* (April 1919): 3–4; White, *Improved Dwellings for the Laboring Classes*, 9. See also Worthington, *The Dwellings of the Poor*, x; Veiller, *Housing Reform*, 30. For international conversations among reformers, see Rodgers, *Atlantic Crossings*. For excellent accounts of the public importance of private domesticity, see Ryan, *Empire of the Mother*; Blackmar, *Manhattan for Rent*, 87.
46. Wood, "Report of the Committee on Housing," 1. See also Harkness, "Real Estate Speculation and Juvenile Delinquency," 13.
47. "A writer," quoted in Embree, "Housing of the Poor in Chicago," 360. See also Wright, *Moralism and the Model Home*, especially 234.
48. Chicago Relief and Aid Society, *First Special Report*, 8.
49. *Chicago Times*, October 18, 1871.
50. Charles Cleaver, "One of the Oldest Residents of Chicago," in *History of Chicago from 1833 to 1892*, 49, 62. For statistical evidence of boarders, see Groth, *Living Downtown*, 56.
51. On the industrial-era economics of the cult of domesticity, see Boydston, *Home and Work*.
52. Clark, *Housing and Homes*, 1. Calder quotes a bumper sticker: "I owe, I owe, it's off to work I go" (*Financing the American Dream*, 299, 303).
53. Butterworth, *Zig-Zag Journeys in the White City*, 130–31; Abbott, *Tenements of Chicago*, 314, 335; Groth, *Living Downtown*, chapter 7. Groth notes that hotels also allow gay and single people to find shelter, and allow gamblers, sailors, politicians, and other migratory workers to preserve their mobility. "In the long run, the ecologically and culturally aberrant idea about housing may prove to be the single-family house on an open lot, not the more social way of living downtown in a hotel" (*Living Downtown*, 17).
54. Abbott, *Tenements of Chicago*, 337. The same passage appears verbatim in Wilson, "Chicago Families in Furnished Rooms," 108.
55. Wilson, "Chicago Families in Furnished Rooms," 103, 115, 13–14.
56. Engels, *The Housing Question*, 45, 18, 29, 41–42. On 29–30, Engels approvingly quotes *La Emancipacion* (Madrid, March 16, 1872): "The cleverest leaders of the ruling class have always directed their efforts towards increasing the number of small property owners in order to build an army for themselves against the proletariat. . . . [They] sought to stifle all revolutionary spirit in their workers by selling them small dwellings to be paid for in annual installments, and at the same time to chain the workers by this property to the factory." A century later,

from the other end of the political spectrum, housing developer William Levitt famously declared, "No man who owns his own house and lot can be a communist. He has too much to do." William Levitt (1948), quoted in Hayden, *Redesigning the American Dream*, 8. See also Lawrence Veiller (1920), quoted in Hayden, *Redesigning the American Dream*, 17; Herbert Hoover (1931), quoted in Groth, *Living Downtown*, 254. See Wright, *Moralism and the Model Home*, 125.

57. Citizens' Association of Chicago, *Report*, 18.
58. "Report of the Fifth Annual Banquet of the Chicago Real Estate Board," *Chicago Real Estate and Building Journal* 30, no. 6 (1888): 62.
59. Chicago *Tribune*, November 3, 1871, quoted in Sawislak, *Smoldering City*, 95.
60. Police Commissioner Thomas Brown (1871), quoted in Sawislak, *Smoldering City*, 64.
61. Gay, "Chicago and the Relief Committee," 171, 172.
62. Einhorn, *Property Rules*, 250, 264–65. While one-quarter of Chicagoans owned property, this proportion increased to nearly one-half on the far North Side.
63. See "They Thirst for Gore," *Chicago Times*, January 15, 1872. According to the Census of 1880, 81 percent of North Side residents were foreign-born. The correct German spelling would be *Nord Seit*, but the English-language press seemed more concerned with mocking German pronunciation than achieving correct spelling. For insurance issues for the working-class, see Sawislak, *Smoldering City*, 77–79.
64. J. W. Foster, "A Glance at Chicago's History," *Lakeside Monthly* 7, no. 37 (1872): 10.
65. *New Chicago*, 24. Sawislak makes this point about insurance in *Smoldering City*, as does "The North Side Incendiaries," *Chicago Tribune*, January 16, 1872.
66. Resolutions from a January 13 mass meeting at Alderman Carney's house, reprinted under the headline "North-Side Stupidity," *Chicago Times*, January 14, 18727. Urban historian Christine Rosen has calculated that brick houses cost twice as much as wooden ones (*The Limits of Power*, 99).
67. *Chicago Times*, January 14, 1872; *Chicago Tribune*, January 15, 1872.
68. Resolutions of a January 13 meeting at Alderman Carney's house, reprinted under the headline, "North-Side Stupidity."
69. See Einhorn, *Property Rules*, 128–33.
70. "Great Demonstration," *Illinois Staats-Zeitung*, January 16, 1872, translated for the author by Anna Souchuk.
71. "Communism," *Chicago Tribune*, January 16, 1872; "Hesing's Mob," *Chicago Times*, January 16, 1872.
72. "Hesing's Mob." See also "Great Demonstration."
73. "Communism." The *Chicago Times* reported that only six or seven policemen were there to monitor this crowd; the *Chicago Tribune* reported eight to ten police were present.
74. "Hesing's Mob."
75. "Communism." The *Chicago Times* reported a similar statement: "It is impossible to do any business to-night, I declare the council adjourned." Fear about the floors breaking is one of the few details where the German-language account concurs with the English. "Hesing's Mob."
76. "The Incidents of Monday Evening," *Illinois Staats-Zeitung*, January 17, 1872, translated by Souchuk; "The Fire Ordinance and Mr. U. C. Hesing," *Illinois Staats-Zeitung*, January 18, 1872, translated by Souchuk; "Hesing's Mob."
77. It was not strictly binary: the rival newspapers did make some attempts to understand each other. Both English-language newspapers printed interviews with Anton Hesing of the *Staats-Zeitung*, even as they opined that he should be tried

by a grand jury for the crime of leading a mob. See "Monday Night's Riot," *Chicago Tribune*, January 17, 1872; "The Fire-Bugs," *Chicago Times*, January 17, 1872. The *Tribune* even printed a rough translation of the *Staats-Zeitung*'s account of the Monday night march. The next Saturday, when a few North Siders held a public meeting in favor of fire limits, the *Times* reported it under the headline "They Are Not All Idiots" (January 21, 1872).

78. "Hesing's Mob."

79. "They Thirst for Gore."

80. "The Fire-Bugs"; *Chicago Tribune*, January 17, 1872; *Chicago Tribune*, January 17, 1872; *Chicago Republican*, November 13, 1871, quoted in Sawislak, *Smoldering City*, 125. "The North Side Incendiaries," *Chicago Tribune*, January 15, 1872.

81. "Huts and Palaces," *Illinois Staats-Zeitung*, January 15, 1872, translated by Souchuk; "The Fire Boundaries," *Illinois Staats-Zeitung*, January 10, 1872, translated by Souchuk.

82. "Huts and Palaces"; "The Fire Boundaries."

83. "The Incidents of Monday Evening." The penultimate verb is indecipherable, but *herd* would be consistent with the language of the time.

84. "Hesing's Mob"; "Communism." English-language newspapers also compared the North Side protestors to the Southerners who had recently rebelled in the Civil War, and even to the "Ku Kluxers," who resisted legal rules.

85. "The Common Council," *Chicago Tribune*, January 18, 1872. "Peace Restored," *Chicago Times*, January 18, 1872, reported 125 policemen. The *Times* also reported the council meetings under the headlines "An Almost Interminable Discussion of the Proposed Ordinance," "A Body Which Is Fond of Amending Everything but Its Own Manners," and "The Fire Limits," January 20, 1872. "The Fire Boundaries."

86. "The Fire . . . A Mass of Shanties Are Kindling-Wood for Burning a Few Palaces," *Chicago Tribune*, July 15, 1874.

87. "Yesterday's Fire: A Cheap Penalty for Amazing Folly," *Chicago Tribune*, July 15, 1874.

88. "Grand Mass-Meeting at McKormick's Hall Yesterday," *Chicago Tribune*, July 19, 1874. The *Tribune* advised "every man who has a dollar at stake" to attend: "The Meeting Tonight," July 18, 1874. "The Fire," *Chicago Tribune*, July 21, 1874. Editorials, *Chicago Tribune*, July 21, 1874. The issue did not end in 1874. When Chicago annexed suburbs in 1889, 1890, 1895, 1897, and 1914, each annexation included a debate about whether to extend the city's fire limits to the newly expanded city limits. As we shall see in the next chapter, the Town of Lake, an industrial suburb on Chicago's South Side, stayed outside the fire limits for decades after being annexed within the city limits.

89. William D. Kerfoot advertisement, *Real Estate and Building Journal* 8, no. 13 (1872): 103; S. E. Gross advertisement (ca. 1880), in Broadsides—Real Estate, Chicago History Museum. Einhorn discusses other fire limits in *Property Rules*, 129. In the twentieth century George Sanchez noted that Mexican Americans moved to unincorporated Belvedere, outside Los Angeles, to avoid city regulations about lot size, sewage disposal, and taxes for city services. George Sanchez, *Becoming Mexican American: Ethnicity, Culture and Identity in Chicano Los Angeles, 1900–1945* (New York: Oxford University Press, 1993), 201. Similarly Adam Rome observes that twentieth-century tract-house developers often took advantage of "power vacuums," building in areas with fewer environmental and urban planning regulations, instead of building less sprawling infill projects (*The Bulldozer in the Countryside*, 266).

90. Chamberlin, *Chicago and Its Suburbs*, 204.
91. *Real Estate and Building Journal* 8, no. 11 (1872): 84. *Real Estate and Building Journal* 8, no. 24 (1872): 185.
92. *Lakeside Monthly*, October 1872, 57; "Protection for the Centre of the City," *Chicago Tribune*, July 17, 1874.
93. "They Thirst for Gore"; "The Fire-Bugs."
94. Frank Gilbert, "The Rebuilding of the City," *Lakeside Monthly Magazine* 8, no. 46 (1872): 281; W. A. Croffatt, "Reconstruction," *Lakeside Monthly Magazine* 7, no. 37 (1872): 57. See also Sawislak, *Smoldering City*, 203–6.
95. Mayor Joseph Medill speech, quoted in Sawislak, *Smoldering City*, 197. For union activity in the year after the fire, see Sawislak, *Smoldering City*, 163–216.
96. *Industrial Chicago*, 3: 593. Similarly on the ten-year anniversary of the fire, the *New York Times* declared, "No monument has ever been erected to commemorate the event, and really Chicago needs none but herself." "Chicago's Recovery," *New York Times*, October 12, 1881. *Land Owner*, October 1872, quoted in Sawislak, *Smoldering City*, 163; Maitland, *Old and New Chicago*, 21; "Editor's Historical Record," *Harper's New Monthly Magazine* 46, no. 271 (1872): 149. See also Andrew Shulman, "One Year After," *Lakeside Monthly Magazine* 8, no. 46 (1872): 247.
97. John Greenleaf Whittier, "Chicago," quoted in Maitland, *Old and New Chicago*, 15.
98. Hoyt, *One Hundred Years of Land Values in Chicago*, 102–3.
99. *New Chicago*, 21, which also contains a thorough description of post-fire buildings. Colbert and Chamberlin, *Chicago and the Great Conflagration*, 206. They added that the fire "can not be construed otherwise than as a timely reminder of the power of God, working through the elements, as a hint to fear Him, love our fellow-men, subdue our pride, and make our walls of brick" (370).
100. *New Chicago*, 31–32.
101. Gilbert, "The Rebuilding of the City," 292; Shulman, "One Year After," 243, 245. Urban renewal usually refers to post-1945 uses of eminent domain to remove slum housing from cities, but similar practices have a longer history. In the 1910s, for example, 16,500 New Yorkers were displaced for Penn Station. In Chicago in the 1890s, thousands were evicted so that small parks could replace their tenements. "It was strange to find people so attached to homes that were so lacking in all the attributes of comfort and decency," a reformer declared, surprised that anyone wanted to live in homes she considered indecent. Quoted in Fogelson, *Downtown*, 331.
102. Boorstin, "The Balloon-Frame House," 148–52; "The Ruined City," Chicago dispatch to *New York Times*, October 11, 1871; Foster, "A Glance at Chicago's History," 8. Because many of the poor lacked both sewers and cellars, and because some owned their homes but not the land their homes stood on, house-moving was quite frequent in 1870s Chicago.
103. Wade, *Chicago's Pride*, 156. Wade reports that the O'Leary family moved in 1879 "to escape prying reporters and to give their youngest child, James Patrick O'Leary, a normal childhood. The father, an unskilled laborer, soon became a fixture in the Irish-owned saloons at the Stockyards, but he refused to talk about the Chicago fire." Glen Holt and Dominic Pacyga reprint a photograph of the O'Leary Saloon in this neighborhood (*Chicago*, 133).
104. Wilkie, *Ordinances of the Building and Health Departments of the City of Chicago*, Article IX, section 1071, p. 44. As noted in chapter 1, the Town of Lake was exempt from most of these ordinances, even after its annexation. Pierce, *A History of Chicago*, 3: 52–53, 92–93, 73–74, 98.

105. *Lakeside Monthly*, January 1872, quoted in Rosen, *Limits of Power*, 145. See also Chamberlin, *Chicago and Its Suburbs*, 91. For Chicago's commercial reorganization, see Rosen, *Limits of Power*, 112–76. For "rational" or "unbalanced" planning, see Rosen, *Limits of Power*, 159; Jacobs, *The Life and Death of Great American Cities*, 215.

106. Olmsted, quoted in Fogelson, *Downtown*, 21. See also Johnson, "The Natural History of the Central Business District," 583; *New Chicago*, 24; "The Effect of the Fire upon Real Estate," *Lakeside Monthly Magazine* 8, no. 46 (1872): 262.

3. LAKE AND JUNGLE: THE ASSEMBLY-LINE FACTORY AS A FORCE FOR SUBURBANIZATION

1. Samuel Eberly Gross (Firm), *Tenth Annual Illustrated Catalogue*, 62–63.

2. Gross's ad has been reprinted in Wright, *Moralism and the Model Home*, 43; Hayden, *Redesigning the American Dream*, 23; Clark, *The American Family Home*, 98; Hayden, *Building Suburbia*, 7. Gross is also discussed in Jackson, *Crabgrass Frontier*, 135; Clark, "Own Your Own Home," 135–53; Margaret Garb, "Selling Home Ownership: Samuel Eberly Gross and the Easy Payment Plan" in *Building the American Dream*. While Emily Clark and Garb examine how Gross commodified middle-class domesticity and sold it to workers, Ann Durkin Keating considers Gross's other elite subdivisions in *Building Chicago*, 27–28, 70–71.

3. Samuel Eberly Gross (Firm), *Tenth Annual Illustrated Catalogue*, 60. *Dinner* was a traditional term for the midday meal that we now call lunch. Kenneth Jackson has memorably defined suburbs as spaces with a long enough journey to work to make it difficult for workers to go home for lunch, but Lake is not the only suburb where residents could actually eat lunch at home. Half of the original adult male residents of Long Island's Levittown worked in defense industry factories nearby, not in the central city, yet few would argue that Levittown was not a suburb (Jackson, *Crabgrass Frontier*, 4). Baxandall and Ewen, *Picture Windows*, 143. In Herbert Gans's ethnography of Levittown (now Willingboro), New Jersey, 8 percent of residents reported that their primary reason for moving was to be closer to work (*The Levittowners*, 35).

4. Samuel Eberly Gross (Firm), *Tenth Annual Illustrated Catalogue*, 60–64.

5. Mary E. McDowell, "City Waste" (1927), in *McDowell Symposium*, 1, 2. See also Jablonsky, *Pride in the Jungle*, 14–24. Despite his usual advertising acumen, developer Samuel Eberly Gross had a penchant for naming streets and towns after himself, names that were soon changed by the citizens of Grossville, Grossdale, and Gross Avenue. In 1937 Gross Avenue was renamed McDowell, after University of Chicago Settlement House head Mary McDowell. For "Whisky Point," see Holt and Pacyga, *Chicago*, 121–26, 132. For hair fields, see Herbert Phillips, "Mary McDowell as We Knew Her in the Yards," in *McDowell Symposium*, 120–21. For photographs and an extended account of Bubbly Creek, see Washington, *Packing Them In*, 81–96, 104–22.

6. Wade, *Chicago's Pride*, 17, 26, 54, 74.

7. Samuel Eberly Gross (Firm), *Tenth Annual Illustrated Catalogue*, 61; Wade, *Chicago's Pride*, 29, 99; Einhorn, *Property Rules*, 183, 207–14.

8. *Chicago Tribune*, June 29, 1864, quoted in Wade, *Chicago's Pride*, 48. See also Jablonsky, *Pride in the Jungle*, chapter 1; Cronon, *Nature's Metropolis*, chapter 5; Pierce, *A History of Chicago*, 2: 93–95. See also *Industrial Chicago*, 3: 596.

9. Thompson, *Chicago*, 59–60. In 1866, before developments in refrigeration technology, most meatpacking work ceased during the summer, so it is possible that Lake was seen as industrial in the winter but suburban in the summer. It is likely, though, that pollution lingered in the swampy ground and that this was not a space one ordinarily pictures as a suburban retreat.

10. Jablonsky, *Pride in the Jungle*, 10–11; Wade, *Chicago's Pride*, 135. The smell was so strong that Chicago actually passed laws allowing its health department to regulate factories within one mile of the city's limits.

11. Andreas, *History of Cook County*, 654–62.

12. *The Town of Lake Directory*, 28–29, lists major employers, number of employees, and their paydays. House movers were necessary at a time when lots and houses were owned separately, and a lack of plumbing or basements made moving possible.

13. *(Stockyards) Sun*, May 18, 1889, quoted in Wade, *Chicago's Pride*, 274. See also 155, 269, 362, 375.

14. Hoyt, *One Hundred Years*, 143–44.

15. C. B. Berry, *The Other Side, How It Struck Us* (1880), quoted in Wade, *Chicago's Pride*, 119. See also 362, 149, 109.

16. Rudyard Kipling, *From Sea to Sea: Letters of Travel* (1899), reprinted in Pierce, *As Others See Chicago*, 258; Sir John Long, letter of September 1876, reprinted in Pierce, *As Others See Chicago*, 223–24; Sinclair, *Jungle*, 44, 49; *Picturesque Chicago*, 14; Jablonsky, *Pride in the Jungle*, 11.

17. For "disassembly line," see Cronon, *Nature's Metropolis*, 211. For property prices, see Hoyt, *One Hundred Years*, 88–98. Although earlier suburban historians largely ignored industrial suburbs, the new suburban historians have called attention to industrial suburbs. For Chicago, see Harris, "Chicago's Other Suburbs," 401; Ann Durkin Keating, *Chicagoland: City and Suburbs in the Railroad Age* (Chicago: University of Chicago Press, 2005), especially chapter 4; Robert Lewis, *Chicago Made: Factory Networks in the Industrial Metropolis* (Chicago: University of Chicago Press, 2008). For factories' contributions to Los Angeles's sprawl, see Hise, *Magnetic Los Angeles*. For industrial suburbs of Detroit, see Sugrue, *The Origins of the Urban Crisis*, chapter 5.

18. Frank Gilbert, "The Rebuilding of the City," *Lakeside Monthly* 8, no. 46 (1872): 292. Saskia Sassen calls such cities "highly concentrated command points" in *The Global City*, 3.

19. For other causes of early working-class suburbanization, see Andrew Wiese, "Places of Our Own: Suburban Black Towns before 1960," *Journal of Urban History* 19, no. 3 (1993); Andrew Wiese, "The Other Suburbanites: African American Suburbanization in the North before 1950," *Journal of American History* 85, no. 4 (1999): 1495–524. Other studies of early black suburbs have found that some black men's work as railroad porters also helped them live in suburban spots. See Bruce Haynes, *Runyon Heights: The Politics of Race and Space in a Black Middle-Class Suburb* (New Haven, CT: Yale University Press, forthcoming). Census figures in Wade, *Chicago's Pride*, 61, 267. Joseph Greenhut, *Survey* (1893), cited in Wade, *Chicago's Pride*, 362.

20. Mary E. McDowell, "The Foreign Born" (1927), in Hill, *Mary McDowell*, 14.

21. For "Taunleikis," see "Statistical Survey of Town of Lake Chicago Lithuanian Colony," *Lietuva*, September 10, 1909, translated by the Chicago Public Library Omnibus Project, *Chicago Foreign Language Press Survey*, microfiche roll 43, category IIIA. Dreyer's 1870s subdivision seems to have pioneered the "New City" name,

which was also used by the local police station. See Jablonsky, *Pride in the Jungle*, 26, 133. The area's newspaper continued to be known as the *Journal of the Town of Lake* until 1937, when the community, with Saul Alinsky's Neighborhood Council, began to take public pride in its identity as Back of the Yards.

22. Homeownership rates in Abbott and Breckenridge, "Housing Conditions in Chicago, part III," 461, 433. According to the U.S. census, in 1890, 28.7 percent of Chicago homes were owned; in 1900, 25.1 percent; in 1910, 26.2 percent; and in 1920, 27.0 percent. See Abbott, *The Tenements of Chicago*, 54, 366. Nineteenth-century homeownership rates were similarly about one-quarter of Chicago families, according to Einhorn, *Property Rules*, 264.

23. Montgomery, *The American Girl in the Stockyards District*, 19–20.

24. Finlay, "A Survey of Social Problems and Social Services in the Town of Cicero, Illinois," 10; "A Visit to the States," *London Times*, October 21 and 24, 1887, reprinted in Pierce, *As Others See Chicago*, 231; J. H. Van Vlissingen, "Development of Manufacturing Suburbs," *Chicago Tribune*, January 19, 1902. Graham Romeyn Taylor also observed this in his classic, *Satellite Cities*, 1. John Appleton emphasized factories' need for large blocks of inexpensive land, which he asserts were not available in central Chicago from 1880 onward ("The Iron and Steel Industry of the Calumet District," 92–94). As early as 1874 Everett Chamberlin explained, "The policy of locating manufactories in the suburbs for cheapness of fabrication, has been pursued here as in other cities, owing to their exemption from municipal taxation, smaller cost of ground, cheapness of living, room for ample unobstructed facilities" (*Chicago and Its Suburbs*, 364). Recently Jefferson Cowie has observed that industrial suburbanization preceded and foreshadowed corporate globalization as capital migrated in search of pliable laborers and accommodating governments (*Capital Moves*, 2).

25. Robert Lewis, "Industry and the Suburbs," in *Manufacturing Suburbs*, 7.

26. Chamberlin, *Chicago and Its Suburbs*, 415–16. Kenneth Jackson writes that Riverside "set the sociological and architectural pattern for hundreds of communities that developed in the twentieth century" (*Crabgrass Frontier*, 85). Robert Fishman adds, "If there is a single plan that expresses the idea of the bourgeois utopia, it is Olmsted's Riverside" (*Bourgeois Utopia*, 129).

27. Chamberlin, *Chicago and Its Suburbs*, 416.

28. Runnion, *Out of Town*, 16–17.

29. *Land Owner: Journal of Real Estate Building and Improvement* 4, no. 8 (1872): 125.

30. *Land Owner* 5, no. 9 (1873): 155.

31. Samuel Eberly Gross (Firm), *Chicago—The Mid-Continent Metropolis*, 1.

32. Samuel Eberly Gross (Firm), *Tenth Annual Illustrated Catalogue*, 36.

33. Samuel Eberly Gross (Firm), *Chicago—The Mid-Continent Metropolis*, 4.

34. *Land Owner: Journal of Real Estate Building and Improvement* 4, no. 8 (1872): 125.

35. Samuel Eberly Gross (Firm), *Tenth Annual Illustrated Catalogue*, 2.

36. Andreas, *History of Chicago*, 3: 451; *Real Estate and Building Journal* 26, no. 32 (1884): 377; *Real Estate and Building Journal* 26, no. 33 (1884): 387.

37. For tax problems, see "Reviewers Find More Property," *Chicago Tribune*, August 6, 1901; "Gross Submits a Tax Problem," *Chicago Tribune*, July 23, 1902; "Seek S. E. Gross' Assets: Creditors File Petition," *Chicago Tribune*, February 27, 1904; "S. E. Gross Hiding; Hunted Two Years," *Chicago Tribune*, May 26, 1907. In the United States, Gross won his suit against the producers of the play version of *Cyrano*, receiving a token $1, while losing his suit against Rostand in France. See "Says 'Cyrano' Is Plagiarism," *Chicago Tribune*, January 6, 1899; "Mr. Gross as a Literary

Source," *Chicago Tribune*, February 9, 1910; "Recall 'Piracy' of Cyrano from Chicago Author," *Chicago Tribune*, January 22, 1951. For bankruptcy, see "S. E. Gross'
Fortune Is Gone," *Chicago Tribune*, April 3, 1908; "Telling Why Gross Failed," *Chicago Tribune*, April 4, 1908; "Gross Lots under Hammer," *Chicago Tribune*, May 12,
1909; Obituary, *Chicago Tribune*, October 25, 1913; *The Biographical Dictionary*,
78–82. For a photograph of Gross's Lake Shore Drive residence, see Moses and
Kirkland, *The History of Chicago*, 2: 586.

38. Dreiser, *Jennie Gerhardt*, 333. For car shop booms, see Chamberlin, *Chicago and
Its Suburbs*, 217; Hoyt, *One Hundred Years*, 176; W. N. Mitchell and M. J. Jucius,
"Industrial Districts of the Chicago Region and the Influence on Plant Location,"
Journal of Business of the University of Chicago 6, no. 2 (1933): 139–56. On Toll-
eston boom, see Monchow, *Seventy Years of Real Estate Subdividing*, 21–23, 90;
Hoyt, *One Hundred Years*, 176; Taylor, *Satellite Cities*, chapter 6, 254. This boom
was followed by a bust when the stockyards announced they would not move after all. Perhaps that bust influenced Dreiser's misunderstanding of the real estate
risks of the neighborhood near stockyards. See *Illustrations of Greater Chicago*,
76–77.

39. *Land Owner* 5, no. 8 (1873): 130.

40. Chamberlin, *Chicago and Its Suburbs*, advertisement after 422.

41. On problems facing poorer suburbs, see Orfield, *Metropolitics*, 15. For recent photographs of Harvey, Ford Heights, and Robbins, Illinois, see Vergara, *American
Ruins*, 92–93, 151, 179, 189.

42. Antanas Kaztauskis, "The Life Story of a Lithuanian," as told to Ernest Poole, reprinted in Holt, *The Life Stories of Undistinguished Americans*, 14–15.

43. Sinclair, *The Jungle*, 56, 59. "It seemed probably, in view of the circumstances,
that the old lady regarded it rather as feeding the chickens than as cleaning the
rooms" (34–35).

44. Sinclair, *Jungle*, 58–60. This pattern resembles other working-class suburbs. Barbara Kelly notes that it was William Levitt's unfinished, expandable attics that
allowed Levittowners to live affordably while doing enough of their own home
improvement to enter the middle class via their own sweat equity (*Expanding the
American Dream*, 166). Becky Nicolaides interviewed suburban residents of Los
Angeles who chose to forgo services in order to save money on taxes (*My Blue
Heaven*, 137).

45. Sinclair, *Jungle*, 81, 101, 86, 122.

46. Sinclair, *Jungle*, 213–14. For other associations between housing and manliness,
see 54, 61.

47. For charges of exaggeration, see "Literature: The Jungle," *Chicago Tribune*, February 26, 1906; "Find 'The Jungle' 95 Percent Lies," *Chicago Tribune*, May 5,
1906. For impact on meatpacking, see Upton Sinclair, "The Boycott on the Jungle," letter to the editor, *New York Times*, May 18, 1906; "The Jungle Hunt to
Produce Game: Roosevelt Determined to Get Hide Either of Packers or of Author
of Charges against Them," *Chicago Tribune*, April 11, 1906; "Beef Trust Beaten,"
New York Times, May 27, 1906; Ronald Gottesman, introduction to Sinclair, *The
Jungle*, xxiv.

48. "Jurgis Rudkus and 'The Jungle,'" *New York Times Book Review*, March 3, 1906.

49. Wade, *Chicago's Pride*, 270, 376.

50. Miller, "Rents and Housing Conditions in the Stockyards District of Chicago," 8,
29, 14. Relying on oral histories, Thomas Jablonsky reports that decaying animal
carcasses in the creek caused the bubbles: "Local legend claims that the diameter

of these bubbles had to be measured in feet. . . . In calmer moments residents recall bubbles five to eight inches across. . . . Even today, where the south fork ends north of Thirty-ninth Street alongside a city pumping station, an endless multitude of greasy bubbles defines the surface of the waterway. Its consistency is like crankcase oil" (*Pride in the Jungle*, 19).

51. Sanborn Map Company, *Chicago: Volume 9* (New York: Sanborn-Perris Map Co., 1894), maps 48 and 49; Sanborn Map Company, *Chicago: Volume 13* (New York: Sanborn Map Co., 1925), maps 48 and 49; Sanborn Map Company, *Chicago Packing Houses: Union Stock Yards* (New York: Sanborn-Perris Map Co., 1901), n.p.

52. H. G. Wells, *The Future in America* (1906), reprinted in Quaife, *The Development of Chicago*, 259–60.

53. For "democratization of the American dream," see Harris, "Chicago's Other Suburbs," 397, though Harris does point out that working-class suburbanizers sacrificed municipal services and sometimes their health. Bigott, *From Cottage to Bungalow* emphasizes gentility while ignoring mortgage foreclosures, racial strife, and other less positive aspects of working-class suburbia.

54. Glickman, *A Living Wage*. For more on workers' loss of control during these years, see Montgomery, *The Fall of the House of Labor*.

55. See Berger, *Working Class Suburb*. For an ethnographic discussion of the fluidity of class status in suburbia, see Judith Stacey, *Brave New Families* (Berkeley: University of California Press, 1998), 30–35.

4. "BETTER THAN A BANK FOR A POOR MAN": WORKERS' STRATEGIES FOR HOME FINANCING

1. Samuel Eberly Gross (Firm), *Tenth Annual Illustrated Catalogue*, 73. The same letter, with the word *gentlemen* substituting for *sir*, appeared five years earlier in Samuel E. Gross (Firm), *The Gross Cottages, Houses, and Lots*, 29. For other exhortations to upward mobility through real estate investments, see Chamberlin, *Chicago and Its Suburbs*; Putney, *Real Estate Values and Historical Notes of Chicago*; *Chicago Times*, March 7, 1874, quoted in Pierce, *A History of Chicago* 3: 207; "Old Settler" broadside (1874), in Broadsides—Real Estate, Chicago Historical Museum. Potter Palmer made his first fortune by marketing dry goods, then vastly increased this fortune by creating the State Street commercial district as well as the Lake Shore Drive residential district. See "Potter Palmer's Chicago," *Chicago History* 5, no. 10 (1959–60): 289–300. When Altgeld arrived in Chicago in 1875, he was too poor to rent a bedroom, so he slept on his office floor, saved his money, and invested it in suburban subdivisions that made his fortune. See Ginger, *Altgeld's America*, 64

2. *Lots in Winslow, Jacobson and Tallman's Subdivision for Sale Cheap*, 3. Winslow was the president of the Scandinavian National Bank, Jacobson the vice president, and Tallman a cashier at Trader's National Bank. *Land Owner* 7, no. 1 (1875): 10. For the prevalence of owner-building in working-class suburbs elsewhere, see Harris, *Unplanned Suburbs*; Nicolaides, *My Blue Heaven*.

3. "Real Estate," *Chicago Tribune*, April 21, 1889; Work, "Negro Real Estate Holders of Chicago," 18, 24; Hoyt, *One Hundred Years of Land Values*, 167, 101; *Real Estate and Building Journal* 30, no. 27 (1888): 324; *Chicago Tribune*, June 6, 1926, quoted in Hughes, "The Growth of an Institution," 30; *Alarm*, October 11, 1884, 1, 4. Dynamite instructions in *Alarm*, June 27, 1885, 1. "To ARMS! An Appeal to the Wage Slaves of America" appeared in *Alarm*, June 13, 1885, 1.

"Well-attended" socialist meetings in the working-class suburbs of the Town of Lake and Lake View are reported in *Alarm* on February 21, 1884, 3 and March 20, 1886, 1.

4. *Land Owner* 6, no. 1 (1874): 3; Monchow, *Seventy Years of Real Estate Subdividing*, 52; *Land Owner* 4, no. 8 (1872): 127.
5. *Chicago Tribune*, January 1, 1887, reprinted in Pierce, *History of Chicago*, 3: 207. See also Nichols, *Pay Dirt in Chicago*.
6. See "Chicago Real Estate," *Chicago Tribune*, April 21, 1889; "Chicago Real Estate," *Chicago Tribune*, November 17, 1887.
7. Bruton, "A Study of Tenement Ownership by Immigrant Workingmen," 21, 38, 9–10; *Real Estate and Building Journal, Intermediate Edition* 2, no. 16 (1888): n.p.; Abbott and Breckinridge, "Housing Conditions in Chicago," 461, 433. In the stockyards homeownership rates were 49 percent, twice the rate of Chicago overall.
8. Chicago Title and Trust Company, *One Hundred Years of Land Values*, Chicago Historical Museum.
9. Hoyt, *One Hundred Years of Land Values*, 276.
10. *Land Owner* 7, no. 6 (1875): 89; Dickens, *The Life and Adventures of Martin Chuzzlewit*; Simpson and Burton, *The Valuation of Vacant Land in Suburban Areas*, 5, 4.
11. Chicago Real Estate Exchange, *Catalogue of 200 Residence Lots*, 2–4.
12. For Point du Sable, see Work, "Negro Real Estate Holders of Chicago," 5; Chicago Commission on Race Relations, *The Negro in Chicago*, 139. Drake and Cayton, *Black Metropolis*, 31, repeat a supposed Potawatomie saying: "The first white man to settle at Chickagou was a Negro." For blacks expecting their property value to depreciate, see Work, "Negro Real Estate Holders of Chicago," 37.
13. Work, "Negro Real Estate Holders of Chicago," 37.
14. Ericsson and Myers, *Sixty Years a Builder*, 45, 99, 68. For another example of early immigrants dealing in land, see the letters of Nikolaus Schwenck, 1850s and 1860s, in Keil and Jentz, *German Workers in Chicago*, 28.
15. For average wages, see Sennett, *Families against the City*, 85. There was apparently little wage inflation in these years. Chicago's Immigrant Commission Study of 1904–14 found that one-third of immigrant families earned less than $500 annually, while another one-third earned less than $750. On large real estate loans, see James, *The Growth of Chicago Banks*, 396. Balloon plan in Calder, *Financing the American Dream*, 66, 281. "Typical mortgages" in Feasel, "The Financing of Urban Residential Construction," 23, 34. Bank avoidance in Breckinridge, *New Homes for Old*, 36–37; Bruton, "A Study of Tenement Ownership by Immigrant Workingmen *in Chicago* (unpublished M.A. dissertation for the University of Chicago School of Social Service Administration, 1924), 32.
16. Ad in *The Merchants and Manufacturers of Chicago: Being a Complete History of our Mercantile and Manufacturing Interests, and their Progress since the Fire* (Chicago: J.M. Wing & Co., 1873), 166. Canal terms in Henry L. Turner, "Chicago Real Estate" in *Industrial Chicago, vol. 4: The Commercial Interests* (Chicago: Goodspeed Publishing Co., 1894), 16.
17. See Bruton, *Tenement Ownership*, 30 as well as Beryl Satter, *Family Properties: Race, Real Estate, and the Exploitation of Black Urban America* (New York: Metropolitan Books, 2009), especially 4–13. Satter estimates that in the 1950s, approximately 85 percent of Chicago properties sold to blacks were sold on contract, earning spectacular profits for speculators and stripping many blacks of their savings. George Lipsitz adds that the cumulative effect of decades of housing policies favoring white people affects not only family savings and inherited

wealth but also health, education, and access to jobs, creating "fatal couplings of place and race in our society" (*How Racism Takes Place*, 4).

18. Bruton, "A Study of Tenement Ownership by Immigrant Workingmen," 36, 7–8.
19. Pierce, *History of Chicago*, 3: 206.
20. Bruton, "A Study of Tenement Ownership by Immigrant Workingmen," 27–28.
21. E. G. Pauling, secretary of the Garden City Equitable Loan and Building Association, quoted in "Chicago Building Societies," *Chicago Tribune*, March 25, 1883; *Charter and By-Laws of the Mechanics and Traders Savings, Loan and Building Association of Chicago Illinois* (Chicago: J. M. W. Jones, 1889), 23; Building and Loan Associations, Miscellaneous Pamphlets, Chicago History Museum; Wrigley, *The Working Man's Way to Wealth*, 3, 43, 5. Wrigley's popular book went through at least six printings in the 1860s and 70s. See Bodfish, *History of Building and Loan Associations in the United States*, 4, 11.
22. *Charter and By-Laws of the Mechanics and Traders Savings, Loan and Building Association of Chicago*, 10; *Charter and By-Laws of the Unions Savings, Loan and Building Association of Chicago Illinois* (Chicago: Brown, Pettibone & Kelly, 1882), 22, in Building and Loan Associations, Miscellaneous Pamphlets, Chicago History Museum. This sentence appears verbatim in at least two later pamphlets: *The Citizen's Building and Loan* (1884), and the *Mechanics' and Traders' Savings and Loan Association* (1889), in Building and Loan Associations, Miscellaneous Pamphlets, Chicago History Museum.
23. *Pamphlet of Citizens' Building and Loan Association* (1885), in Building and Loan Associations, Miscellaneous Pamphlets, Chicago History Museum; *Charter and By-Laws of the Mechanics and Traders Savings, Loan and Building Association of Chicago*, 11. See also Chicago Historical Museum's file on Building and Loan Associations, Miscellaneous Pamphlets, especially Citizens' Building & Loan (1884), 5; Union Savings & Loan (1882), 23. Bodfish, *History of Building and Loan Associations in the United States*, 147; *Pamphlet of Citizens' Building and Loan Association* (1885).
24. James, *The Growth of Chicago Banks*, 448, 518, 50; Hoyt, *One Hundred Years of Land Values*, 125, 138; McCullough, *Eighth Annual Report*, viii.
25. *Directory of the Building, Loan, and Savings Associations of Chicago and Cook County*; Bodfish, *History of Building and Loan Associations in the United States*, 377. See also Cohen, *Making a New Deal*, 76, 233, 274.
26. Hughes, "The Growth of an Institution," 49; "Value of Their Property," *Chicago Tribune*, March 7, 1886, reprinted in the *Chicago Foreign Language Press Survey*, roll 1.
27. "Chicago Building Societies Which Represent an Investment of $5,000,000," *Chicago Tribune*, March 25, 1883; Abbott, *The Tenements of Chicago* 391n12; Bruton, "A Study of Tenement Ownership by Immigrant Workingmen," 30, 33, 16. See also Work, "Negro Real Estate Holders of Chicago," 15, 19.
28. "Caution," Letters column, *Real Estate and Building Journal Intermediate News* 11, no. 23 (1888): 8. "Strange to say, the craze in this direction seems to have taken possession principally of the poorer and lower order of our foreign born element," he added. See also *Real Estate and Building Journal* 30, no. 29 (1888): 338; "Poor People's Banks," *Chicago Tribune*, January 16, 1889. Bodfish, *History of Building and Loan Associations in the United States*, 375, declares that in Illinois the "wild-cat" Nationals gave "a consequent blot to the fair name of building and loan which took some years to erase."
29. For bank failures, see Nell Painter, *Standing at Armageddon: The United States, 1877–1919* (New York: Norton, 1987), 116. For unemployment, see Addams, *Twenty Years at Hull House*, 121; Menand, *The Metaphysical Club*, 289–316. Gore, *Second Annual Auditor's Report: 1893*, preface.

30. Henry S. Rosenthal, quoted in Bruton, "A Study of Tenement Ownership by Immigrant Workingmen," 30; Bruton, "A Study of Tenement Ownership by Immigrant Workingmen," 28; Gore, *Third Annual Report*, 5.

31. McCullough, *Seventh Annual Report*, vi–vii; McCullough, *Eleventh Annual Report*, viii–xi.

32. Hoyt, *One Hundred Years of Land Values*, 42, 76. My calculation of 20 percent is unreliable because 6 percent of charity-seeking homeowners does not necessarily mean that 6 percent of all homeowners used building and loans; 4,094 houses owned by building and loan associations in 1898 does not necessarily mean that all 4,094 foreclosures happened in one year, and the population of 1900 did not necessarily live equally divided, five people to a household. Still, it is my best attempt to put into perspective Chicago's turn-of-the-century housing market.

33. E. P. Beach, "The Selection of Loans," reprinted in *Proceedings of the Building Association League of Illinois*, 41. For Chicago's rapidly increasing special-assessment levies, see Pierce, *History of Chicago*, 3: 337; R. A. Gates, "Forfeitures and Lapses," reprinted in *Proceeds of the Building Association League of Illinois*, 56.

34. Blue Island Land and Building Company, *Suburban Homes*, 9–10. For rental rates as a proportion of property value, see Citizen's Association Committee on Tenement Houses, *Report* (1884) quoted in Pierce, *History of Chicago*, 3: 270.

35. *Land Owner* 4, no. 8 (1872): 127.

36. "Interview with Male in the Technical Branch," August 21, 1930, *Hawthorne Study Microfiche* 184, quoted in Cohen, *Making a New Deal*, 32. See also "Suburban Real Estate," *Chicago Tribune*, April 11, 1880; "Real Estate," *Chicago Tribune*, June 20, 1880. "The incessant noise of a large city" and "jarring of the brain and spinal cord by continual treading on the stone and brick pavements" were believed to endanger urban residents' nervous systems, along with "bad ventilation and impure air, imperfect drainage, damp cellars [and] insufficient nourishment," according to Dr. Walter B. Platt, "The City's Injurious Influences," *Hyde Park Herald*, October 28, 1887.

37. "Our Chicago Suburbs—Ravenswood," *Land Owner* 6, no. 3 (1874): 39. The term *school villages* comes from Morken, "The Annexation of Morgan Park to Chicago," 3. Quote from a Ravenswood resident in *Land Owner* 6, no. 3 (1874): 39. This article contrasts Ravenswood with other suburbs that were only "a patch of oozing marsh, quaking with ague, or a blank, treeless, shrubless prairie, sprinkled with third- and fourth-rate cottages and shanties and, yclept, with some euphonious name, as park, elyseum, or paradise."

38. A.E.H., *The House That Lucy Built*, 3.

39. A.E.H., *House That Lucy Built*, 4–5.

40. A.E.H., *House That Lucy Built*, 7, 8, 9.

41. For southern laundresses, see Tera W. Hunter, *To 'Joy My Freedom: Southern Black Women's Lives and Labors after the Civil War* (Cambridge, MA: Harvard University Press, 1997), 57–58; Jones, *Labor of Love, Labor of Sorrow*, 125–26. For the West, see Susan Lee Johnson, "Domestic Life in the Diggings," in Valerie Matsumoto and Blake Allmendinger, eds., *Over the Edge: Remapping the American West* (Berkeley: University of California Press, 1999), 107–33. For the technology of laundering, see Nye, *Electrifying America*, 303–4.

42. A.E.H., *House That Lucy Built*, 12–13.

43. A.E.H., *House That Lucy Built*, 10–13.

44. A.E.H., *House That Lucy Built*, 13.

45. See Margaret Garb's extended discussion of this advertisement in "Selling Home Ownership: Samuel Eberly Gross and the Easy Payment Plan" in "Building the American Dream."

46. Bruton, "A Study of Tenement Ownership by Immigrant Workingmen," 21. See also 9–10.

47. Ozog, "A Study of Polish Home Ownership in Chicago," 52, 57, 63, 103. In Ozog's sample group, 6 percent had shops in their homes, and 12 percent took in boarders, a practice that had subsided by the time of his study. Earlier, before homeownership, 56 percent of Ozog's sample had taken in boarders. See also Bruton, "A Study of Tenement Ownership by Immigrant Workingmen," 9–10, 21, 38. For "peasant" land hunger, see Hughes, "The Growth of an Institution," 14–15; Breckinridge, *New Homes for Old*, 105; Hoyt, *One Hundred Years of Land Values*, 104. For a more recent example, see Slayton, *Back of the Yards*, 31. For Chicago's reliance on property taxes, see Einhorn, *Property Rules*; Pierce, *History of Chicago*, 3: 333. For the power of ethnic wards, see Sawislak, *Smoldering City*, 259.

48. Van Holst, *Modern American Homes*, Plate 100, a two-family house in Oak Park. Similarly, many contemporary zoning codes permit home businesses or ignore home boarders, so long as the neighborhood appears to have only single-family residences. See Baxandall and Ewen, *Picture Windows*, 246–49. For contemporary rules enforcing hidden vegetable gardens, see McKenzie, *Privatopia*, 13.

49. On becoming "real Americans" through property ownership, see Abbott, *Tenements of Chicago*, 381; Bruton, "A Study of Tenement Ownership by Immigrant Workingmen," 19. "Insulting the Bohemians," *Svornost*, January 29, 1885, translated by *Chicago Foreign Language Press Survey*, roll 1. *Daily Jewish Courier*, July 17, 1914, translated by *Chicago Foreign Language Press Survey*, roll 38.

50. "Number of Lithuanian Home Owners Increasing," *Lietuvia*, October 15, 1909, translated by the *Chicago Foreign Language Press Survey*, microfilm roll 43, category I-F; *Lietuvia*, December 11, 1908, translated by *Chicago Foreign Language Press Survey*, roll 38; *Lietuvia*, June 27, 1913, translated by *Chicago Foreign Language Press Survey*, roll 43.

51. As Laura Wexler points out, the nineteenth-century discourse of sentimental domesticity, institutionalized in the early twentieth century, functioned to "dehumanize" anyone who did not have a sentimental home, making them seem uncivilized, even savages. Workers might try to claim middle-class status through their houses, but that involved playing a dangerous "double-edged, double-jeopardy" game, because elites reserved the right to rule on what was a proper home (*Tender Violence*, especially 101, 105). Extending this idea, Amy Kaplan has analyzed "the imperial reach of domestic discourse" as women's work at home affected America's colonies abroad, calling attention to the significant overlaps between foreign projects and domesticity. In addition to her other work, see Amy Kaplan, "Manifest Domesticity," in Donald E. Pease and Robyn Wiegman, eds., *The Futures of American Studies* (Durham, NC: Duke University Press, 2002), 111–34.

52. Montgomery, *The American Girl in the Stockyards District*, 4; Abbott, *The Tenements of Chicago*, 377–78.

53. Bruton, "A Study of Tenement Ownership by Immigrant Workingmen," 14, 50. The same sentence appears in Abbott, *Tenements of Chicago*, 387.

54. Abbott and Breckinridge, "Housings Conditions in Chicago," 461–62.

55. Abbott and Breckinridge, "Housings Conditions in Chicago," 463.

56. Abbott and Breckinridge, *Delinquent Child and the Home*, 81; Breckinridge, *New Homes for Old*, 107; Mary Eliza McDowell, "Housing" (1921), 3, in Mary Eliza

McDowell Papers, folder 14, "University of Chicago Settlement—Housing," Chicago Historical Museum; Bruton, "A Study of Tenement Ownership by Immigrant Workingmen," 37.

57. Breckinridge and Abbott, *The Delinquent Child and the Home*, 15; Montgomery, *The American Girl in the Stockyards District*, 21; Harkness, "Real Estate Speculation and Juvenile Delinquency," 61.

58. Abbott and Breckinridge, "Housings Conditions in Chicago," 457. See also Breckinridge, *New Homes for Old*, 25–27, 80–81. Abbott, *Tenements of Chicago*, 342, quoted New York's housing reformer Lawrence Veiller: "The lodger evil . . . means the undermining of family life; often the breaking down of domestic standards. It frequently leads to the breaking up of homes and families, to the downfall and subsequent degraded career of young women, to grave immoralities—in a word, to the profanation of the home."

59. Abbott, *Tenements of Chicago*, 379. Becky Nicolaides describes a similar strategy of garage—dwelling owner—builders in *My Blue Heaven*. Abbott and Breckinridge, "Housings Conditions in Chicago," 450.

60. Josefa Humpel Zeman, "The Bohemian People in Chicago," in Addams et al., *Hull House Maps and Papers*, 115, 117.

61. See Jane Addams, "General Comments," in Addams et al., *Hull House Maps and Papers*, 5.

62. Abbott and Breckinridge, "Housings Conditions in Chicago," 463.

63. Dunne, *Mr. Dooley in Peace and in War*, 120.

64. "Excellent Advice" from the Rev. T. DeWitt Talmage, quoted in Samuel Eberly Gross (Firm), *The Gross Cottages, Houses and Lots*, 28.

65. Bigott, *From Cottage to Bungalow*, chapters 6 and 7. Bigott's thesis is that immigrants' working-class homeownership offered a route to American freedom and middle-class gentility, but it is hard to reconcile this with some of his other observations, for instance, that mortality was high because of the extreme economizing that some homeowners subjected themselves to (162). Cicero ceded this track to Stickney in 1900. See Finlay, "A Survey of Social Problems and Social Services," 9–10, 6, 11, 27, 249; Spelman, *The Town of Cicero*, 7.

66. Bigott, *Cottage to Bungalow*, 142. Olivier Zunz observes that "homeownership at the turn of the century was neither particularly middle class nor American" and may well have been "a brake to mobility" (*The Changing Face of Inequality*, 152, 161). Stephan Thernstrom concurs that "ruthless underconsumption" allowed immigrant workers to own homes but at the cost of "sacrifices so great as almost to blur the dichotomy between 'property' and 'poverty'" (*Poverty and Progress*, 136–37, 152–55).

67. Bruton, "A Study of Tenement Ownership by Immigrant Workingmen," 60, 54.

68. Bruton, "A Study of Tenement Ownership by Immigrant Workingmen," 48–49.

69. William Zelosky & Co., *Own Your Home in Beautiful Chicago*, in Chicago Historical Museum.

70. Ozog, "A Study of Polish Home Ownership in Chicago," 137, 65.

5. MAPPING CHICAGO, IMAGINING METROPOLISES: RECONSIDERING THE ZONAL MODEL OF URBAN GROWTH

1. Ericsson and Myers, *Sixty Years a Builder*, 45.

2. Ericsson and Myers, *Sixty Years a Builder*, 45.

3. See comments about Jackson Park circa 1890, quoted in Larson, *The Devil in the White City*, 95.

4. See, for example, *Land Owner* 4, no. 9 (1872): 147.

5. Melani McAlister calls these "cognitive maps" in *Epic Encounters: Culture, Media, and U.S. Interests in the Middle East* (Berkeley: University of California Press, 2001), 4. Katherine Morrissey introduces the term *perceptual regions* in *Mental Territories*, especially 6–8.

6. Perry R. Duis, *Challenging Chicago: Coping with Everyday Life, 1837–1920* (Chicago: University of Illinois Press, 1998), 5. For the Thompson Plat, see Robert A. Holland, *Chicago in Maps 1612–2002* (New York: Rizzoli Press, 2005), 52–53. Peterson, *The Birth of City Planning in the United States*, 9; Edward Benton Talcott, *Chicago, with the Several Additions . . . will be offered for sale* (New York: Peter A. Meisner, 1836), reprinted in Holland, *Chicago Maps*, 64. Ann Durkin Keating explains that in the 1830s, Chicago's "land became real estate." *Chicagoland: City and Suburbs in the Railroad Age* (Chicago: University of Chicago Press, 2005), 35. James Scott explains that the administrative "God's-eye" view of the grid is not for pedestrians or locals but for government bureaucrats, traveling salesmen, tax collectors, and real estate developers who prefer to avoid reliance on local knowledge or local control (*Seeing Like a State*, 56–58). J. B. Jackson calls this an upper-class view that neglects the pedestrian view of diverse vernacular landscapes, grown piecemeal over time ("The Accessible Landscape" [1988], in *Landscape in Sight*, 72). See also Jackson, "The Stranger's Path" (1957), in *Landscape in Sight*, 19–30.

7. Schick, *Chicago and Its Environs*, 419.

8. Runnion, *Out of Town*, 18.

9. "Bird's-Eye Views of the Developing City," in Smith et al., *The Great Chicago Fire*; *Map Showing the Boulevard and Park System and Twelve Miles of Lake Frontage of the City of Chicago* (Chicago: Rand McNally, 1884). See Butler Lowry Real Estate, *Lots in Adjoining Blocks for Sale on East Terms*, Newberry Library; Samuel Eberly Gross, "Second Under the Linden," a bilingual advertisement in the German newspaper *Fackel*, August 11, 1889, reprinted in Keil and Jentz, *German Workers in Chicago*, 137; *Map Showing the Burnt District in Chicago*, 3rd ed. (St Louis: R. P. Studley, 1871,), reprinted in Smith et al., *The Great Chicago Fire*.

10. Chamberlin, *Chicago and Its Suburbs*. See also Keating, *Chicagoland*, 14–17.

11. Thanks to an anonymous reviewer for the *Journal of Urban History* for pointing out the Sidney map of Philadelphia and to Becky Nicolaides for the information that early booster maps of Los Angeles do often contain circles, sometimes centered on "downtown L.A.," though often recentered on specific subdivisions for sale. For Chicago in the center of the circular frame, see, for instance, Edwin Rose, "Black Hawk War Map," unpublished manuscript, 1832; D. B. Cooke, *D. B. Cooke's Great Western Railway Guide* (Chicago: D. B. Cooke, 1855); G. Woolworth Colton, *Map Showing the Location of Galena and Chicago Union Railroad with Its Branches and Connections in Illinois, Wisconsin, Iowa and Minnesota* (Chicago: G. Woolworth Colton, 1862), all reprinted in Holland, *Chicago Maps*, 56, 78–79, 74–75. For suburbs within concentric circles, see Millard and Decker, *LAWNDALE*, in Canadian Centre d'Architecture, back cover; advertisement for Auburn Park, *Chicago Sunday Tribune*, April 14, 1889.

12. *Land Owner* 4, no. 9 (1872): 147.

13. *Land Owner* 4, no. 9 (1872): 147; *The Parks and Property Interests of the City of Chicago*, 27, 34. The parks had the desired effect, dramatically increasing land prices in their vicinity. See Hoyt, *One Hundred Years of Land Values*, 99; Pierce, *A History of Chicago*, 3: 314.

14. Charles M. Muller and Roderick A. Manstein, *Map Showing Territorial Growth of the City of Chicago, to Accompany the Annual Report of the Map Dept.* (Chicago:

Globe, 1891), reprinted in Holland, *Chicago Maps*, 137; George Warrington Stevens, *The Land of the Dollar* (1897), in Pierce, *As Others See Chicago*, 398. For other visitors touring the never fully completed circle of Chicago's park boulevards, see Pierce, *As Others See Chicago*, 229, 303–5, 425, 438–40, 506–7.

15. Stevens, *Land of the Dollar*, 396.
16. See Duis, *Challenging Chicago*, 18, 26; Paul Barrett, *The Automobile and Urban Transit: The Formation of Public Policy in Chicago, 1900–1930* (Philadelphia: Temple University Press, 1983), 9–37.
17. Condit, *The Chicago School of Architecture*, 12.
18. John Leng, *America in 1876* (1877), reprinted in Pierce, *As Others See Chicago*, 220.
19. Paul Bourget, *Outre-Mer Impressions of America* (1895), excerpted in Pierce, *As Others See Chicago*, 384.
20. Johnson, "The Natural History of the Central Business District," 297, 402.
21. As Alison Isenberg explains, "Despite the obvious appeal of living-organism and free-market metaphors . . . the hands of many participants—consumers and protestors as well as businesspeople, government leaders, design consultants, and real estate professionals—have been evident in this history, negotiating the nature of, and the standards for, urban commerce" (*Downtown America*, 2).
22. Edward Hungerford, *The Personality of American Cities* (1912), in Pierce, *As Others See Chicago*, 436.
23. *Chicago Tribune* (1915) and Benjamin Levering (1913) both quoted in Fogelson, *Downtown*, 99–100.
24. See especially Henry Fuller's ambivalent novel, *The Cliff Dwellers*. For "noose," see Moorley, *Old Loopy*; Julian Street, *Abroad at Home* (1914), in Pierce, *As Others See Chicago*, 459. Leader of the Chicago Association of Commerce (1911), quoted in Fogelson, *Downtown*, 99; Barrett, *Automobile and Urban Transit*, 106, 119.
25. Fogelson, *Downtown*, especially chapter 4, 183–217. See also Rae, *City*; Sugrue, *The Origins of the Urban Crisis*.
26. Van Holst, *Modern American Homes*, in Centre Canadienne d'Architecture.
27. Glick, "Winnetka," 27.
28. Hoyt, *One Hundred Years of Land Values*, 203.
29. Bourget, *Outre-Mer Impressions of America*, 385.
30. Emily S. Rosenberg, *Spreading the Dream: American Economic and Cultural Expansion, 1890–1945* (New York: Hill and Wang, 1982), 3–15; Rydell, *All the World's a Fair*; Larson, *The Devil in the White City*; "The Esquimaux Village," in Ives, *The Dream City*.
31. John Wellborn Root, quoted in Larson, *Devil in the White City*, 374; Jon Paterson, *The Birth of City Planning in the United States, 1840–1917* (Baltimore: Johns Hopkins University Press), 57.
32. Burnham (1911), quoted in Reps, *The Making of Urban America*, 496; Smith, *The Plan of Chicago*, 4–6, 14–15, 54.
33. Gerald Danzer, "The *Plan of Chicago* by Daniel H. Burnham and Edward H. Bennett: Cartographic and Historical Perspectives," in Buisseret, *Envisioning the City*, 145–72. For a photograph of Burnham's office penthouse, see Smith, *The Plan of Chicago*, 63. For maps showing this overhead perspective, see "Bird's-Eye Views of the Developing City," in Smith et al., *The Great Chicago Fire*; Holland, *Chicago Maps*, 82–83, 126, 149, 185, 188–89, 196–97, 198. A more unusual bird's-eye perspective looking eastward is in *Land Owner* 6, no. 2 (1874): 1.
34. Burnham and Bennett, *Plan of Chicago*, 1. This plan was a collective, collaborative effort, involving Charles Moore, Jules Guerin, and numerous others who could be considered coauthors, but for simplicity's sake I will refer to it as Burnham's *Plan*.

35. Smith, *The Plan of Chicago*, 4–6, 14–15, 54.
36. Burnham and Bennett, *Plan*, plate 34, p 31.
37. Burnham and Bennett, *Plan*, plate 35, p 33.
38. Sally Chappell, "Chicago Issues: The Enduring Power of a Plan," in *The Plan of Chicago*, 15.
39. Speaker at the Commercial Club, January 18, 1910, quoted in Moody, *Wacker's Manual*, 65. As Carl Smith has pointed out, "The *Plan* itself was forward-looking, but in some respects the publicity techniques the planners used to generate support . . . were even more innovative and modern" (*The Plan of Chicago*, 74); see also 76–85, 111–29.
40. Moody, *Wacker's Manual*, xv. For distribution of this primer, see Miller, *Here's the Deal*, 12.
41. Walter D. Moody, *Wacker's Manual of the Plan of Chicago: Municipal Economy, especially prepared for study in the public schools of Chicago* (Chicago: Chicago Plan Commission, 1913), 11; Moody, *Wacker's Manual*, 81.
42. Moody, *Wacker's Manual*, 50; "Chicago—The Great Central Market," reprinted in Moody, *Wacker's Manual*, 101.
43. Moody, *Wacker's Manual*, 26, 38, 63, 75.
44. Miller, *Here's the Deal*, 13.
45. Walter D. Moody, *Chicago's Greatest Issue*, 9–10, Centre Canadienne d'Architecture.
46. Smith, *The Plan of Chicago*, 133.
47. In his well-researched assessment of the *Plan*, Carl Smith finds no definitive evidence that Burnham made this memorable statement (*The Plan of Chicago*, 98).
48. Chicago Zoning Commission, *Zoning Chicago*, 4, 3, 5.
49. Joseph Schweiterman and Dana Caspall, *The Politics of Place: A History of Zoning in Chicago* (Chicago: Lake Claremon Press, 2006), 17, 28; Herbert Hoover, quoted on 25.
50. Hornstein, *A Nation of Realtors*, 105–8; Frederick Morrison Babcock, *The Appraisal of Real Estate* (New York: Macmillan, 1924), 23–24, 208–9.
51. Dennis Smith, *The Chicago School: A Liberal Critique of Capitalism* (1988), quoted in Davis, *Ecology of Fear*, 363. Actually, as Burgess's student Amos Hawley observed, "human ecology has had a rather grudging acceptance in the discipline of sociology," rarely mentioned in many textbooks, as most sociologists preferred to focus on structural factors instead of ecological metaphors about populations' collective adaptations to their environment (*Human Ecology*, 7). Burgess's zonal model has lingered longer with urban historians.
52. Ernest Burgess, "The Growth of the City: An Introduction to a Research Project," in Burgess et al., *The City*, 52. Dorothy Ross argues that this abstract universalizing, severing social science from history, was a mark of American social science and a loss to both social science and history (*The Origins of American Social Science*, especially xii–xvi, 274–76).
53. Burgess, "The Growth of the City," 54–56.
54. Burgess, "The Growth of the City," 56.
55. Roderick McKenzie, "The Ecological Approach to the Study of Human Community," in Burgess et al., *The City*, 78, 77, note I; Burgess, "The Growth of the City," 54, 57.
56. Burgess, "The Growth of the City," 48, 53, 50; McKenzie, "The Ecological Approach to the Study of Human Community," 78; Ross, *Origins of American Social Science*, 359, 364. Andrew Ross argues that this biological language took on its own "reproductive life," repeatedly naturalizing phenomena that are social (*The Chicago Gangster Theory of Life*, 118).

57. Ernest Burgess, "Residential Segregation in American Cities," *Annals of the American Academy of Political and Social Science*, Vol. 140 (Nov. 1928), 115.
58. Faris and Dunham, *Mental Disorders in Urban Areas*, 36, 170.
59. Frederick M. Babcock, *The Valuation of Real Estate* (New York: McGraw-Hill, 1932), 2, 47, 58, 18–19, 68.
60. Babcock, *Valuation*, 60–61, 3, 91.
61. Glick, "Winnetka," 36, 35, 71.
62. Homer Hoyt, "City Growth and Mortgage Risk: Chicago," *Chicago Insured Mortgage Portfolio* (1937), in Homer Hoyt, *According to Hoyt: Fifty Years of Homer Hoyt, 1916 to 1966* (Chicago: Homer Hoyt Associates, 1967), 585.
63. Hoyt, *According to Hoyt*, 592–93.
64. Hoyt, *According to Hoyt*, 593.
65. Hoyt, *According to Hoyt*, 588.
66. Walter Firey, *Land Use in Central Boston* (1947; New York: Greenwood Press, 1968), 4, 13.
67. James T. Farrell, *The Young Manhood of Studs Lonigan* (1934) in *Studs Lonigan: A Trilogy*, 407–8.
68. Farrell, *Young Manhood*, 408. Farrell is using an older definition of *jazz* meaning sexual intercourse.
69. Farrell, *Young Manhood*, 134–35.
70. Carla Cappetti, "Ethnographers at Home: The Trilogy of Studs Lonigan," in *Writing Chicago*, 108–44.
71. See Wilson, "Chicago Families in Furnished Rooms"; Harvey Zorbaugh, *The Gold Coast and the Slum: A Sociological Study of Chicago's Near North Side* (Chicago: University of Chicago Press, 1929), xi, 3. Robert Park and Ernest Burgess were editors of Zorbaugh's book, which claims to uphold their theories yet actually shows the long-term stability of the Gold Coast.
72. Reckless, *Vice in Chicago*, 10–11, 120–36.
73. Walter Reckless, "Natural History of Vice Areas in Chicago," PhD dissertation for University of Chicago, 1925, 323. For an accounting of vice in 1911, see Vice Commission of Chicago, *The Social Evil in Chicago*, 72–73.
74. Reckless, *Vice in Chicago*, 130.
75. See, for example, "Ambush, Shoot Dry Sleuth: West Suburbs in Turmoil over Vice War," *Chicago Tribune*, July 8, 1925; "Two Niles Center Saloons Raided by the Sheriff: Vice Activity Shifts from West to North Suburbs," *Chicago Tribune*, July 11, 1917; "Crowe Raids in Suburbs; Seeks Vice Collusion: Seizes Chicago Heights City Records," *Chicago Tribune*, February 1, 1921.
76. Proudfoot, "The Major Outlying Business Centers of Chicago," 49.
77. Proudfoot, "The Major Outlying Business Centers of Chicago," 4.
78. Proudfoot, "The Major Outlying Business Centers of Chicago," 12, 2.
79. Clove, *The Park Ridge–Barrington Area*, 32–34. Clove credits the concept of a neighborhood "life cycle" to L. Elden Smith, "Measuring the Neighborhood Risk," *Insured Mortgage Portfolio* 2 (February 1938): 9–11, 22–23.
80. Copeland, "The Limits and Characteristics of Metropolitan Chicago," 3–4. For the overlaps between nature and culture, see, for instance, Cronon, *Nature's Metropolis*. For ideas of print culture and popular maps disseminating ideas of "imagined communities," see Benedict Anderson, *Imagined Communities* (London: Verso, 1983).
81. Copeland, "The Limits and Characteristics of Metropolitan Chicago," figure 58.
82. Copeland, "The Limits and Characteristics of Metropolitan Chicago," 5.

83. Copeland, "The Limits and Characteristics of Metropolitan Chicago," 231, 235.
84. Copeland, "The Limits and Characteristics of Metropolitan Chicago," 54, 65.
85. Copeland, "The Limits and Characteristics of Metropolitan Chicago," 67.
86. Gary, Indiana; Milwaukee, Wisconsin; and Chicago and its inner-ring suburbs formed the three nuclei.
87. Harris and Lewis, "Constructing a Fault(y) Zone," 624. For "industrial garden," see Self, *American Babylon*, especially 8–9, 28–32. For brownstoners, see Suleiman Osman, *The Invention of Brownstone Brooklyn: Gentrification and the Search for Authenticity in Postwar New York* (New York: Oxford University Press, 2011).
88. Firey, *Land Use in Boston*, 324–40.
89. Jackson, *Crabgrass Frontier*.

6. THE MORTGAGES OF WHITENESS: CHICAGO'S RACE RIOTS OF 1919

1. "Ghastly Deeds of Race Rioters Told," *Chicago Defender*, August 2, 1919. Official counts of the Chicago Commission on Race Relations are in their report, *The Negro in Chicago*, hereafter CCRR, which relied on statistics from hospitals and churches as well as the coroner and police. It is the most widely accepted count, but there were others. The *Chicago Defender* reported forty dead and "more than 500 wounded, many of them fatally" (August 2, 1919). The *Chicago Tribune* estimated thirty-three dead, 306 "hurt," two thousand homeless, and up to $500,000 in lost property (August 4, 1919). As the riot still simmered, on August 1, 1919, eighty-one leaders of forty-eight civic organizations met at the Union League Club to discuss what was happening and how to prevent its ever happening again. They called on Illinois governor Frank Lowden, who appointed six blacks and six whites to the Chicago Commission on Race Relations, with sociologist Graham Romeyn Taylor as its executive secretary. The members of the commission included Robert Abbott, owner and publisher of the *Chicago Defender*; Edgar Bancroft, a lawyer and trustee of the Tuskegee Institute; William Scott Bond, a realtor and trustee of the University of Chicago; Edward Osgood Brown, president of the Chicago branch of the NAACP; George Hall, the vice president of the Chicago Urban League; George Jackson, a realtor; Harry Eugene Kelly, a lawyer; Victor Lawson, editor of the *Chicago Daily News*; Adelbert Roberts, the grand master of the Colored Odd Fellows of America; Julius Rosenwald, president of Sears Roebuck; Francis Shepardson, Illinois's former superintendent of education; and Lacey Kirk Williams, a Baptist minister.
2. Sandburg, *Chicago Race Riots*, 4.
3. Potawatomie saying in Drake and Cayton, *Black Metropolis*, 31. See also CCRR, 139; Work, "Negro Real Estate Holders of Chicago," 5.
4. "Migration of the Talented Tenth," in C. G. Woodson, *A Century of Negro Migration* (1918), quoted in Drake and Cayton, *Black Metropolis*, 53. For an overview of the gradual formation of the first ghetto, see Work, "Negro Real Estate Holders of Chicago," 13; Hirsch, *Making the Second Ghetto*, 3–15. For suburbs, see Wiese, *Places of Their Own*, especially 15, 23, 61–65, 118–23.
5. David Katzman, in *Before the Ghetto: Black Detroit in the Nineteenth Century* (1973) calls this process "the push of discrimination" along with "the pull of ethnocentrism" (quoted in Grossman, *Land of Hope*, 127). Specific statistics for 1900 are in Work, "Negro Real Estate Holders of Chicago," 28. Statistics for 1910 are in Grossman, *Land of Hope*, 123. Statistics for 1930 are in Cohen,

Making a New Deal, 34. See also Drake and Cayton, *Black Metropolis*, 12. The boundaries of the Black Belt extended in those decades from Thirty-fifth Street south to Fifty-fifth Street and beyond, but the dramatic increase in the percentage of blacks living there is due less to this boundary extension and more to increasing racial segregation in the first decades of the twentieth century.

6. Herbst, "The Negro in the Slaughtering and Meat Packing Industry," 46, 53–56, xiv; Cohen, *Making a New Deal*, 35.

7. For "greenhorns," see Herbst, "The Negro in the Slaughtering and Meat Packing Industry," xiv. Headline quoted in Drake and Cayton, *Black Metropolis*, 61. For the best accounts of the Great Migration to Chicago, see Grossman, *Land of Hope*; Wilkerson, *The Warmth of Other Suns*.

8. Wilson, *Mary McDowell*, 169.

9. Realtor survey cited in Grossman, *Land of Hope*, 135. Boarders in CCRR, 155, 165. On kitchenettes, see Wilson, *Mary McDowell*, 177; CCRR, 185; Tuttle, *Race Riot*, 162. Richard Wright, *Twelve Million Black Voices*, quoted in Stange, *Bronzeville*, xxiii. See also Drake and Cayton, *Black Metropolis*, 61.

10. *Chicago Defender*, October 20, 1917, quoted in Grossman, *Land of Hope*, 145.

11. CCRR, 216; Work, "Negro Real Estate Holders of Chicago," 9. The terms *rustic suburb* and *domestic service suburb* and the list of African American suburbs come from Wiese, *Places of Their Own*, 61, 64, 122. CCRR adds Glencoe to Wiese's list (CCRR 136–37).

12. "Chicago Heights Quiet in Spite of Riot Rumors," *Chicago Tribune*, August 7, 1920; "Autoists Tell of Traps Set in Specialville," *Chicago Tribune*, August 1, 1926; "More Officials Admit Graft in Motorists' Fines," *Chicago Tribune*, July 16, 1926; "Specialville, Noted for Raids, Changes Name to Dixmoor," *Chicago Tribune*, October 25, 1929. Lilydale in CCRR, 224–25.

13. CCRR, 608, 138–39. Even booster literature described the houses of Robbins as "pioneer shacks" (McCoo, *Say It with Pictures*, 64).

14. Wiese, *Places of Their Own*, 122, 121, 114. Other African American suburbs in this area included Phoenix, West Harvey, and Markham.

15. CCRR, 137.

16. CCRR, 155–56.

17. See Harris, "Chicago's Other Suburbs."

18. In 1917 in *Buchanan v. Warley*, the U.S. Supreme Court invalidated Kentucky's racist zoning ordinance, and Chicago did not yet have the state authority to enact any zoning. In the 1920s many wealthier Chicago neighborhoods would develop restrictive covenants. But in the first few years after World War I bombing was the strategy used to keep neighborhoods white. See Tuttle, *Race Riot*, 161, 173. Temperature in CCRR, 11. Earlier riots of summer 1919 in CCRR, 1–3.

19. Wilson, *Mary McDowell*, 173.

20. For the power of workers to maneuver despite surveillance, see James Scott, *Domination and the Arts of Resistance: Hidden Transcripts* (New Haven, CT: Yale University Press, 1990). For the significant switch from issues of production to issues of consumption, see Glickman, *A Living Wage*.

21. "Scab race" quoted in Grossman, *Land of Hope*, 218. See also 208–45; Cohen, *Making a New Deal*, 33–36, 45–46; Tuttle, *Race Riot*, 156. Although some African American workers respected picket lines and joined unions, many others saw few reasons to do so, since few unions welcomed them. Blacks were not the only group to enter into stockyard work by breaking strikes; Poles first began as scab

laborers during the stockyards strike of 1886, and women first worked as strike-breakers in 1894. See Pacyga, *Polish Immigrants*, 44, 54, 172. Alma Herbst explains that blacks were not the only scabs in the stockyards strike of 1904, but they were "conspicuous," thus gaining the enmity of strikers ("The Negro in the Slaughtering and Meat Packing Industry," 53–56).

22. Cohen, *Making a New Deal*, 12; "32,000 Threaten Strike at Yard," *Chicago Tribune*, August 8, 1919. See also "Labor Council Blames Packers for Race Riots," *Chicago Tribune*, August 18, 1919; Sandburg, *Chicago Race Riots*, 74. In 1919 the union attracted 30 percent of black stockyards workers and more than 90 percent of white; James Grossman has argued this was a half-hearted welcome into what was clearly a "white man's union" (*Land of Hope*, 241).

23. *Chicago Daily Tribune*, August 7, 1919, quoted in Tuttle, *Race Riot*, 64. CCRR, 6, 36–38. For an elegant argument for the multicausality of another, later riot, see James Goodman, *Blackout* (New York: Farrar, Straus and Giroux, 2003).

24. CCRR, 6, 10–11, 18, 22; Grossman, *Land of Hope*, 219–20. Before some Chicago streetcar crossings were raised, the death rate from streetcar accidents was six hundred people a year, almost two a day. This statistic does not include those who were merely maimed and left armless or legless (Cronon, *Nature's Metropolis*, 373).

25. "Ghastly Deeds of Race Rioters Told," *Chicago Defender*, August 2, 1919; CCRR, 6, 32.

26. CCRR, 7. Lizabeth Cohen discusses the threat of starvation in *Making a New Deal*, 149. For relief efforts, see CCRR, 41, 44–47.

27. On the activities of Ragen's Cots during the riots, see CCRR, 12–17. On the role of Father Brian, see McGreevy, *Parish Boundaries*, 3. Monday's activity in Wilson, *Mary McDowell*, 175. Tuesday's in CCRR, 14, which also mentions the connections between Ragen's Colts and the New City police substation.

28. Relying on oral histories, Thomas Jablonsky describes Ragen's Colts as "a Canaryville-based Irish gang" who beat up Poles around Sherman Park in the years after World War I" (*Pride in the Jungle*, 90). For sports scores, see "Beloit Ousted from Top Berth by Ragen Colts: Meets Its First Reverse in Chicago League," *Chicago Tribune*, May 28, 1917; "Sportsman Subjugate Ragens, 7–6" in *Sportsman Bag*, June 1, 1923, a newsletter sponsored by Hull House, reproduced in Thrasher, *The Gang*, 67. "Clubwomen See Fighting Girls End Wild Dance," *Chicago Tribune*, March 22, 1915; "New Year Ball of Ragen Colts Branded as Orgy: Investigators Charge the Dance Was 'Vilest' Ever Attended," *Chicago Tribune*, January 3, 1918; "Ragen Colts, on Pleasure Bent, Get Corralled," *Chicago Tribune*, February 4, 1922; "K.C. Foe Chased by Ragen Colts: Orator Flees with Air Full of Chairs," *Chicago Tribune*, February 1, 1922; "Two Young Men Tell How Blows Killed Stranger: 'Annoyed Girl' Their Reason for Deed," *Chicago Tribune*, August 16, 1922. Headquarters is photographed in Thrasher, *Gang*, 459. "Sheldon Gang Member Shot at Ragen Colts," *Chicago Tribune*, February 1, 1927; "Two Wounded in Gun Duel of Ragen's Colts," *Chicago Tribune*, July 16, 1917; "Row between 2 Clubs Causes Shooting," *Chicago Tribune*, October 25, 1920. Jane Addams testified in CCRR, 55: "The politician used to take care of the young voter and the boy nearly a voter, but now he comes down to boys of thirteen and fourteen and fifteen and begins to pay their rent and gives them special privileges and keeps the police off when they are gambling. The whole boy problem is very much mixed up with these—I won't call them gangs, but they are clubs with more or less political affiliations."

29. Thrasher, *Gang*, 459, 456, 477. Interview 242 describes an unnamed Democratic club with so many resemblances to Ragen's Colts that it is listed in the index as "Ragen's Colts" (458).

30. See CCRR, 3; "City Hall Politics Caused Riots—Hoyne," *Chicago Tribune*, August 24, 1919; "Stop Exploiting of Negro Votes, Pulpits Demand," *Chicago Tribune*, August 4, 1919. Democratic newspaper quoted in Grossman, *Land of Hope*, 177. For census counts of the black population of Chicago, see Hirsch, *Making the Second Ghetto*, 17. Smith and Lewis, *Chicago*, 393–94. For the historic class and ethnic rivalries underlying disputes over temperance, see Sawislak, *Smoldering City*, chapter 5, "Laws and Order."

31. CCRR, 12. The coroner's jury declared, "These clubs are here, they are popular, they take the place of the disappearing saloon and poolroom. Properly governed and controlled, they should be encouraged and fostered and, when necessary, disciplined" (17).

32. Thrasher, *Gang*, 46–47, 62, 65. See also "Clubs Closed by Riots Seek to Open Again," *Chicago Tribune*, August 23, 1919; "Three Athletic Clubs Raided on South Side," *Chicago Tribune*, September 12, 1919; CCRR, 12–17.

33. Thrasher, *Gang*, 26, 28, 57, 3, 80.

34. Lending credence to McGreevy's argument in *Parish Boundaries*, Thrasher reported finding few gangs in Jewish neighborhoods (*Gang*, 10, 12).

35. "Father Brian, who had charge of these boys, taught them how to box and how to build themselves up physically," according to testimony to the grand jury investigating the riots (quoted in CCRR, 16). For Wentworth as riot's "deadline," see CCRR, 37, 115. For the parishes, see Koenig, *A History of the Parishes*, 38, 216, 59. Langston Hughes recalled being beaten as a teenager for crossing Wentworth Avenue in the 1920s: see Grossman, *Land of Hope*, 118. For continuing struggles over Wentworth Avenue in the 1940s, see Hirsch, *Making the Second Ghetto*, 52. Wentworth was also geographically central to other parishes: St. George Church was located near Thirty-ninth and Wentworth, and St. Anne's was at Wentworth and Fifty-fifth (now Garfield Boulevard). See McGreevy, *Parish Boundaries*, 13, 2, 19–21. See also Eileen M. McMahon's examination of St. Sabina's parish on Chicago's southwest side, *What Parish Are You From?* For "structural rootedness," see Gamm, *Urban Exodus*, 129.

36. Pacyga, *Polish Immigrants*, 134–46. In 1930, when University of Chicago sociologists identified seventy-two "community areas" in Chicago, the community of Kenwood was—and still is—exactly congruous with the parish of St. Ambrose, signifying how much community and parish identities could overlap (Koenig, *History of the Parishes*, xv–xvii). After 1916 Chicago's Archbishop George Mundelein opposed national, non-English-speaking parishes and opened only fifteen more. Parishes in the former Town of Lake included the German parish of St. Augustine, built in 1879, the Polish parish of St. Joseph in 1886, the Bohemian parish of Saints Cyril and Methodius in 1892, the French parish of St. John the Baptist in 1892, the Slovakian parish of St. Michael the Archangel in 1898, the Lithuanian parish of Holy Cross in 1904, the Byzantine Rite Catholic church of St. Mary in 1905, a second Polish parish of St. John of God in 1906, the Ukrainian Catholic Church of the Nativity in 1906, and a third Polish parish of Sacred Heart in 1910, in addition to five largely Irish parishes. This dizzying record of church development reveals a dense, rapidly growing multiethnic neighborhood in which a date of national parish formation usually signifies the date that an immigrant group had arrived in significant numbers (Koenig, *History of the Parishes*, 855–56, 970).

37. Rev. Matthew Schmitz message to parishioners, quoted in Koenig, *History of the Parishes*, 94.

38. Rev. Vincent Schrempp, *Pfarbotte* (parish magazine), February 1925, quoted in Koenig, *History of the Parishes*, 95.
39. As Gamm explains, "It was in the 1920s . . . that middle-class white ethnics forged their paths from urban neighborhoods to the suburbs. It was in the 1920s that Jewish neighborhoods began their long unraveling, and it was in the 1920s that Catholic neighborhoods began their resistance to the new forces promoting suburbanization" (*Urban Exodus*, 27).
40. Tuttle, *Race Riot*, 176. On varied responses, see Koenig, *History of the Parishes*, especially 108–9, 357–58. After 1945 the Archdiocese of Chicago formally advocated peaceful racial succession and welcomed black children into Catholic schools, as some individual parishes had begun to do earlier, while others violently resisted integration (Koenig, *History of the Parishes*, xvii–xxi). The challenge of neighborhood succession was not limited to Catholics. Chicago's oldest white Baptist church reported in 1918, "Our church has been greatly handicapped in the past year by the great influx of colored people and the removal of many Whites." Membership declined so drastically that church leaders believed "the church was face to face with catastrophe. No eloquent preaching, no social service, could save a church in a community that was nearly 100 percent Negro." This is a particularly racist sentiment, considering the number of blacks who were traditionally Baptist. The First Baptist Church was eventually sold to blacks. See Drake and Cayton, *Black Metropolis*, 63–64.
41. Italian and Slavic couples in South Deering, quoted in Hirsch, *Making the Second Ghetto*, 186. On later parish struggles, see McGreevy, *Parish Boundaries*, 187–92, 98–99. "What parish are you from?" rioters in Englewood asked strangers in 1949, in order to identify Jews, communists, and University of Chicago students. Members of Visitation Parish had noticed nine African Americans in the home of a Jewish labor organizer, and this led crowds of three thousand to ten thousand people to gather outside that home, lingering for days, with the tacit encouragement of their parish priest and to the dismay of Catholic liberals from other neighborhoods. The nine blacks had been attending a union meeting, but local rumors reported they might have been buying the house. Thirteen people were injured and fifty-four arrested in one week in November 1949. The parish's official history reports with subtle racist pride, "Although other parts of Englewood underwent racial change in the 1950s, the neighborhood around 55th [later Garfield] and Halsted remained a white enclave for nearly twenty more years." See McGreevy, *Parish Boundaries*, 94–95; Hirsch, *Making the Second Ghetto*, 93; Koenig, *History of the Parishes*, 972–74. In 1963 three black families did move into this parish, triggering a week of racial strife in which 154 people were arrested in scuffles that injured seven policemen. After that, white families rapidly moved away. New priests and nuns began new programs for the black and Puerto Rican families of their parish, but the transition from an Irish Catholic enclave was so rocky that Visitation High School was relocated, southeastward, to make it "more accessible" to white students who had moved away.
42. Wilson, *Mary McDowell*, 175. Bubbly Creek rumors in CCRR, 32–33.
43. Koenig, *History of the Parishes*, 366, 872.
44. "Negroes Didn't Set Fires, Say Their Aldermen," *Chicago Tribune*, August 3, 1919. See also "Ruins and Desolation of Belgian War Zone Recalled by Fire 'Back of the Yards,'" *Chicago Tribune*, August 3, 1919; "Blame Negroes for Fire," *Chicago Tribune*, August 5, 1919.
45. "Negroes Didn't Set Fires, Say Their Aldermen."

46. Grand jury report quoted in CCRR, 16, 21. "I.W.W. Also Suspected," *Chicago Tribune*, August 3, 1919.
47. Jablonsky, *Pride in the Jungle*, 97; Koenig, *History of the Parishes*, 872, 366.
48. Armour superintendent quoted in CCRR, 20–21. *Narod Polski*, January 19, 1921, *Naujienos*, June 3, 1914, quoted in Jablonsky, *Pride in the Jungle*, 90–91. Pacyga, *Polish Immigrants*, 219. Rev. Louis Grudzinski called the riots a "black pogrom," as quoted in Pacyga, *Polish Immigrants*, 220. On July 30, 1919, the *Dwiennik Zwiazkowy* newspaper ran a front-page cartoon showing Uncle Sam hypocritically protesting Jewish pogroms in Poland, with the caption, "On the Occasion of the Black Pogrom in America." See Pacyga, *Polish Immigrants*, 222, 226.
49. "Upset Plan to Put Negroes Back in Yards," *Chicago Tribune*, August 3, 1919; "Negroes Return to Yards Today Guarded by Host: Labor Protests Move to Place Police in Packing Plants," *Chicago Tribune*, August 7, 1919; "32,000 Threaten Strike at Yard," *Chicago Tribune*, August 8, 1919). See also Grossman, *Land of Hope*, 225; Pacyga, *Polish Immigrants*, 247; Cohen, *Making a New Deal*, 46–51. Cohen argues that the burning of Lithuanian homes in Back of the Yards left "black-white relations permanently seared" (37).
50. The local newspaper was named *Journal Town of Lake* until 1937. Local police were houses in the New City substation, echoing the name that Samuel Eberly Gross had used for his subdivision. Both Town of Lake and New City were names used by residents who preferred to avoid the potentially pejorative Stockyards District, Packingtown, and Jungle. In 1937 the Back of the Yards Neighborhood Council changed the name of the local journal and helped foster a greater pride in the name Back of the Yards. See Jablonsky, *Pride in the Jungle*, 133. *Sanborn Fire Insurance Map of Chicago* (New York: Sanborn Map Co., 1925), 13: 43, 44.
51. For the residents of Hermitage, Wood, Honore, Lincoln (Wolcott), along Forty-third, Forty-fourth, and Forty-fifth Streets, see *Polk's Chicago*, especially 368, 379, 511, 953–54. For Lithuanian names, see William R. Schmalstieg, "Lithuanian Names," *Lituanas: Lithuanian Quarterly Journal of Arts & Sciences* 28, no. 3 (1982). At 4337 S. Lincoln, John and Emily Janusik lived with Frank and Rose Kalata in a building that none of them owned, but their nearest neighbors with recognizably Lithuanian names were five blocks away, at 4801 S. Lincoln, where Sophie and F. W Jasota rented rooms above Gertrude and Adam Potocki's soft drink store. Wood Street had a few more Lithuanian names, along with the Lopez, Martinez, Ortiz, and Ybarra families, who were almost certainly Mexican, on a street dominated by Polish names like Grserzczak, Kowalski, Lukachekski, Mrowka, Opszarny, Strna, Wojdyla, and Zawodniak.
52. See *Polk's Chicago*, especially pages 368, 379, 511, 953–54. Lizabeth Cohen discusses the challenges facing small ethnic grocers in these years in *Making a New Deal*, 106–20. Conveniently Chicago's street numbering system after 1911 reveals the cross-street in the street number: the 4300 block of Hermitage is the block just south of the intersection of Hermitage and Forty-third Street.
53. It transitioned quickly after that. In 1980 this area was only 57.5 percent white, and today it is about 33 percent white, 33 percent Hispanic, and 33 percent black. See Jablonsky, *Pride in the Jungle*, 150.
54. "Race Feud May Result," *Chicago Tribune*, November 3, 1903; "Court Blocks Morgan Park Negro Invasion," *Chicago Tribune*, August 2, 1917; CCRR, 608, 137–38. Woodlawn in Tuttle, *Race Riot*, 161.
55. L. M. Smith, identified as the leader of the "Kenwood Improvement Association," quoted in Sandburg, *Chicago Race Riots*, 18–19.

56. Kenwood and Hyde Park Property Owners Association, *Property Owners Journal* (1920s), quoted in Freund, *Colored Property*, 16.
57. Kenwood and Hyde Park Property Owners Association, *Property Owners Journal* (1920s), quoted in Freund, *Colored Property*, 14.
58. CREB and NAREB quoted in Freund, *Colored Property*, 15; Satter, *Family Properties*, 40. In Robert Self's excellent analysis, this was "segregation's consequence: racism rationalized as economic calculation" (*American Babylon*, 160).
59. *Chicago Property Owner's Journal*, December 13, 1919, quoted in CCRR, 121.
60. W. E. B. DuBois, *Black Reconstruction in the United States* (1935), quoted in Roediger, *The Wages of Whiteness*, 12.
61. Garb, *City of American Dreams*, especially introduction and 202.
62. "Segregation to Prevent Race Riots Is Urged," *Chicago Tribune*, August 6, 1919.
63. Alderman Schwartz, quoted in CCRR, 210.
64. L. M. Smith quoted in Sandburg, *Chicago Race Riots*, 18–19. CCRR, 122; Drake and Cayton, *Black Metropolis*, 79, 178–79, 184.
65. CCRR, 194.
66. CCRR, 194–204, 609.
67. Lawsuit of the Chicago Contract Buyers' League, quoted in Satter, *Family Properties*, 12–13. For Mortgage Banker's Association, see 43.
68. For "blight," see Smith quoted in Sandburg, *Chicago Race Riots*, 18–19. Meeting announcement, October 1918, quoted in CCRR, 118. At a similar meeting on May 5, 1919, "the sentiment was expressed that the Negro invasion of the district was the worst calamity that had struck the city since the Great Fire" (CCRR, 119).
69. Daniel Martinez HoSang calls this the "language of political whiteness," a language in which "whiteness functions as an absentee referent," never having to speak its name. Paraphrasing Mark Brillant, HoSang concludes that "housing proved to be the shoal where racial liberalism would run aground," as the realtor-led "suburban counterrevolution" of the 1960s and 1970s twisted the language of civil rights freedoms to fight against fair housing, affordable housing, and property taxes (*Racial Propositions*, especially 266 and 54). For "suburban counterrevolution," see also Self, *Babylon*, chapters 7 and 8; Daniel HoSang, "Racial Liberalism and the Rise of the Sunbelt West: The Defeat of Fair Housing on the 1964 California Ballot," in Michelle Nickerson and Darren Dochuk, eds., *Sunbelt Rising: The Politics of Place, Space, and Region* (Philadelphia: University of Pennsylvania Press, 2011).
70. See Freund, *Colored Property*; David Freund, "Marketing the Free Market: State Interventions and the Politics of Prosperity in America" in Kruse and Sugrue, *The New Suburban History*.
71. For probationary whiteness, see Jacobson, *Whiteness of a Different Color*. More recently Thomas Guglielmo has argued against Jacobson in *White on Arrival*, pointing out that ethnic Italians "did not need to become white" because they were already white in "critical ways," including naturalization law, the courts, unions, employers, neighbors, and realtors. My own research shows a pattern more consistent with Jacobson's: there was a flexible racism against probationary white ethnics that was never as rigid as the later racism against blacks. Ethnoracial ladder of property values in Drake and Cayton, *Black Metropolis*, 174–75. Roediger, *Working toward Whiteness*, 8; Eric Lott, *Love and Theft: Blackface Minstrelsy and the American Working Class* (New York: Oxford University Press, 1995).
72. Freund, *Colored Property*, 38–41. See also Roediger, *Working toward Whiteness*, especially 8–9, 157–77.

73. Reverend Daniel Cantwell, "Postscript on the Cicero Riot" (1951), quoted in Hirsch, *Making the Second Ghetto*, 194.
74. Jack Homer, "Cicero Nightmare" (1951), quoted in Hirsch, *Making the Second Ghetto*, 194.
75. Hirsch, *Making the Second Ghetto*, 196. Among the many accounts of the Back of the Yards Neighborhood Council, a good introduction is Thomas Jablonsky, "The Neighborhood Council," in *Pride in the Jungle*, 134–46. Horwitt, *Let Them Call Me Rebel*, 313–16, 367, 415.
76. "Lowden Asks Better Conditions," *Chicago Tribune*, August 5, 1919.

CONCLUSION: THE CITY OF THE TWENTIETH CENTURY

1. Hirsch, *Making the Second Ghetto*, 9; Drake and Cayton, *Black Metropolis*, 202–5.
2. Hunt, *Blueprint for Disaster*, 44–45, 59, 79. See also Lipsitz, *How Racism Takes Place*, especially 1–37; Satter, *Family Properties*.
3. Hirsch, *Making the Second Ghetto*, 91–92, 41–58, 72–76.
4. Wiese, *Places of Their Own*, 268.
5. On suburbanizing and then globalizing industries, see Cowie, *Capital Moves*. On Schaumberg as an edge city, see Garreau, *Edge City*, 5, 28, 76.
6. For the property-owner politics of school busing, see HoSang, *Racial Propositions*, especially chapter 4; Matthew Lassiter, *The Silent Majority: Suburban Politics in the Sunbelt South* (Princeton, NJ: Princeton University Press, 2005). For the property-owner politics on multiple sides of the civil rights movement, see Self, *American Babylon*. For property tax revolts, see Nicolaides and Wiese, *The Suburb Reader*, chapter 13. For suburbanization as a spur to environmentalism, see Rome, *The Bulldozer in the Countryside*.
7. David Streitfeld and Gretchen Morgenson, "Building Flawed American Dreams: Helping Low-Income Families Buy Homes and Watching the Failures," *New York Times*, October. 19, 2008; *Real Estate and Building Journal*, December. 30, 1876, quoted in Chicago Title and Trust Company, *One Hundred Years of Chicago Land Values* (1933), Chicago History Museum.
8. As David Harvey explains, "Fixed capital in the built environment is both immobile and long-lived. It expresses the power of dead labor over living by committing the latter to certain patterns of use for an extended time" (*Spaces of Capital*, 83).
9. "The Most Practical Philanthropist," *Knights of Labor* (September 7, 1889), 1-4, quoted in Clark, "Own Your Own Home," 149.

SELECTED BIBLIOGRAPHY

ARCHIVES

Centre Canadienne d'Architecture, Montreal

Millard and Decker, *LAWNDALE: Property for Sale in This Beautiful Suburb*. Booklet. Chicago: Lakeside, 1875.

Moody, Walter D. *Chicago's Greatest Issue: An Official Plan*. Booklet. Chicago: Chicago Plan Commission, 1911.

Van Holst, H. V. *Modern American Homes*. Booklet. Chicago: American School of Correspondence, 1913.

Chicago History Museum, Chicago

A.E.H. *The House That Lucy Built, or, A Model Landlord*. Chicago: Samuel Eberly Gross Firm, 1886.

Andreas, Alfred Theodore. *History of Chicago from the Earliest Period to the Present Time*. Chicago: A. T. Andreas, 1884–86.

Andreas, Alfred Theodore. *History of Cook County Illinois from the Earliest Period to the Present Time*. Chicago: A. T. Andreas, 1884.

Angle, Paul, ed. *The Great Chicago Fire, Described in Seven Letters by Men and Women Who Experienced Its Horrors*. Chicago: Chicago Historical Society, 1946.

The Biographical Dictionary and Portrait Gallery of Representative Men of Chicago, Minnesota Cities, and the World's Columbian Exposition. Chicago: H. C. Cooper Jr., 1892.

Blue Island Land and Building Company. *Suburban Homes: Morgan Park*. Chicago: American Hebrew Publication Society, 1886.

Broadsides—Real Estate.

Building and Loan Associations. Miscellaneous pamphlets.

Chicago Blue Book of Selected Names, 1890. Chicago: Chicago Directory, 1890.

Chicago Blue Book of Selected Names, for the Year Ending 1915. Chicago: Chicago Directory, 1914.

Chicago Real Estate Exchange. *Catalogue of 200 Residence Lots in Bates' New Re-Subdivision of Part of the Celebrated Normal Park*. Chicago: N.p., 1881.

The Chicago Society Directory and Ladies' Visiting and Shopping Guide. Chicago: Ensign, McClure, 1876.

Chicago Title and Trust Company. Miscellaneous pamphlets.

Chicago Title and Trust Company. *One Hundred Years of Land Values*.

Cleaver, Charles. *History of Chicago from 1833 to 1892*. Chicago: Author, 1892.

Directory of the Building, Loan, and Savings Associations of Chicago and Cook County, Illinois. Chicago: American Building Association News Co., 1895.

Ericsson, Henry, with Lewis E. Myers. *Sixty Years a Builder: The Autobiography of Henry Ericsson*. Chicago: A. Kroch & Sons, 1942.

Flinn, John J. *Chicago: The Marvelous City of the West. A History, an Encyclopedia, and a Guide*. Chicago: Flynn and Sheppard, 1891.

Gore, David. Second Annual Report of the Auditor of Public Accounts of Building and Loan Associations of the State of Illinois: 1893. Springfield, IL: Ed F. Hartman, State Printer, 1894.

Gore, David. *Third Annual Report of the Auditor of Public Accounts of Building and Loan Associations of the State of Illinois: 1894*. Springfield, IL: Ed F. Hartman, State Printer, 1895.

Illustrations of Greater Chicago. Chicago: J. M. Wing, 1875.

Industrial Chicago, vol. 3: *The Manufacturing Interests*. Chicago: Goodspeed, 1894.

Industrial Chicago, vol. 4: *The Commercial Interests*. Chicago: Goodspeed, 1894.

Kirkland, Caroline. *A Matchless Outlook: The Most Beautiful Residence District in the World Today*. Pamphlet. Chicago: *Chicago Tribune*, May 1, 1927.

Mary Eliza McDowell Papers.

McCoo, F. A. *Say It with Pictures: Achievements of the Negro in Chicago Illinois for the Past Twenty-five Years, Shown for the Inspiration of the Negro Everywhere*. Chicago: F. A. McCoo, 1933.

McCullough, J. S. *Eighth Annual Report of the Auditor of Public Accounts of Building, Loan and Homestead Associations of the State of Illinois*. Springfield, IL: Phillips Brothers, State Printers, 1899.

McCullough, J. S. *Eleventh Annual Report of the Auditor of Public Accounts of Building, Loan and Homestead Associations of the State of Illinois*. Springfield, IL: Phillips Bros., State Printers, 1902.

McCullough, J. S. *Seventh Annual Report of the Auditor of Public Accounts of Building, Loan and Homestead Associations of the State of Illinois: 1898*. Springfield, IL: Phillips Brothers, State Printers, 1899.

McDonald, R. H. *R. H. McDonald's Illustrated History and Map of Chicago, with a History of the Great Fire*. New York: R. B. Thompson, 1872.

The Merchants and Manufacturers of Chicago: Being a Complete History of Our Mercantile and Manufacturing Interests, and Their Progress since the Fire. Chicago: J. M. Wing, 1873.

Moses, John, and Joseph Kirkland, eds. *The History of Chicago*. Chicago: Munsell, 1895.

Our Suburbs: A Resume of the Origin, Progress, and Present State of Chicago's Environs. Chicago: George R. Clarke, 1873.

The Parks and Property Interests of the City of Chicago. Chicago: Western News, 1869.

Picturesque Chicago. Chicago: Chicago Engraving, 1879.

Picturesque Chicago. Chicago: Chicago Engraving, 1882.

Polk's Chicago: Numerical Street and Avenue Directory. Chicago: R. L. Polk, 1928.

Proceedings of the First Annual Meeting of the National Board of Real Estate Agents at the Briggs Houses, Chicago, October 12–14, 1870. Chicago: Land Owner Press, 1870.

Proceedings of the Building Association League of Illinois at Its Annual Meeting Held at Galesburg, June 1894. Chicago: American Building Association News, 1894.

Putney, M. H. *Real Estate Values and Historical Notes of Chicago from the Earliest Period to the Present Time*. Chicago: N.p., 1900.

Reversed Directory of the Elite of Chicago. Chicago: H. A. Pierce, 1880.

Runnion, Jason B. *Out of Town: Being a Descriptive, Historical, and Statistical Account of the Suburban Towns and Residences of Chicago*. Chicago: Western News, 1869.

Samuel Eberly Gross (Firm). *Chicago—The Mid-Continent Metropolis*. Chicago: N.p., 1895.

Samuel Eberly Gross (Firm). *The Gross Cottages, Houses, and Lots*. Chicago: Samuel E. Gross, 1886.

Samuel Eberly Gross (Firm). *Tenth Annual Illustrated Catalogue of S. E. Gross' Famous City Subdivisions and Suburban Towns on Easy Monthly Payments*. Chicago: Samuel E. Gross, 1891.

Schick, Louis. *Chicago and Its Environs: A Handbook for the Traveler*. Chicago: L. Schick, 1891.

Spelman, Walter Bishop. *The Town of Cicero: History, Advantages and Government*. Cicero, IL: J. Sterling Morton High School, Vocational Department, Division of Printing, 1922.

Standing files—Chicago (Boosterism).

Thompson, J. S. *Chicago: A Stranger and Tourists' Guide*. Chicago: Religious Publishing Association, 1866.

The Town of Lake Directory. Chicago: R. R. Donnelley & Sons, 1886.

Wilkie, D. O. *Ordinances of the Building and Health Departments of the City of Chicago and the Annexed Towns of Lake View, Hyde Park, and the Town of Lake*. Chicago: George K. Hazlitt, 1891.

William Zelosky & Co. *Own Your Home in Beautiful Chicago*. Circa 1920.

Newberry Library, Chicago

Butler Lowry Real Estate. *Lots in Adjoining Blocks for Sale on East Terms*. Chicago: circa 1888.

Johnson, Henry, *North Chicago: Its Advantages, Resources, and Probably Future, Including a Sketch of Its Outlying Suburbs*. Chicago: Henry C. Johnson, 1873.

Lots in Winslow, Jacobson and Tallman's Subdivision for Sale Cheap. Chicago: C. W. Dunkley, 1872.

Map collection.

Joseph Regenstein Library, University of Chicago

Appleton, John Bargate. "The Iron and Steel Industry of the Calumet District—A Study in Economic Geography." PhD dissertation, University of Chicago, 1925.

Bruton, Mary Frances. "A Study of Tenement Ownership by Immigrant Workingmen in Chicago." PhD dissertation, University of Chicago, 1924.

Clove, Robert Charles. *The Park Ridge–Barrington Area: A Study of Residential Land Patterns and Problems in Suburban Chicago*. Chicago: University of Chicago Libraries Private Edition, based on a dissertation for the Department of Geography, 1942.

Copeland, Lewis. "The Limits and Characteristics of Metropolitan Chicago." Master's thesis, University of Chicago, 1937.

Feasel, Fred. "The Financing of Urban Residential Construction." PhD dissertation, University of Chicago, 1920.

Finlay, Frank David. "A Survey of Social Problems and Social Services in the Town of Cicero, Illinois." PhD dissertation, University of Chicago, 1937.

Glick, Clarence Elmer. "Winnetka: A Study of a Residential Suburban Community." PhD dissertation, University of Chicago, 1928.

Harkness, Reuben Elmore Earnest. "Real Estate Speculation and Juvenile Delinquency." PhD dissertation, University of Chicago Divinity School, 1915.

Herbst, Alma. "The Negro in the Slaughtering and Meat Packing Industry in Chicago." PhD dissertation, University of Chicago, 1930.

Johnson, Earl Shepard. "The Natural History of the Central Business District." PhD dissertation, University of Chicago, 1944.

Miller, Alice Mae. "Rents and Housing Conditions in the Stockyards District of Chicago." PhD dissertation, University of Chicago, 1923.

Morken, W. Hubert. "The Annexation of Morgan Park to Chicago: One Village's Response to Urban Growth." PhD dissertation, University of Chicago, 1968.

Ozog, Julius John. "A Study of Polish Home Ownership in Chicago." PhD dissertation, University of Chicago, 1942.

Proudfoot, Malcolm. "The Major Outlying Business Centers of Chicago." PhD dissertation, University of Chicago, 1936.

Reckless, Walter. *Vice in Chicago*. Chicago: University of Chicago Press, 1933.

Wilson, Evelyn Heacox. "Chicago Families in Furnished Rooms." PhD dissertation, University of Chicago, 1929.

Work, Monroe Nathan. "Negro Real Estate Holders of Chicago." PhD dissertation, University of Chicago, 1903.

Sterling Memorial Library, Yale University

Map collection.

PUBLISHED WORKS

Abbott, Edith. *The Tenements of Chicago, 1908–1935*. Chicago: University of Chicago Press, 1936.

Abbott, Edith, and Sophonisba Breckinridge, eds. "Housings Conditions in Chicago, part III: The Twenty-Ninth Ward Back of the Yards." *American Journal of Sociology* 11, no. 4 (January 1911): 433–68.

Addams, Jane. *Twenty Years at Hull-House*. New York: Signet Classic, 1981. First published 1910.

Addams, Jane, et al. *Hull-House Maps and Papers*. New York: Thomas Y. Crowell, 1895.

Algren, Nelson. *Chicago: City on the Make*. New York: Doubleday, 1951.

The Biographical Dictionary and Portrait Gallery of Representative Men of Chicago, Minnesota Cities, and the World's Columbian Exposition. Chicago: H. C. Cooper Jr., 1892.

Blackmar, Elizabeth. *Manhattan for Rent, 1785–1850*. Ithaca, NY: Cornell University Press, 1989.

Blumin, Stuart. *The Emergence of the Middle Class: Social Experience in the American City, 1760–1900*. Cambridge, UK: Cambridge University Press, 1989.

Bodfish, H. Morton. *History of Building and Loan Associations in the United States*. Chicago: U.S. Building and Loan League, 1931.

Boorstin, Daniel. "The Balloon-Frame House." In *The Americans: The National Experience*. New York: Random House, 1965, 148–52.

Boydston, Jeanne. *Home and Work: Housework, Wages, and the Ideology of Labor in the Early Republic*. New York: Oxford University Press, 1990.

Boyer, M. Christine. *Dreaming the Rational City: The Myth of American City Planning*. Cambridge, MA: MIT Press, 1983.

Breckinridge, Sophonisba. *New Homes for Old*. New York: Harper & Bros., 1921.

Breckinridge, Sophonisba, and Edith Abbott. *The Delinquent Child and the Home*. New York: Russell Sage Foundation, 1912.

Buisseret, David, ed. *Envisioning the City: Six Studies in Urban Cartography*. Chicago: University of Chicago Press, 1998.

Burgess, Ernest, Robert Park, and Roderick McKenzie, eds. *The City*. Chicago: University of Chicago Press, 1925.

Burnham, Daniel, and Edward Bennett. *Plan of Chicago*. Chicago: Commercial Club, 1909.

Butterworth, Hezekiah. *Zig-Zag Journeys in the White City, with Visits to the Neighboring Metropolis*. Boston: Estes & Lauriat, 1894.

Calder, Lendol. *Financing the American Dream: A Cultural History of Consumer Credit*. Princeton, NJ: Princeton University Press, 1999.

Cappetti, Carla. *Writing Chicago: Modernism, Ethnography, and the Novel*. New York: Columbia University Press, 1993.

Chamberlin, Everett. *Chicago and Its Suburbs*. Chicago: T. A. Hungerford, 1874.

Chappell, Sally, ed. *The Plan of Chicago: 1909–1979*. Chicago: Art Institute of Chicago, 1979.

Chicago Commission on Race Relations. *The Negro in Chicago: A Study of Race Relations and a Race Riot*. Chicago: University of Chicago Press, 1922.

Chicago Foreign Language Press Survey. Chicago: Works Progress Administration, Chicago Public Library Omnibus Project, 1942.

Chicago Relief and Aid Society. *First Special Report of the Chicago Relief and Aid Society*. Chicago: Culver, Page, Hoyne, 1871.

Chicago Relief and Aid Society. *Report of the Chicago Relief and Aid Society to the Common Council of the City of Chicago*. Chicago: Horton & Leonard, January 1872.

Chicago Zoning Commission. *Zoning Chicago*. Chicago: N.p., April 1922.

Citizens' Association of Chicago. *Report of the Committee on Tenement Houses*. Chicago: George K. Hazlitt, 1884.

Clark, Charles Eugene. *Housing and Homes: An Address at the Fourth Annual Convention of the Illinois League of Local Building and Loan Associations*. Decatur, IL: N.p., October 1919.

Clark, Clifford Edward, Jr. *The American Family Home, 1800–1960*. Chapel Hill: University of North Carolina Press, 1986.

Clark, Emily. "Own Your Own Home: S. E. Gross, the Great Domestic Promoter." In Eleanor Thompson, editor, *The American Home: Material Culture, Domestic Space, and Family Life*. Winterthur, DE: Winterthur Museum, 1998, 135–53.

Cohen, Lizabeth. *A Consumers' Republic: The Politics of Mass Consumption in Postwar America*. New York: Knopf, 2003.

Cohen, Lizabeth. *Making a New Deal: Industrial Workers in Chicago, 1919–1934*. London: Cambridge University Press, 1990.

Colbert, Elias, and Everett Chamberlin. *Chicago and the Great Conflagration*. Cincinnati: C. F. Vent, 1871.

Condit, Carl W. *The Chicago School of Architecture: A History of Commercial and Public Building in the Chicago Area, 1875–1925*. Chicago: University of Chicago Press, 1964.

Cowie, Jefferson. *Capital Moves: RCA's Seventy-Year Quest for Cheap Labor*. New York: New Press, 1999.

Creese, Walter L. "Riverside: The Greatest American Suburb." In *The Crowning of the American Landscape*. Princeton, NJ: Princeton University Press, 1985, 219–40.

Cromie, Robert. *The Great Chicago Fire*. New York: McGraw-Hill, 1958.

Cromley, Elizabeth Collins. *Alone Together: A History of New York's Early Apartments*. Ithaca, NY: Cornell University Press, 1990.

Cronon, William. *Nature's Metropolis: Chicago and the Great West*. New York: Norton, 1991.

Cuff, Dana. *The Provisional City: Los Angeles Stories of Architecture and Urbanism*. Cambridge, MA: MIT Press, 2000.

Davis, Mike. *Ecology of Fear: Los Angeles and the Imagination of Disaster*. New York: Vintage Books, 1998.

Davis, Mike. *Magical Urbanism: Latinos Reinvent the U.S. City*. London: Verso, 2000.

d'Eramo, Marco. *The Pig and the Skyscraper, Chicago: A History of Our Future*. Translated by Graeme Thomson. London: Verso, 2002.

Deutsch, Sarah. *Women and the City: Gender, Space, and Power in Boston, 1870–1940*. New York: Oxford University Press, 2000.

Dickens, Charles. *The Life and Adventures of Martin Chuzzlewit*. London: Oxford University Press, 1951. First published 1844.

Dixon, Chris *Perfecting the Family: Antislavery Marriages in Nineteenth-Century America*. Amherst: University of Massachusetts Press, 1997.

Douglass, Harlan. *The Suburban Trend*. New York: Century, 1925.

Downing, Andrew Jackson. *The Architecture of Country Houses*. New York: Dover, 1969. First published 1850.

Drake, St. Clair, and Horace R. Cayton. *Black Metropolis: A Study of Negro Life in a Northern City*. New York: Harcourt, Brace & World, 1965. First published 1945.

Dreiser, Theodore. *Jennie Gerhardt: A Novel*. New York: Harper, 1911.

Dreiser, Theodore. *Sister Carrie*. New York: Signet Classic, 1980. First published 1900.

Duany, Andres, Elizabeth Plater-Zyberk, and Jeff Speck. *Suburban Nation: The Rise of Sprawl and the Decline of the American Dream*. New York: Farrar, Straus and Giroux, 2000.

Dunne, Finley Peter. *Mr. Dooley in Peace and in War*. Boston: Small, Maybard, 1905.

Ebner, Michael. *Creating Chicago's North Shore: A Suburban History*. Chicago: University of Chicago Press, 1988.

Edel, Matthew, Elliot Sclar, and Daniel Luria. *Shaky Palaces: Homeownership and Social Mobility in Boston's Suburbanization*. New York: Columbia University Press, 1994.

Einhorn, Robin. *Property Rules: Political Economy in Chicago, 1833–1872*. Chicago: University of Chicago Press, 2001.

Elshtain, Jean Bethke, ed. *The Jane Addams Reader*. New York: Basic Books, 2002.

Embree, Frances Buckley. "The Housing of the Poor in Chicago." *Journal of Political Economy* 8, no. 3 (1900).

Engels, Friedrich. *The Housing Question*. Moscow: Progress, 1970. First published 1872.

Faris, Robert E., and Warren Dunham. *Mental Disorders in Urban Areas: An Ecological Study of Schizophrenia and Other Psychoses*. Chicago: University of Chicago Press, 1939.

Farrell, James T. *Studs Lonigan: A Trilogy*. New York: Penguin, 2001. First published 1932–35.

Fishman, Robert. *Bourgeois Utopias: The Rise and Fall of Suburbia*. New York: Basic Books, 1987.

Fogelson, Robert M. *Downtown: Its Rise and Fall, 1880–1950*. New Haven, CT: Yale University Press, 2001.

Freund, David. *Colored Property: State Policy and White Racial Politics in Suburban America*. Chicago: University of Chicago Press, 2007.

Fuller, Henry. *The Cliff Dwellers*. New York: Irvington, 1981. First published 1893.

Fuller, Henry. *With the Procession*. Chicago: University of Chicago Press, 1965. First published 1895.

Gamm, Gerald. *Urban Exodus: Why the Jews Left Boston and the Catholics Stayed*. Cambridge, MA: Harvard University Press, 1999.

Gans, Herbert. *The Levittowners: Ways of Life and Politics in a New Suburban Community.* New York: Columbia University Press, 1982. First published 1967.

Garb, Margaret. "Building the American Dream: A History of Home Ownership and Housing Reform, Chicago, 1871–1919." PhD dissertation, Columbia University, 2001.

Garb, Margaret. *City of American Dreams: A History of Home Ownership and Housing Reform in Chicago, 1871–1919.* Chicago: University of Chicago Press, 2005.

Garreau, Joel. *Edge City: Life on the New Frontier.* New York: Random House, 1991.

Ginger, Ray. *Altgeld's America: The Lincoln Ideal versus Changing Realities.* New York: Funk & Wagnalls, 1958.

Ginzberg, Lori D. *Women and the Work of Benevolence: Morality, Politics, and Class in the Nineteenth-Century United States.* New Haven, CT: Yale University Press, 1990.

Glickman, Lawrence B. *A Living Wage: American Workers and the Making of Consumer Society.* Ithaca, NY: Cornell University Press, 1997.

Gordon, Linda. *Heroes of Their Own Lives: The Politics and History of Family Violence, Boston 1880–1960.* New York: Viking Penguin, 1988.

Gottdiener, M. *The Social Production of Urban Space.* Austin: University of Texas Press, 1994.

Grossman, James. *Land of Hope: Chicago, Black Southerners, and the Great Migration.* Chicago: University of Chicago Press, 1989.

Groth, Paul. *Living Downtown: The History of Residential Hotels in the United States.* Berkeley: University of California Press, 1994.

Guglielmo, Thomas. *White on Arrival: Italians, Race, Color, and Power in Chicago, 1890–1945.* Oxford: Oxford University Press, 2003.

Harris, Richard. "Chicago's Other Suburbs." *Geographical Review* 84, no. 4 (1994): 394–410.

Harris, Richard. *Unplanned Suburbs: Toronto's American Tragedy, 1900 to 1950.* Baltimore: Johns Hopkins University Press, 1996.

Harris, Richard, and Robert Lewis. "Constructing a Fault(y) Zone: Misrepresentations of American Cities and Suburbs, 1900–1950." *Annals of the Association of American Geographers* 88, no. 4 (1998): 622–39.

Harris, Richard, and Robert Lewis. "The Geography of North American Cities and Suburbs, 1900–1950: A New Synthesis." *Journal of Urban History* 27, no. 3 (2001): 262–92.

Harvey, David. *Spaces of Capital: Towards a Critical Geography.* New York: Routledge, 2001.

Hawley, Amos. *Human Ecology: A Theoretical Essay.* Chicago: University of Chicago Press, 1986.

Hayden, Dolores. *Building Suburbia: Green Fields and Urban Growth, 1820–2000.* New York: Pantheon Books, 2003.

Hayden, Dolores. *The Grand Domestic Revolution: A History of Feminist Designs for American Homes, Neighborhoods, and Cities.* Cambridge, MA: MIT Press, 1981.

Hayden, Dolores. *The Power of Place: Urban Landscape as Public History.* Cambridge, MA: MIT Press, 1995.

Hayden, Dolores. *Redesigning the American Dream: The Future of Housing, Work, and Family Life.* New York: Norton, 1984.

Haynes, Bruce. *Red Lines, Black Spaces: The Politics of Race and Space in a Black Middle-Class Suburb.* New Haven, CT: Yale University Press, 2001.

Hill, Caroline M., ed. *Mary McDowell and Municipal Housekeeping: A Symposium.* Chicago: Millar, 1937.

Hirsch, Arnold. *Making the Second Ghetto: Race and Housing in Chicago, 1940–1960.* Cambridge, UK: Cambridge University Press, 1983.

Hise, Greg. *Magnetic Los Angeles: Planning the Twentieth-Century Metropolis.* Baltimore: Johns Hopkins University Press, 1997.

Holt, Glen, and Dominic Pacyga. *Chicago: A Historical Guide to the Neighborhoods. The Loop and South Side.* Chicago: Chicago Historical Society, 1979.

Holt, Hamilton, ed. *The Life Stories of Undistinguished Americans as Told by Themselves.* New York: Routledge, 1990.

Hornstein, Jeffrey M. *A Nation of Realtors: A Cultural History of the Twentieth-Century American Middle Class.* Durham, NC: Duke University Press, 2005.

Horwitt, Sanford. *Let Them Call Me Rebel: Saul Alinsky—His Life and Legacy.* New York: Knopf, 1989.

HoSang, Daniel Martinez. *Racial Propositions: Ballot Initiatives and the Making of Post-war California.* Berkeley: University of California Press, 2010.

Hoyt, Homer. *One Hundred Years of Land Values in Chicago.* University of Chicago Libraries, Private Edition, based on a dissertation submitted to the University of Chicago Department of Economics, 1933.

Hughes, Everett Charington. "The Growth of an Institution: The Chicago Real Estate Board." PhD dissertation, University of Chicago, 1931.

Hunt, D. Bradford. *Blueprint for Disaster: The Unraveling of Chicago Public Housing.* Chicago: University of Chicago Press, 2009.

Isenberg, Alison. *Downtown America: A History of the Place and the People Who Made It.* Chicago: University of Chicago Press, 2004.

Ives, Halsey. *The Dream City: A Portfolio of Photographic Views of the World's Columbian Exposition.* St. Louis, MO: M. D. Thompson, 1893–94.

Jablonsky, Thomas. *Pride in the Jungle: Community and Everyday Life in Back of the Yards Chicago.* Baltimore: Johns Hopkins University Press, 1993.

Jackson, J. B. *Landscape in Sight: Looking at America.* Edited by Helen Lefkowitz Horowitz. New Haven, CT: Yale University Press, 1997.

Jackson, Kenneth T. *Crabgrass Frontier: The Suburbanization of the United States.* New York: Oxford University Press, 1985.

Jackson, Shannon. *Lines of Activity: Performance, Historiography, Hull-House Domesticity.* Ann Arbor: University of Michigan Press, 2000.

Jacobs, Jane. *The Life and Death of Great American Cities.* New York: Modern Library, 1993. First published 1961.

Jacobson, Matthew Frye. *Barbarian Virtues: The United States Encounters Foreign Peoples at Home and Abroad, 1876–1919.* New York: Hill and Wang, 2000.

Jacobson, Matthew Frye. *Whiteness of a Different Color: European Immigrants and the Alchemy of Race.* Cambridge, MA: Harvard University Press, 1998.

James, F. Cyril. *The Growth of Chicago Banks,* vol. 1: *The Formative Years.* New York: Harper & Brothers, 1938.

Jones, Jacqueline. *Labor of Love, Labor of Sorrow: Black Women, Work and the Family, from Slavery to the Present.* New York: Basic Books, 1985.

Jurca, Catherine. *White Diaspora: The Suburb and the Twentieth-Century American Novel.* Princeton, NJ: Princeton University Press, 2001.

Keating, Ann Durkin. *Building Chicago: Suburban Developers and the Creation of a Divided Metropolis.* Columbus: Ohio State University Press, 1988.

Keil, Hartmut, and John B. Jentz, eds. *German Workers in Chicago: A Documentary History of Working-Class Culture from 1850 to World War I.* Urbana: University of Illinois Press, 1988.

Kelly, Barbara M. *Expanding the American Dream: Building and Rebuilding Levittown*. Albany: State University of New York Press, 1993.

Koenig, Harry. *A History of the Parishes of the Archdiocese of Chicago, Published in Observance of the Centenary of the Archdiocese*. Chicago: Archdiocese of Chicago, 1980.

Kruse, Kevin, and Thomas Sugrue, eds. *The New Suburban History*. Chicago: University of Chicago Press, 2006.

Latham, Michael. *Modernization as Ideology*. Chapel Hill: University of North Carolina Press, 2000.

Larson, Erik. *The Devil in the White City*. New York: Crown, 2003.

Leach, Neil, ed. *The Hieroglyphics of Space: Reading and Experiencing the Modern Metropolis*. London: Routledge, 2002.

Leach, Neil, ed. *Rethinking Architecture*. London: Routledge, 1997.

Lees, Andrew *Cities Perceived: Urban Society in European and American Thought, 1820–1940*. Manchester, UK: Manchester University Press, 1985.

Lefebvre, Henri. *The Production of Space*. Translated by Donald Nicholson-Smith. Oxford: Blackwell, 2001. First published 1974.

Lewis, Robert, ed. *Manufacturing Suburbs: Building Work and Home on the Metropolitan Fringe*. Philadelphia: Temple University Press, 2004.

Lewis, Sinclair. *Babbitt*. New York: Bantam Books, 1922.

Lipsitz, George. *How Racism Takes Place*. Philadelphia: Temple University Press, 2011.

Lipsitz, George. *The Possessive Investment in Whiteness: How White People Profit from Identity Politics*. Philadelphia: Temple University Press, 2006.

Luzerne, Frank. *Through the Flames and Beyond, or Chicago as It Was and as It Is*. New York: Wells & Co., 1872.

Maitland, James. *Old and New Chicago: Pen and Pencil Sketches of the Garden City*. Chicago: Hockney and Lane, 1879.

Marchand, Roland. *Creating the Corporate Soul*. Berkeley: University of California Press, 1988.

Marsh, Margaret. *Suburban Lives*. London: Rutgers University Press, 1990.

Mason, Karen. "Mary McDowell and Municipal Housekeeping." In Lucy Murphy and Wendy Venet, eds. *Midwestern Women: Work, Community, and Leadership at the Crossroads*. Bloomington: Indiana University Press, 1997.

Mayer, Harold, and Richard Wade. *Chicago: Growth of a Metropolis*. Chicago: University of Chicago Press, 1969.

McGreevy, John T. *Parish Boundaries: The Catholic Encounter with Race in the Twentieth-Century Urban North*. Chicago: University of Chicago Press, 1996.

McKenzie, Evan. *Privatopia: Homeowner Associations and the Rise of Residential Private Governments*. New Haven, CT: Yale University Press, 1994.

McMahon, Eileen. *What Parish Are You From? A Chicago Irish Community and Race Relations*. Lexington: University Press of Kentucky, 1995.

McShane, Clay. *Down the Asphalt Path: The Automobile and the American City*. New York: Columbia University Press, 1994.

Menand, Louis. *The Metaphysical Club: A Story of Ideas in America*. New York: Farrar, Straus and Giroux, 2001.

Meyerowitz, Joanne. *Women Adrift: Independent Wage Earners in Chicago, 1880–1930*. Chicago: University of Chicago Press, 1988.

Miller, Donald. *City of the Century: The Epic of Chicago and the Making of America*. New York: Simon and Schuster, 1996.

Miller, Ross. *American Apocalypse: The Great Fire and the Myth of Chicago*. Chicago: University of Chicago Press, 1990.

Miller, Ross. *Here's the Deal: The Making and Breaking of a Great American City*. Evanston, IL: Northwestern University Press, 1996.

Mills, C. Wright. *White Collar: The American Middle Classes*. Oxford: Oxford University Press, 1951.

Mintz, Sidney. *Sweetness and Power: The Place of Sugar in Modern History*. New York: Penguin Books, 1985.

Monchow, Helen Corbin. *Seventy Years of Real Estate Subdividing in the Region of Chicago*. Chicago: Northwestern University Press, 1919.

Montgomery, David. *The Fall of the House of Labor: The Workplace, the State, and American Labor Activism, 1865–1925*. Cambridge, UK: Cambridge University Press, 1987.

Montgomery, Louise. *The American Girl in the Stockyards District*. Chicago: University of Chicago Press, 1913.

Moody, Walter D. *Wacker's Manual of the Plan of Chicago: Municipal Economy*. 4th ed. Chicago: Chicago Plan Commission, 1924.

Moorley, Christopher. *Old Loopy: A Love Letter to Chicago*. Chicago: Argus Book Shop, 1935.

Morrissey, Katherine. *Mental Territories: Mapping the Inland Empire*. Ithaca, NY: Cornell University Press, 1997.

Moskowitz, Marina. *Standard of Living: The Measure of the Middle Class in Modern America*. Baltimore: Johns Hopkins University Press, 2004.

Mosley, Stephen. *The Chimney of the World: A History of Smoke Pollution in Victorian and Edwardian Manchester*. Cambridge, UK: White Horse Press, 2001.

Mumford, Lewis. *The City in History*. New York: Harcourt, Brace, Jovanovich, 1961.

New Chicago: A Full Review of Reconstruction, for the Year. Chicago: Horton & Leonard, 1872.

Nichols, Hi. *Pay Dirt in Chicago*. Chicago: John's, 1933.

Nicolaides, Becky. *My Blue Heaven: Life and Politics in the Working-Class Suburbs of Los Angeles, 1920–1965*. Chicago: University of Chicago Press, 2002.

Nicolaides, Becky, and Andrew Wiese, eds. *The Suburb Reader*. New York: Routledge, 2006.

Norris, Frank. *The Pit*. New York: Doubleday, Page, 1903.

Nye, David. *Electrifying America: Social Meanings of a New Technology, 1880–1940*. Cambridge, MA: MIT Press, 1997.

Nye, David. *Narratives and Spaces: Technology and the Construction of American Culture*. New York: Columbia University Press, 1997.

Odem, Mary. *Delinquent Daughters: Protecting and Policing Adolescent Female Sexuality in the United States, 1885–1920*. Chapel Hill: University of North Carolina Press, 1994.

Orfield, Myron. *Metropolitics: A Regional Agenda for Community and Stability*. Washington, DC: Brookings Institute Press, 1997.

Pacyga, Dominic. *Polish Immigrants and Industrial Chicago: Workers on the South Side, 1880–1922*. Columbus: Ohio State University Press, 1991.

Palen, J. John. *The Suburbs*. New York: McGraw-Hill, 1995.

Peterson, Jon A. *The Birth of City Planning in the United States, 1840–1917*. Baltimore: Johns Hopkins University Press, 2003.

Pierce, Bessie Louise, ed. *As Others See Chicago: Impressions of Visitors, 1673–1933*. Chicago: University of Chicago Press, 1933.

Pierce, Bessie Louise. *A History of Chicago*. New York: Knopf, 1940–41.

Pierce, Bessie Louise. *A History of Chicago*. Vol. 2: *From Town to City, 1848–1871*. New York: Knopf, 1940.

Pierce, Bessie Louise. *A History of Chicago*. Vol. 3: *The Rise of a Modern City, 1871–1893*. New York: Knopf, 1957.

Quaife, Milo Milton, ed. *The Development of Chicago, 1674–1914, Shown in a Series of Contemporary Original Narratives*. Chicago: Caxton Club, 1916.

Radford, Gail. *Modern Housing for America: Policy Struggles in the New Deal Era*. Chicago: University of Chicago Press, 1996.

Rae, Douglas. *City: Urbanism and Its End*. New Haven, CT: Yale University Press, 2003.

Reps, John W. *The Making of Urban America: A History of City Planning in the United States*. Princeton, NJ: Princeton University Press, 1965.

Rodgers, Daniel. *Atlantic Crossings: Social Politics in a Progressive Age*. Cambridge, MA: Harvard University Press, 1998.

Roe, E. P. *Barriers Burned Away*. New York: Dodd & Mead, 1872.

Roediger, David. *The Wages of Whiteness: Race and the Making of the American Working Class*. New York: Verso, 1991.

Roediger, David. *Working toward Whiteness: How America's Immigrants Became White. The Strange Journey from Ellis Island to the Suburbs*. New York: Basic Books, 2005.

Rome, Adam. *The Bulldozer in the Countryside: Suburban Sprawl and the Rise of American Environmentalism*. London: Cambridge University Press, 2001.

Rosen, Christine Meisner. *The Limits of Power: Great Fires and the Process of City Growth in America*. London: Cambridge University Press, 1986.

Ross, Andrew. *The Chicago Gangster Theory of Life: Nature's Debt to Society*. New York: Verso, 1994.

Ross, Dorothy. *The Origins of American Social Science*. Cambridge, UK: Cambridge University Press, 1992.

Ryan, Mary P. *Civic Wars: Democracy and Public Life in the American City during the Nineteenth Century*. Berkeley: University of California Press, 1997.

Ryan, Mary P. *Cradle of the Middle Class: The Family in Oneida County, New York, 1790–1865*. London: Cambridge University Press, 1981.

Ryan, Mary P. *The Empire of the Mother: American Writing about Domesticity, 1830–1860*. New York: Haworth Press, 1982.

Rydell, Robert. *All the World's a Fair: Visions of Empire at American International Expositions*. Chicago: University of Chicago Press, 1984.

Sandburg, Carl. *Chicago Poems*. New York: Henry Holt, 1916.

Sandburg, Carl. *Chicago Race Riots, July 1919*. New York: Harcourt, Brace, and Howe, 1919.

Sassen, Saskia. *The Global City: New York, London, and Tokyo*. Princeton, NJ: Princeton University Press, 1991.

Satter, Beryl. *Family Properties: Race, Real Estate, and the Exploitation of Black Urban America*. New York: Metropolitan Books, 2009.

Sawislak, Karen. *Smoldering City: Chicagoans and the Great Fire, 1871–1874*. Chicago: University of Chicago Press, 1995.

Schulten, Susan. *The Geographical Imagination in America, 1880–1950*. Chicago: University of Chicago Press, 2001.

Schultz, Rima Lunin, et al. "Urban Experience in Chicago: Hull-House and Its Neighbors, 1889–1963." University of Illinois at Chicago, www.uic.edu/jaddams/hull/urbanexp/.

Scott, James. *Seeing Like a State: How Certain Schemes to Improve the Urban Condition Have Failed*. New Haven, CT: Yale University Press, 1998.

Self, Robert O. *American Babylon: Race and the Struggle for Postwar Oakland*. Princeton, NJ: Princeton University Press, 2005.

Sennett, Richard *Families against the City: Middle Class Homes in Industrial Chicago*. Cambridge, MA: Harvard University Press, 1970.

Sies, Mary Corbin, and Chris Silver, eds. *Planning the Twentieth-Century American City*. Baltimore: Johns Hopkins University Press, 1996.

Simpson, Hebert D., and John E. Burton. *The Valuation of Vacant Land in Suburban Areas, Chicago Area*. Chicago: Institute for Economic Research, Northwestern University, 1931.

Sinclair, Upton. *The Jungle*. New York: Penguin Classics, 1974. First published 1905.

Sklar, Kathryn Kish. *Catharine Beecher: A Study in American Domesticity*. New York: Norton, 1978.

Slayton, Robert A. *Back of the Yards: The Making of a Local Democracy*. Chicago: University of Chicago Press, 1986.

Smith, Carl. *The Plan of Chicago: Daniel Burnham and the Remaking of the American City*. Chicago: University of Chicago Press, 2006.

Smith, Carl. *Urban Disorder and the Shape of Belief: The Great Chicago Fire, the Haymarket Bomb, and the Model Town of Pullman*. Chicago: University of Chicago Press, 1995.

Smith, Carl, et al. *The Great Chicago Fire and the Web of Memory*. Chicago Historical Society and Northwestern University, http://www.chicagohs.org/fire/.

Smith, Henry Justin, and Lloyd Lewis. *Chicago: The History of Its Reputation*. New York: Harcourt, Brace, 1929.

Spinney, Robert G. *City of Big Shoulders: A History of Chicago*. DeKalb: Northern Illinois University Press, 2000.

Spurlock, John. *Free Love: Marriage and Middle-Class Radicalism in America, 1825–1860*. New York: New York University Press, 1988.

Stange, Maren. *Bronzeville: Black Chicago in Pictures*. New York: New Press, 2003.

Stilgoe, John R. *Borderlands: Origins of the American Suburb, 1820–1939*. New Haven, CT: Yale University Press, 1988.

Soja, Edward. *Postmodern Geographies: The Reassertion of Space in Critical Social Theory*. London: Verso, 1989.

Sugrue, Thomas. *The Origins of the Urban Crisis: Race and Inequality in Postwar Detroit*. Princeton, NJ: Princeton University Press, 1996.

Taylor, Graham Romeyn. *Satellite Cities: A Study of Industrial Suburbs*. New York: D. Appleton, 1915.

Terkel, Studs. *Chicago*. New York: Pantheon Books, 1985.

Thernstrom, Stephan. *Poverty and Progress: Social Mobility in a Nineteenth-Century City*. Cambridge, MA: Harvard University Press, 1964.

Thrasher, Frederic. *The Gang: A Study of 1313 Gangs in Chicago*. Chicago: University of Chicago Press, 1927.

Trachtenberg, Alan. *The Incorporation of America: Culture and Society in the Gilded Age*. New York: Hill and Wang, 1982.

Tuttle, William M. *Race Riot: Chicago in the Red Summer of 1919*. Chicago: University of Illinois Press, 1970.

Vanneman, Reeve, and Lynn Weber Cannon. *The American Perception of Class*. Philadelphia: Temple University Press, 1987.

Veiller, Lawrence. *Housing Reform: A Hand-book for Practical Use in American Cities*. New York: Russell Sage Foundation, 1910.

Veiller, Lawrence. *The Tenement House Problem*. New York: N.p., 1905.

Vergara, Camilo José. *American Ruins*. New York: Monacelli Press, 1999.

Vice Commission of Chicago. *The Social Evil in Chicago*. Chicago: Gunthrop-Warren, 1911.

Wade, Louise Carroll. *Chicago's Pride: The Stockyards, Packingtown, and Environs in the Nineteenth Century*. Chicago: University of Illinois Press, 1987.

Waldie, D. J. *Holy Land: A Suburban Memoir*. New York: St. Martin's Press, 1996.

Warner, Sam Bass. *Streetcar Suburbs: The Process of Growth in Boston (1870–1900)*. Cambridge, MA: Harvard University Press, 1978.

Washington, Sylvia Hood. *Packing Them In: An Archeology of Environmental Racism in Chicago, 1865–1954*. Lanham, MD: Lexington Books, 2005.

Weiss, Marc. *Rise of the Community Builders: The American Real Estate Industry and Urban Land Planning*. New York: Columbia University Press, 1987.

Wexler, Laura. *Tender Violence: Domestic Vision in an Age of U.S. Imperialism*. Chapel Hill: University of North Carolina Press, 2000.

White, Alfred Treadway. *Improved Dwellings for the Laboring Classes: The Need and the Way to Meet It on Strict Commercial Principles*. New York: N.p., 1877.

Wiese, Andrew. *Places of Their Own: African American Suburbanization in the Twentieth Century*. Chicago: University of Chicago Press, 2004.

Wilkerson, Isabel. *The Warmth of Other Suns: The Epic Story of America's Great Migration*. New York: Vintage, 2010.

Williams, Raymond. *The Country and the City*. Oxford: Oxford University Press, 1973.

Wilson, Howard. *Mary McDowell: Neighbor*. Chicago: University of Chicago Press, 1928.

Worthington, T. Locke. *The Dwellings of the Poor and Weekly Wage-Earners in and around Towns*. New York: Charles Scribner & Sons, 1893.

Wright, Gwendolyn. *Building the Dream: A Social History of Housing in America*. Cambridge, MA: MIT Press, 1981.

Wright, Gwendolyn. *Moralism and the Model Home: Domestic Architecture and Cultural Conflict in Chicago, 1873–1913*. Chicago: University of Chicago Press, 1980.

Wrigley, Edmund. *The Working Man's Way to Wealth. A Practical Treatise on Building Associations: What They Are and How to Use Them*. Philadelphia: James K. Simon, 1869.

Zunz, Olivier. *The Changing Face of Inequality: Urbanization, Industrial Development, and Immigrants in Detroit, 1880–1920*. Chicago: University of Chicago Press, 1982.

INDEX